Th. Flik · H. Liebig

16–Bit-
Microprocessor Systems

Structure, Behavior, and Programming

Translated by G. Bisiani

With 188 Figures and 27 Tables

Springer-Verlag
Berlin Heidelberg New York Tokyo

Dr.-Ing. Thomas Flik
Prof. Dr.-Ing. Hans Liebig

Institut für Technische Informatik,
Technische Universität Berlin
Franklinstrasse 28/29, 1000 Berlin 10, FRG

Gigliola Bisiani

917 Bellefonte Ave., Pittsburgh, PA 15232, USA

ISBN-13: 978-3-540-15164-7   e-ISBN-13: 978-3-642-93285-4
DOI: 10.1007/978-3-642-93285-4

Library of Congress Cataloging in Publication Data
Flik, Th., 1943-. 16–bit microprocessor systems. Translation of: 16–Bit-Mikroprozessor-
systeme. Bibliography: p. Includes index. 1. Microprocessors. I. Liebig, Hans. II. Title.
III. Title: Sixteen–bit microprocessor systems. QA76.5.F44613 1985   001.64   85-8056

© Springer-Verlag Berlin Heidelberg 1985

Foreword

In the last few years, a large number of books on microprocessors have appeared on the market. Most of them originated in the context of the 4-bit and the 8-bit microprocessors and their comparatively simple structure. However, the techno-logical development from 8-bit to 16-bit microprossors led to processor components with a substantially more complex structure and with an expanded functionality and also to an increase in the system architecture's complexity.

This books takes this advancement into account. It examines 16-bit micro-processor systems and describes their structure, their behavior and their programming. The principles of computer organization are treated at the component level. This is done by means of a detailed examination of the characteristic functionality of microprocessors. Furthermore the interactions between hardware and software, that are typical of microprocessor technology, are introduced. Interfacing techniques are one of the focal points of these considerations.

This puplication is organized as a textbook and is intended as a self-teaching course on 16-bit microprocessors for students of computer science and communications, design engineers and users in a wide variety of technical and scientific fields. Basic knowledge of boolean algebra is assumed. The choice of material is based on the 16-bit microprocessors that are currently available on the market; on the other hand, the presentation is not bound to any one of these microprocessors.

The first chapter introduces the behavior, the basic structure and the assembly language programming of a simple 16-bit microprocessor system. The reader that is already familiar with the basics of computer organization and assembly language programming can skip this chapter. - The second chapter deals only with those hardware characteristics of a 16-bit microprocessor that are needed for programming and lays the foundation for the third chapter, where several important programming techniques are described. - The fourth chapter focuses on the problems of the system structure, in particular on the flow of signals between the miroprocessor and the various system components. - Chapters 5 and 6 tackle the most common interfacing techniques. Along with the principles of I/O organization and data transmission, several interfacing components and their interfacing to microprocessor systems are discussed in detail.

Chapter 7 plays the role of an appendix, where the characteristics of 16-bit microprocessors (Motorola MC 68000, Zilog Z 8000, Intel 8086 and their successors) are illustrated. This, together with the suggested references, provides microprocessor

VI

users with an overview that is useful in their selection of a manufacturer.

We gratefully acknowlegde the assistance of Renate Kirchmann, Hildegard Klimmeck, Ingrid Kunkel, Rolf Malinowski and Dipl.-Math. Horst Seyferth during the realization of this book. In particular we would like to thank Dr. Jürgen Wazeck of Bosch Elektronik, Berlin for his cooperation; and Gigliola Bisiani, Pittsburgh who translated the book into English and carefully prepared the final version.

Berlin, July 1985   Th. Flik and H. Liebig

Table of Contents

1 Introduction to the Structure and the Programming of a Microprocessor

Microprocessor systems are general purpose programmable digital computers of small to medium capacity. Their advantages lie in the miniaturization of the components, in the low hardware costs and in the possibility to adapt the hardware to the problem at hand in a modular way. Thanks to these qualities, microprocessors are now used in new fields of application, which were precluded to conventional digital computers or had to be tackled by employing custom systems with very high design and production costs.

A starting point for the development of microprocessors is the technology, originated in 1948 with the discovery of the transistor, that allows the integration of complex logical switching circuits on semiconductor chips of a few mm^2. Thus in 1959, Fairchild, a semiconductor company, managed to place several transistors on a chip. By means of this technological advancement, the integration density could be increased and the switching times abbreviated thus increasing the capacity of the devices as well.

At the end of the Sixties, logic components became more complex in their function, but at the same time more specific, which increasingly limited their range of application. Datapoint, an American company producing so-called intelligent terminals, developed a simple programmable processor for terminal control in 1969 and commissioned the two semiconductor companies Intel and Texas Instruments to integrate it on a single chip. Intel succeeded in producing the component; nevertheless, it could not be employed for the intended application because of its low processing speed. Thus, Intel decided to market this processor as a programmable logic device. The two available versions had processing capacities of respectively 4 and 8 bits and were called Intel 4004 and Intel 8008. The age of microprocessors had begun.

In the meantime, 1-bit, 4-bit and above all 8-bit microprocessors have become rather popular in the fields of control, feedback control and mathematical computation. This development was supported by the production of entire families of microprocessors with a large number of additional components, that considerably facilitated the design of microprocessor systems. However, the drawback of these processors rested on their low performance when executing numerical problems. The new versions of 8-bit microprocessors solve this difficulty by means of multiplication and division instructions as well as operations with 16-bit and 32-bit operands.

The first 16-bit microprocessor, Texas Instruments' TMS 9900 [1], appeared on the market in 1977, and was successfully followed by Intel 8086 [2], Zilog Z8000 [3] and Motorola MC68000 [4] over the period 1978 - 1980. 16-bit microprocessors appear to have a substantially higher performance than 8-bit processors, but their structure is also more complex. On the one hand, this allows the introduction of microprocessors in applications typical of minicomputers, whereas on the other hand the system design is more complex and leads to bigger and more expensive systems.

A trend towards microprocessors with a capacity that is higher than 16 bits emerges from the technological advancements in the production of semiconductor components. At present, 32-bit microprocessors are already available on the market; they will substitute the 16-bit digital computing devices that were built with conventional technology. Despite this development, low performance microprocessors will retain the application areas for which their capabilities are sufficient.

In this book, we will be only concerned with 16-bit microprocessors; in particular, the first chapter will provide some introductory clarification. Section 1.1 will deal with the representation of information, Section 1.2 with the structure and behavior of 16-bit microprocessor systems and Section 1.3 with machine programming and assembly language level.

1.1 Representation of Information

1.1.1 Information Units

In the case of digital systems, the information is represented in binary form. The smallest unit of information is the bit (binary digit). A bit can take on two values, that we will define 0 and 1. When implemented, they are represented, for instance, as two different voltages on a signal line or as two different magnetization states on an information carrier. Several bits are combined into bigger information units. Thus, a so-called half byte is composed of 4 bits and one byte consists of 8 bits. In the case of microprocessors, a 16-bit unit is called word, a 32-bit unit is a double word. In the representation of information units, we will enumerate the individual bits from right to left starting with zero (Figure 1.1). Accordingly, bit 0 will be defined as the Least Significant Bit (LSB) and the bit with the highest index as the Most Significant Bit (MSB).

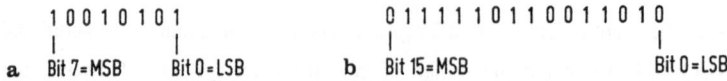

Fig. 1.1. Units of information. a) byte, b) word

1.1.2 Number Representation

In the decimal number system, the ten digits 0 through 9 are used for the representation of numbers; they are weighted by the 10th power of their position. Thus, the value of a number results from the sum of the weighted digits, for example:

$$205 = 2 \cdot 10^2 + 0 \cdot 10^1 + 5 \cdot 10^0$$

Binary Numbers. In the binary number system, only the two binary digits 0 and 1 are available for the representation of numbers, and they are weighted by the power of 2 of their position. As with decimal numbers, the value of a number results from the sum of the weighted digits. In the following example, in order to differentiate between number systems, the basis of a number is indicated by an index: .

$$11001101_2 = 1 \cdot 2^7 + 1 \cdot 2^6 + 1 \cdot 2^5 + 1 \cdot 2^4 + 1 \cdot 2^3 + 1 \cdot 2^2 + 1 \cdot 2^1 + 1 \cdot 2^0 = 205_{10}.$$

Number Conversion. The sum of the weighted digits also indicates the procedure for the conversion from binary to decimal numbers. Thus, the decimal value for the above example is 205. In order to convert a decimal number into a binary number, it has to be decomposed into its power of 2 components. A common procedure is to divide the decimal number by 2 and note the remainder; then the same procedure is to be repeated with the result until the result is zero. The remainder, which can have values 0 and 1, creates the binary number starting with the lowest bit (see also [6]). The above example can be broken up into:

```
205:2 = 102, remainder 1
102:2 =  51, remainder 0
 51:2 =  25, remainder 1
 25:2 =  12, remainder 1
 12:2 =   6, remainder 0
  6:2 =   3, remainder 0
  3:2 =   1, remainder 1
  1:2 =   0, remainder 1   →   11001101.
```

16-bit microprocessors perform operations with binary numbers in byte, word or often double word format, where binary numbers with a smaller number of digits than required are adapted to a larger format by means of so-called leading zeros. Since a unit of information in the representation is limited to n bits, the value of a number is restricted to the range between 0 and $2^n - 1$ in the case of binary numbers. If this range is exceeded in an arithmetic operation, the result is still within the range limits; its value, however, is not correct, and the microprocessor signals an arithmetic overflow by setting the Carry bit (C). Figure 1.2a illustrates the occurrence of arithmetic overflow with an example of 8-bit binary numbers on the number ring.

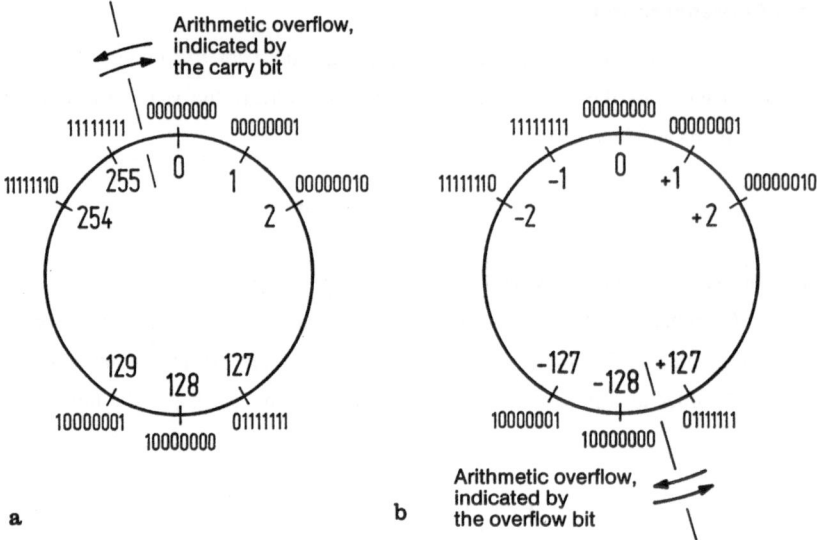

Fig. 1.2. Number ring. a) 8-bit binary, b) 8-bit two's complement

Negative Numbers. The most significant bit is used for the representation of the sign in order to distinguish between positive and negative numbers; in the case of positive numbers it is 0, for negative numbers it is 1. The values of the remaining $n-1$ bits are represented in binary code for positive numbers, whereas several representations are possible in the case of negative numbers: sign and magnitude numbers, one's complement numbers and two's complement numbers. Since 16-bit microprocessors are designed for the latter, we will only consider two's complement numbers in this book.

The sum of the positive and negative representation of a two's complement number of n digits adds to 2^n. The conversion from a positive to the corresponding negative number or viceversa (complementing) can be achieved through the bit complement of all n bits and the subsequent addition of 1; for example:

$$+67_{10} = 01000011_2 \qquad \begin{array}{l} \text{bit complement:} \\ \text{addition:} \\ \text{complement:} \end{array} \qquad \begin{array}{l} 10111100 \\ +\ 00000001 \\ 10111101_2 = -67_{10}. \end{array}$$

The value of a two's complement number results from the sum of the weighted digits, where the sign bit is considered a negative weight. For example:

$$10111101_2 = -1 \cdot 2^7 + 0 \cdot 2^6 + 1 \cdot 2^5 + 1 \cdot 2^4 + 1 \cdot 2^3 + 1 \cdot 2^2 + 0 \cdot 2^1 + 1 \cdot 2^0 = -67_{10}.$$

The range of values extends from -2^{n-1} to $+2^{n-1}-1$ in the case of two's complement numbers, where zero is represented as a positive number. An arithmetic overflow, resulting from an arithmetic operation for instance, leads to an (incorrect) number within the range limits (Figure 1.2b). This is indicated by the overflow bit V of the microprocessor.

BCD Numbers. Another possibility of representing numbers in binary form is offered by the digital encoding of decimal numbers in binary coded decimals (BCD). In this case, the single decimal digits are substituted by 4-digit binary numbers and lined up according to Table 1.1. For example:

$$205_{10} = 0010\ 0000\ 0101_{BCD}.$$

Table 1.1. BCD code

Decimal code	BCD code
0	0 0 0 0
1	0 0 0 1
2	0 0 1 0
3	0 0 1 1
4	0 1 0 0
5	0 1 0 1
6	0 1 1 0
7	0 1 1 1
8	1 0 0 0
9	1 0 0 1

Table 1.2. ASCII code (USASCII [27])

Bit position

7 6 5 4 3 2 1	0 0 0	0 0 1	0 1 0	0 1 1	1 0 0	1 0 1	1 1 0	1 1 1
0 0 0 0	NUL	DLE	SP	0	@*	P	'**	p
0 0 0 1	SOH	DC1	!	1	A	Q	a	q
0 0 1 0	STX	DC2	"*	2	B	R	b	r
0 0 1 1	ETX	DC3	#*	3	C	S	c	s
0 1 0 0	EOT	DC4	$	4	D	T	d	t
0 1 0 1	ENQ	NAK	%	5	E	U	e	u
0 1 1 0	ACK	SYN	&	6	F	V	f	v
0 1 1 1	BEL	ETB	'*	7	G	W	g	w
1 0 0 0	BS	CAN	(	8	H	X	h	x
1 0 0 1	HT	EM	)	9	I	Y	i	y
1 0 1 0	LF	SUB	*	:	J	Z	j	z
1 0 1 1	VT	ESC	+	;	K	[*	k	{*
1 1 0 0	FF	FS	,*	<	L	*	l	|*
1 1 0 1	CR	GS	−	=	M	]*	m	}*
1 1 1 0	SO	RS	.	>	N	^*	n	~*
1 1 1 1	SI	US	/	?	O	_	o	DEL

1.1.3 Symbol Representation

The ASCII code (American Standard Code of Information Interchange) is most common means of representing symbols such as letters, digits and special symbols of an alphabet in microprocessor systems. Each symbol is represented by a 7-bit code (Table 1.2). If the code for a symbol is completed with an eighth bit, for example a zero at the beginning or an extra bit for code check, the symbol becomes as long as a byte.

1.1.4 Hexadecimal and Octal Representation

Reading binary coded information, like numbers, symbols or other bit combinations, is usually difficult for humans and, because of multiple digit numbers, hard to grasp. For this reason, binary information is usually represented in a condensed form when outside a microprocessor system, e.g.

on a printer output. Most of the time, we will adopt the hexadecimal representation, where each bit combination is given as a number in the basis 16 number system. The decimal digits 0 through 9 and the letters A through F are used as hexadecimal digits with values 0 through 15. When the bit combination is to be translated into hexadecimal representation, bits are divided from right to left in a sequence of 4-bit units, and each unit is associated with the hexadecimal digit that corresponds to the 4-bit binary number. For example:

1100 1010 1111 0101 = CAF5

Table 1.3 shows the correspondence of hexadecimal digits to 4-bit binary numbers.

Table 1.3. Hexadecimal code

4-bit binary code	Hexadecimal code
0 0 0 0	0
0 0 0 1	1
0 0 1 0	2
0 0 1 1	3
0 1 0 0	4
0 1 0 1	5
0 1 1 0	6
0 1 1 1	7
1 0 0 0	8
1 0 0 1	9
1 0 1 0	A
1 0 1 1	B
1 1 0 0	C
1 1 0 1	D
1 1 1 0	E
1 1 1 1	F

Another common compact representation is the octal code. In this case, each bit combination is represented by a digit in the basis 8 number system. The decimal digits 0 through 7 are used for the representation of digits, and 3-bit units are combined. For example:

1 100 101 011 110 101 = 145365.

For an in-depth study of information representations see for example [5-7].

1.2 Introduction to the Hardware Structure

1.2.1 Hardware Components of a Microprocessor System

The basic structure of a microprocessor system consists of three hardware components: the actual microprocessor for the processing of mathematical quantities (operands, results) controlled by a program, the main memory (working memory) for the storage of mathematical quantities and of the program, and the I/O unit for the input and output of data (programs and mathematical quantities) (Figure 1.3).

The microprocessor itself includes a control unit and a data processing unit. The control unit manages the microprocessor as well as the main memory and the I/O unit. It reads instructions from the main memory, interprets them and controls their execution. The operands that have to be processed are read from the main memory or by means of an I/O unit into the data processing unit. The results are made available to the main memory or to an I/O unit. Thus, the data processing unit plays the role of a translator between operands and results by executing logical and arithmetic operations on the operands.

The main memory includes a large number of single memory cells organized in byte or word format; it is useful to think of these cells as arranged in sequential order. For selecting a given cell, memory locations are numbered; i.e., each memory location can be unequivocally identified by a number. This number is called address. Addresses as well can be represented as 0/1 combinations; with 16 bits one can, for example, encode a maximum of $2^{16} = 65536 = 64$ K addresses. The limits of the available address space of the main memory, and therefore its memory cell capacity, are thus indicated by the address length (K stands for "one thousand": 1 K $= 2^{10} = 1024$).

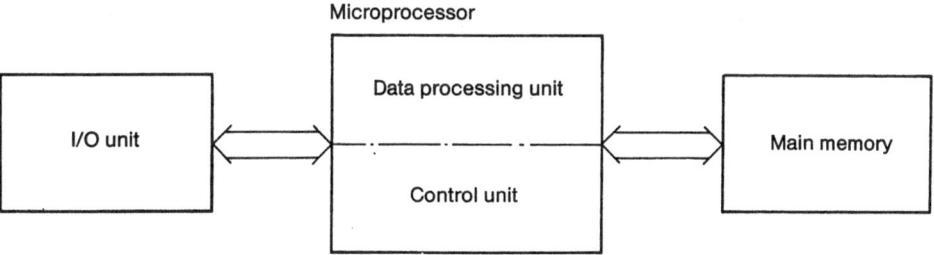

Fig. 1.3. Components of a microprocessor system

Address

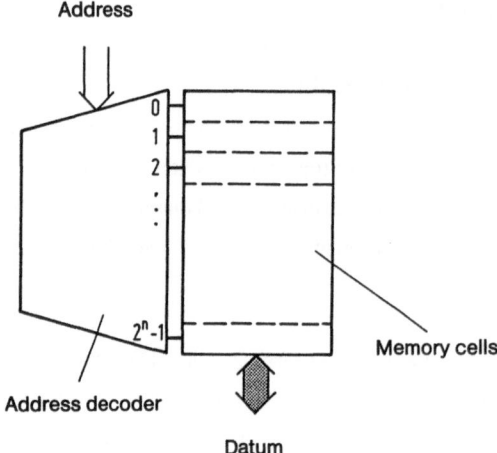

0
1
2
:
:
2^n-1

Memory cells

Address decoder

Datum

Fig. 1.4. Random access memory (RAM)

Figure 1.4 introduces the symbolic representation of a memory. The rectangular field defines the writeable and readable memory cells, and the trapezoid stands for the address decoder, which selects just one memory cell when an address is applied. These memories, whose cells can be all accessed in the same amount of time, are also called Random Access Memories (RAM's).

The microprocessor itself only possesses very few memory cells when compared to the main memory. Some of these cells are designated to particular purposes within the processor and are not directly available for machine and assembly programming. Other processor memory cells can be accessed like main memory cells. Such single memory cells, which can also be found in other system components, are often called registers; several registers linked together to form a small memory are called register files. Although registers and memory cells do not differ in their functionality, we would like to keep the conceptual distinction between registers as single memory cells and big memories.

The I/O unit represents the interface between the microprocessor system and the peripherals (for example an I/O device). It is thus called interface unit or just interface. Its simplest form includes an addressable register for the temporary storage of the data to be transported. More complex interfaces take over control functions for the data transmission. For example, they allow the synchronization between an often much slower peripheral device and the fast working microprocessor hardware.

1.2.2 Basic System Structure

In Figure 1.3 there are connection paths, that are independent from each other and connect the single components of a microprocessor system; these paths generally indicate the transfer of information. In reality, we distinguish between three types of information for which separate connection paths are usually implemented:

1. data, which includes instructions, operands and results;

2. addresses for the selection of memory cells and registers; and

3. signals for the control of the information exchange between the individual components.

The cost for the connecting paths would greatly increase with the number of components in a situation similar to what portrayed in Figure 1.3. Thus, data, address and signal control paths are built only once and are made available to all components for information transmission. These connecting paths are also called buses, or respectively data bus, address bus and control bus. If combined they are called system bus. A bus is a collection of functionally related signal lines that connect at least two components of a digital system for the exchange of information. These components can be single registers, or complete functional units, such as microprocessors, memories and I/O units.

Figure 1.5 shows a bus-oriented microprocessor system. The data bus is represented by a shaded double line, the address bus by a clear double line. The control bus is indicated by two single thick lines, where each line represents several control circuits. In the future we will retain this convention and we will omit additional characterization of buses in the figures.

Unlike Figure 1.3, Figure 1.5 presents several memory units and several I/O units, which indicate the modularity of a bus-oriented microprocessor system. In this rather simple, but basic system

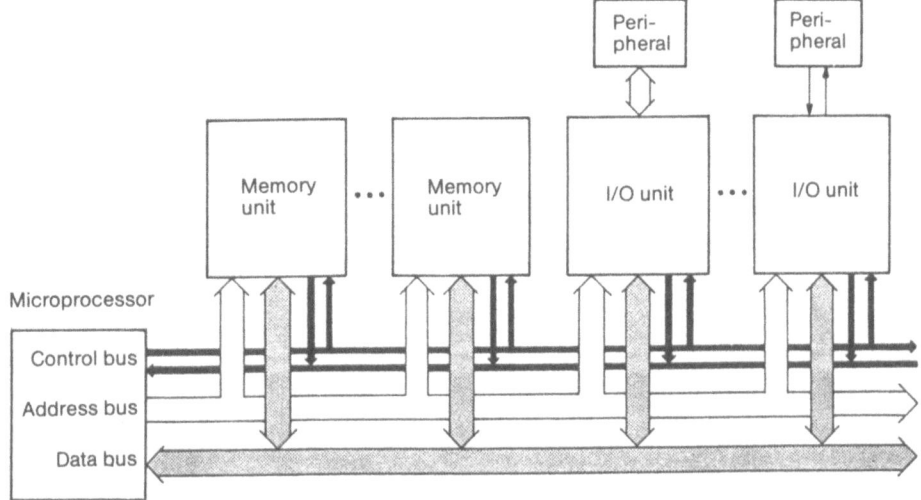

Fig. 1.5. Bus-oriented microprocessor system

configuration, the microprocessor is the only active component, i.e. it is the only device that can control the bus system. The memory and I/O units behave passively. Only two of the system components (a sender and a receiver) are simultaneously connected to the common data bus, so as to avoid conflicts during data transfer.

As shown in Figure 1.5, the data bus allows data transfers in both directions; it can be switched in the direction of the transfer. Such a bus is known as a bidirectional bus. On the contrary, the address bus allows transfers only in one direction; such a bus is called unidirectional. Most of the signal lines of the control bus are unidirectional, some of them are bidirectional. According to their function, the unidirectional control lines permit the signal flow to either go towards or away from the microprocessor.

The advantages of a bus-oriented microprocessor system lie in the low cost and easy extensibility of the general purpose connection paths. The single components of the microprocessor system will be briefly discussed below.

1.2.3 The Microprocessor

The behavior of a microprocessor system is specified by a sequence of instructions stored as a program in the main memory and processed by the microprocessor. The possible processor operations are determined by its instruction set. The most important instructions are those for data transfer, for arithmetic and logical operations, and instructions for so-called program branches.

Instruction Formats. For a dyadic operation that combines two operands and achieves one result, we need four specifications:

    1. Type of operation (op code),

    2. Address of the first operand (first source address),

    3. Address of the second operand (second source address),

    4. Address of the results (destination address).

If these four specifications are combined in one instruction, we have a three-address instruction format corresponding to Figure 1.6.

To quote an example, 8-bits for the op code and 16 bits for each address result·in a 56-bit long instruction. In relation to a memory word length of 16 bits, a similar instruction would use four memory cells when storing a program, where 8 bits would go unused in one cell.

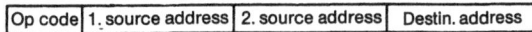

Fig. 1.6. Format of a three-address instruction

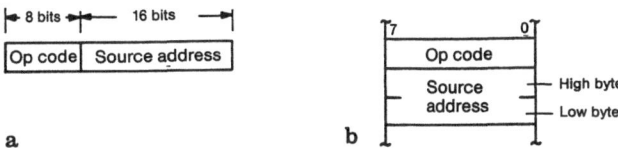

a   b

Fig. 1.7. One-address instruction of an 8-bit microprocessor:
a) general purpose format, b) byte-oriented memory representation

In order to shorten the size of an instruction, the number of addresses in the instruction, for instance, can be reduced. Moreover, there are two possibilities, implicit and hidden addressing, that can be often used in combination and can be found in both 8-bit and 16-bit microprocessors.

One-Address Instructions. 8-bit microprocessors are equipped with a special register, the accumulator, that is addressed as the source of one of the two operands whenever there is a dyadic operation. At the same time, this register is used as the destination for the result, so that the operand that was originally stored in the accumulator is lost. The address of the accumulator is not given explicitly in the instruction, but it is implicitly contained in the op code (implicit addressing); in addition, two addresses coincide thanks to the double function of the accumulator (hidden addressing). Besides the op code, the source address of the second operand is also indicated in the instruction as a memory address. Special load and store instructions allow the operand transfer between the accumulator and other registers or memory cells. Figure 1.7a shows such a one-address instruction format for an 8-bit microprocessor. In a byte-organized memory typical of an 8-bit microprocessor, this instruction uses three consecutive memory cells (Figure 1.7b).

One of the drawbacks of one-address instructions, when carrying out a two-operand operation, is that they need three instructions altogether:

1. load the accumulator with the content of a memory cell (first operand),

2. combine the content of the accumulator with the content of a memory cell (second operand),

3. store the content of the accumulator (result) in a memory cell.

Two-Address Instructions. Instead of the typical one-address instruction accumulator, 16-bit microprocessors have a set of 8 or 16 general purpose processor registers. Each one of them can, among other things, assume the function of the accumulator. Moreover, a register address is

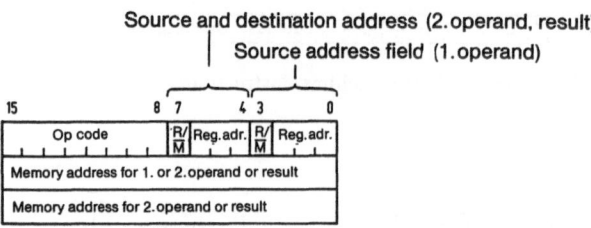

Fig. 1.8. Two-address instruction format of a 16-bit microprocessor

needed in the instruction for the selection of one register. This should require less bits than are needed by a memory address, 3 bits in the case of 8 registers. Since the registers are generally more accessible this way, they are also called general purpose registers, and the register file is called general purpose register set.

We will base the following observations on a rather simple version of a microprocessor with 8 general purpose registers. Addresses are explicitly indicated, although source and destination share one address. Thus, we have an instruction format with two explicit address fields (two-address instruction), that can select the general purpose register set (processor internal addresses), the main memory or other peripheral units (processor external addresses) in all possible combinations (Figure 1.8).

An instruction contains two address fields, and one bit $(R/\overline{M})$ decides if the address is processor internal $(R/\overline{M} = 1)$ or processor external $(R/\overline{M}=0)$. The processor internal 3-bit register addresses and the $R/\overline{M}$ bits are directly stored in the first instruction word. The processor external 16-bit addresses are placed in the memory cells that follow the first instruction word. Hence the instructions consist of one, two or three words. With these we can create the following instruction types, that are relative to the source and destination specifications:

1. register-to-register instructions,

2. register-to-memory instructions,

3. memory-to-register instructions,

4. memory-to-memory instructions.

If all the combinations of processor internal and external addresses are possible for source and destination address specifications, the structure of the instruction is also called symmetric. Symmetric instructions facilitate the programming of non-commutative operations, such as subtraction.

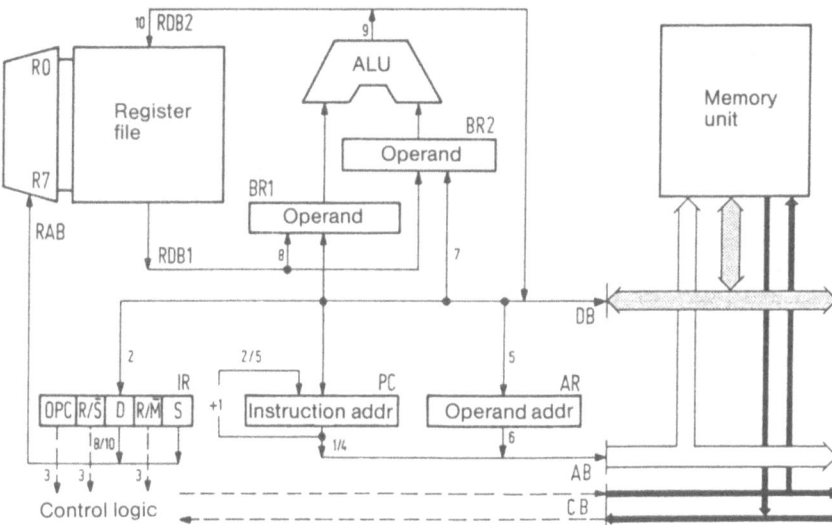

Fig. 1.9. Register structure of a microprocessor (simplified); the numbers refer to Fig. 1.12

Processor Structure. Until now, our considerations were concentrated more on the basic organization, the addressing and the instruction structure of microprocessors. In the following, we will discuss the microprocessor's behavior in detail. To this purpose we need a more precise description of the processor structure, such as depicted in Figure 1.9.

As already mentioned, a microprocessor can be divided into two functional units, the data processing unit and the control unit. The data processing unit consists of the register file and the Arithmetic and Logical Unit (ALU) with the two buffer registers BR1 and BR2. The ALU combines the two 16-bit operands, which are loaded in the buffer register at the beginning of the instruction processing, and generates the result. The register file serves for the temporary storage of operands and results. This allows a quicker operand access by the microprocessor than what would be possible with an external memory.

The control unit includes the Program Counter (PC), which contains the 16-bit address of the next instruction word, the Instruction Register (IR) for the storage of the first 16-bit instruction word, and the Address Register (AR) for the storage of the 16-bit operand addresses that follow the first word of an instruction. The control unit also includes the control logic for the decoding of the instruction op code and for the control of the instruction's execution. The control unit is in charge of reading an instruction, reading the operands, executing the instructions as·well as storing the results. The control logic produces signals for the control of the ALU and of the internal data, address and control signal paths as well as signals for the control of the functional units connected

14

to the external system bus. In addition, it processes control signals from external units, for example the signal that acknowledges a data transfer.

There are several internal buses that connect the register file, the single registers, the ALU and the external system bus. The 16-bit Data Bus (DB), which is connected to the external data bus, supplies the instruction register and the address register with instruction words and transfers the operands between the ALU and the external memories. The addressing of the external memories takes place through the 16-bit Address Bus (AB), that is connected with the external address bus. The 3-bit Register Address Bus (RAB) selects the register file, which in turn is directly connected. by means of the two 16-bit register data buses RDB1 and RDB2, with the ALU or its buffer registers. The operand transfer between the register file and the external data bus occurs through the ALU, which can also assume the role of a bus. In Figure 1.9 the internal Control Bus (CB) is indicated by a broken line and is connected with the external control bus.

Instruction Cycle. The processing of instructions occurs in a repetitive procedure that is called instruction cycle. Each processing step of the instruction cycle is determined by the control unit; these steps are called microinstructions and can include one or more micro-operations. The frequency of the microinstruction steps is controlled by a frequency generator and is called machine clock frequency. The processing that occurs within one period is called machine cycle, and the time for a machine cycle is called machine cycle time. The typical machine cycle times for the present microprocessors are between 1 μs (1 MHz frequency) and 62,5 ns (16 MHz frequency). For a conceptual distinction between the microinstructions that are inaccessible to the programmer of a microprocessor and those that are accessible, the latter are called machine instructions and the instruction cycle is sometimes called machine instruction cycle. Figure 1.10 roughly illustrates an instruction cycle for a two-operand operation.

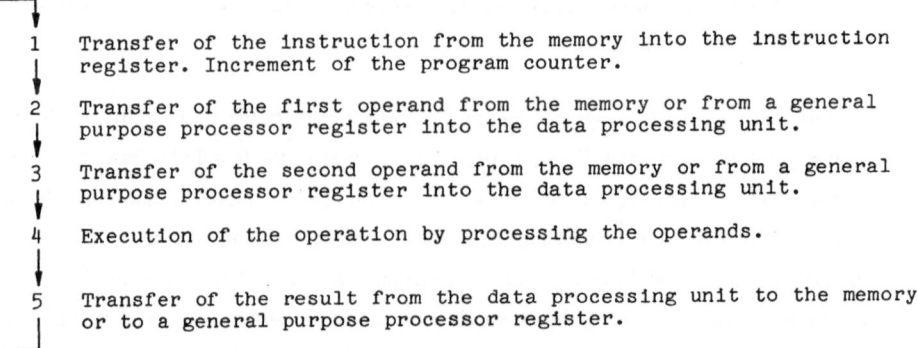

1 Transfer of the instruction from the memory into the instruction
   register. Increment of the program counter.

2 Transfer of the first operand from the memory or from a general
   purpose processor register into the data processing unit.

3 Transfer of the second operand from the memory or from a general
   purpose processor register into the data processing unit.

4 Execution of the operation by processing the operands.

5 Transfer of the result from the data processing unit to the memory
   or to a general purpose processor register.

Fig. 1.10. Instruction cycle (machine instruction cycle)

```
symbolic              binary                hexadecimal

SUB    R5,MADR        0000001011010000      02D0
                      0000000000010000      0010
```

Fig. 1.11. Different ways to write a subtract instruction

The instruction cycle is explained in detail by using a memory-to-register instruction as an example: the subtract instruction SUB R5, MADR. According to the symbolic naming of instructions, we will use SUB for the op code and the two symbolic addresses R5 and MADR for the general purpose register 5 and the memory cell. The instruction has the following effect: The content of the memory cell MADR will be subtracted from the content of the general purpose register 5, and the result will be stored in register 5. Thus, the content of the cell MADR remains unchanged, and the original content of register 5 is substituted by the result.

In Figure 1.11, the subtract instruction is given in symbolic, in binary and in hexadecimal representation. The decimal value 16 was adopted for the symbolic address MADR, and the bit configuration 00000010 as binary code for SUB. - The symbolic denomination is easily understandable to man, whereas the binary denomination corresponds to the representation in the memory and can be unequivocally interpreted by the microprocessor. The hexadecimal alternative is easier to understand than the binary representation, and it saves writing effort when instructions and operands are represented in the machine internal way.

Figure 1.12 introduces the instruction cycle of the subtract instruction arranged according to each single machine cycle and its micro-operations. Transfer operations are defined by the symbol →; for the definition of source and destination we used the acronyms in Figure 1.9, where the cycle numbers that correspond to machine cycles are given in order to clarify the behavior of the processor.

In Figure 1.12 we assume that the access to an external memory cell needs two machine cycles. On the other hand, the access to the register file only needs one machine cycle. A simple, one-step ALU operation like a subtraction also needs one machine cycle. This leads to the conclusion that a memory-to-register subtract instruction uses a total execution time of 10 machine cycles, whereas the register-to-register instruction needs 7, and the memory-to-memory instruction uses 13.

The execution time of an instruction does not only depend on the operand addressing, the type of operation is also important. The execution time increases when instructions require several processing steps in the ALU; this is the case for the multiply instruction for instance.

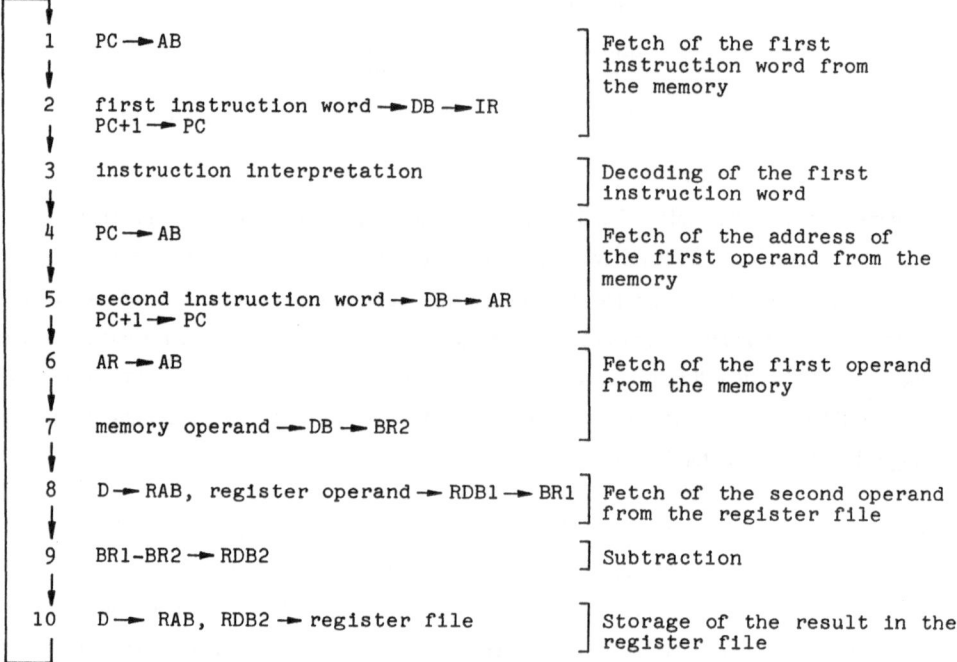

1	PC → AB	Fetch of the first instruction word from the memory
2	first instruction word → DB → IR PC+1 → PC	
3	instruction interpretation	Decoding of the first instruction word
4	PC → AB	Fetch of the address of the first operand from the memory
5	second instruction word → DB → AR PC+1 → PC	
6	AR → AB	Fetch of the first operand from the memory
7	memory operand → DB → BR2	
8	D → RAB, register operand → RDB1 → BR1	Fetch of the second operand from the register file
9	BR1–BR2 → RDB2	Subtraction
10	D → RAB, RDB2 → register file	Storage of the result in the register file

Fig. 1.12. Instruction cycle of the subtract instruction as memory-to-register instruction (for abbreviations see Fig. 1.9)

1.2.4 The Memory

Random access semiconductor memories are often used in microprocessor systems as data and program memories (main memories). In large systems, mass memories (secondary memories) are used as well; their access is sequential and is performed in blocks of data bytes. These memories are for example magnetic tape memories (for instance cassette units), floppy disks and magnetic disk memories (for instance Winchester disks). In the following we would like to focus on the different types of semiconductor memories that can be roughly divided in Random Access Memories (RAM's or read/write memories) and Read Only Memories (ROM's).

Random Access Memories. Random access memories (RAMs) can both be written and read by the microprocessor. The information is stored, depending on the kind of the components, in 1-bit, 4-bit or 8-bit memory cells that can be addressed through a decoding unit (Figure 1.13a). A control logic starts the component activity by means of a chip select line, and sets the data transfer direction through a read/write line. A bidirectional Data Bus Driver (DBD), that can be switched in read or write direction by the control logic, connects the data signals with the memory components.

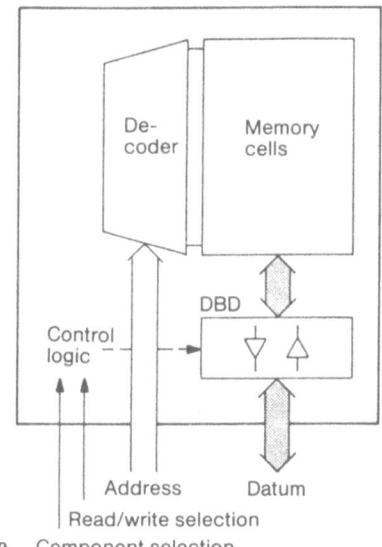 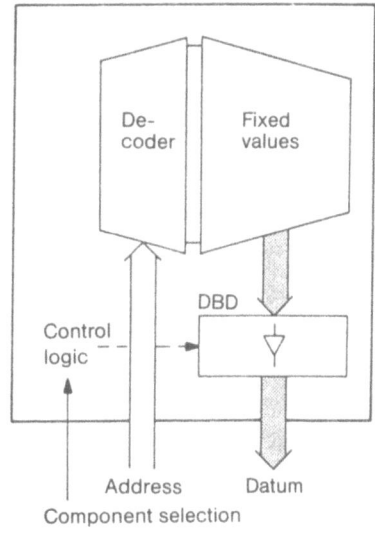

Fig. 1.13. Memory components. a) read/write memory RAM, b) read only memory ROM

There are two ways of storing information in random access memories. In one case, the individual bits are stored in flip flops (static RAM's). Information is stored in the switching state of two transistors, where at different times one is conducting and the other one is open. In the second case (dynamic RAM's) each bit is stored in a capacitor as electric charge (energy memory). Since charge compensations occur within the memory elements, the charge has to be constantly refreshed. In order to achieve this, an additional memory control is necessary in microprocessor systems (refresh unit). When compared to static RAM's, dynamic random access memories have the advantage of possessing a larger storage capacity per memory component (at present 64 K bits for static RAM's and 256 K bits for dynamic RAM's).

Read Only Memories. The information stored in Read Only Memories (ROM's) can be read by the microprocessor, but it cannot be altered. Accordingly, the memory cells (see Figure 1.13b) are fixed values and the data bus driver is a unidirectional amplifier. Furthermore, the read/write line is omitted. Random addressing is implemented by means of a decoder, like in RAM's.

Information is stored in read only memories before the system is started, this is called ROM programming. There are several kinds of ROM programming. In the case of mask-programmable ROM's, the information is stored when the components are fabricated. A mask containing the structure of the binary information is used. Once the information is entered, it cannot be altered any more.

In the case of Programmable ROM's (PROM's) information can be stored by the user with special programming devices. The memory cells are programmable and can be selected by specifying an address. Depending on the bits in the data word, voltage spikes destroy (e.g. fuse) or preserve the links in the memory cells. Another possibility are Erasable Programmable ROM's (EPROM's), which can also be programmed by the user. In this case, the information is stored as electric charge. These charges are erasable at any time by ultra-violet light radiation or by an erasing voltage (Electrically Alterable ROM's, EAROM's). Then, the memory can be programmed again.

ROM's are used for the storage of permanent information (programs, constants), because of their read-only property. On the contrary, RAM's are suited for many applications and are mainly used for the storage of changeable data (variables). In case of power loss, the ROM contents are saved, whereas the RAM contents are lost. An additional power supply against power loss, for instance batteries, is required for the retention of the RAM contents.

1.2.5 I/O Unit

I/O units, with their data buffers, interface the system bus with the peripheral devices, e.g. I/O devices and secondary memories. Apart from their task as data buffer, they also perform control functions for the synchronization of data transfer. In addition, they are used for the exchange of control and status information between the microprocessor and, for example, an industrial process that has to be controlled.

Different operating modes, that can be defined by means of a control word in a control register, are thus possible for an interface component. Its operating state is indicated in a status register. All registers, i.e. data registers, control registers and status registers, can be addressed, written and read as memory cells. This either happens by means of regular memory instructions or through special I/O instructions.

Data transfer between the microprocessor and an interface module is parallel words of 8 or 16 bits, i.e. each data bit has its own system bus data line. Data transmission between the interface module and the peripheral is carried out either bit parallel or bit serial depending on the peripheral. The necessary different synchronization and transmission alternatives are taken into account by means of several interface modules. This choice greatly affects the complexity of a microprocessor system.

The structure and functionality of 16-bit microprocessors are dealt with in detail in Chapter 2, their programming is discussed in Chapter 3, and the connection and management of the main memory, as well as the different I/O units, are described in Chapters 4 through 6. For an in-depth examination of the electrotechnical and logical construction of processors and semiconductor memories, see for instance [8,9].

1.3 Introduction to Assembly Language Programming

1.3.1 Program Representation

The applications of a microprocessor system are defined to a certain extent by its hardware structure, although its function is first defined by the program that it will execute. In the following, we will consider the representation of programs in both external form, that is understandable to man, and machine internal form, that the microprocessor is able to process. To this purpose we will start with a simple task definition and will determine a set of machine instructions that will suffice for the execution of the task.

Program Example. A pulse generator, that sends pulses to a peripheral unit at constant time intervals, is to be built with a microprocessor system. A 16-bit data register is used as I/O device. At the beginning of the program execution, a number, that determines the period length t of the pulse sequence, is made available by the peripheral in this data register (Figure 1.14). After reading the number, the microprocessor first writes a zero in the same register; then, at each pulse interval, it writes a one lasting for the duration of an instruction. The content of the register's bit 0 forms the pulse signal for the peripheral. We give the symbolic address EAREG to the data register and attribute the absolute address $32768 = 2^{15}$ to it.

Figure 1.15 shows the flow chart of the behavior of a program for the solution of this task. Firstly, the time constant t is read from the data register EAREG and is placed in a main memory cell TIMEC; then, the data register is initialized with the value 0 for the following pulse generation (bit $0 = 0$). Pulses are created by repeatedly transferring values 1 and 0 to the data register, which stores the value that was last transferred until it is overwritten by the next transfer. Both values will be

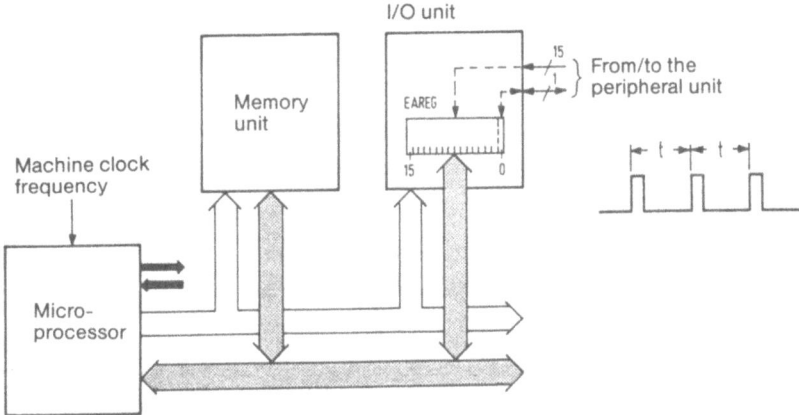

Fig. 1.14. Building a pulse generator with a microprocessor

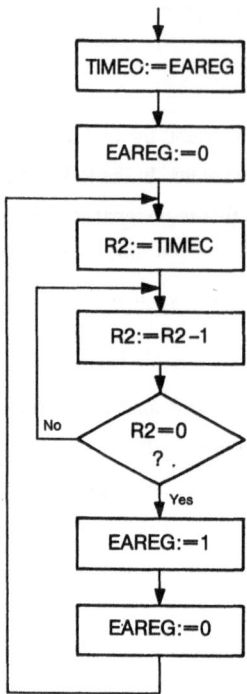

Fig. 1.15. Flow chart for pulse generator

available as constant operands in the memory cells ZERO and ONE. In order to repeatedly transfer these values, the corresponding program portion will be repeated; this is usually called program loop. This loop contains another internal program loop, which is run for as long as indicated by the value of the Time Constant (TIMEC). This means that the time interval t between two pulses is defined by the processing times of the single instructions and the number of loop executions of the internal loop. The instructions' processing times are determined by the number of machine cycles per instruction and by the machine cycle time of the microprocessor.

Symbolic Program Representation. The following list shows a portion of a microprocessor instruction set with the instructions that are needed for the solution of our task. The instructions are given in a symbolic way, as was already done for the subtract instruction, and their functions are briefly described.

MOVE DADR,SADR   Move instruction: transfers the content of the Source Address (SADR) to the Destination Address (DADR).

SUB DADR,SADR   Subtract instruction: subtracts the content of the source address from the content of the destination address and writes the result at the destination address.

CMP ADR1,ADR2   Compare instruction: subtracts the content of ADR2 from the content of ADR1 and stores the information indicating whether the result is bigger, smaller or equal to zero, in a special state register of the processor.

BNE JMPADR   Branch instruction (branch if not equal zero): loads the program counter with the Jump Address (JMPADR) if the state register shows that the state is not equal to zero; otherwise, the next instruction in the program is executed.

JMP JMPADR   Jump instruction: loads the program counter with the Jump Address (JMPADR).

Figure 1.16 shows the machine external representation of the symbolic program corresponding to the flow diagram in Figure 1.15. The internal program loop is closed with the Branch if Not Equal zero instruction (BNE), and the external program loop is closed with the Jump instruction (JMP). The external loop cannot be exited because of the JMP instruction and thus constitutes an infinite loop. The symbolic addresses used in the jump instruction indicate the instructions in the program representing the jump destinations on the left side. The same way, the symbols ZERO, ONE and TIMEC label the constant operands 0 and 1, that are defined at the end of the program, and the storage place for the time constant. The address mappings that are necessary for transferring the program to the internal code can be produced with these labels. As is the case for the symbolic representation, the data area is adjacent to the program area during the subsequent loading of the program in the main memory.

As an example of how to compute the Time Constant (TIMEC), which determines the number of internal loop cycles, we assume a pulse interval of $t=1$ s and a machine cycle time of 1 μs. The number of cycles per instruction shown in Figure 1.16 indicates a running time of 21 machine cycles, i.e. 21 μs, for the internal program loop. This loop will be executed as many times as required by the value of TIMEC, i.e. $21 \cdot$ TIMEC μs. The external loop adds 35 additional machine

```
                symbolic program              number of cycles
                                              per instruction

             MOVE   TIMEC,EAREG                     11
             MOVE   EAREG,ZERO                      11
             MOVE   R1,ZERO                          8
      LABEL1 MOVE   R2,TIMEC                          8
      LABEL2 SUB    R2,ONE                           10
             CMP    R2,R1                             6
             BNE    LABEL2                            5
             MOVE   EAREG,ONE                        11
             MOVE   EAREG,ZERO                       11
             JMP    LABEL1                            5
      TIMEC  ...
      ZERO   0
      ONE    1
```

Fig. 1.16. Pulse generator program in symbolic representation

cycles, i.e. 35 μs, are added. The pulse interval t can thus be calculated as $t = 21 \cdot \text{TIMEC} + 35 \ \mu s$. Therefore, the TIMEC value and the number of internal loop cycles are given by $\text{TIMEC} = (t - 35)/21 \approx 47617$.

Machine Code Representation. Taking our instruction formats as a basis, we want to translate the symbolic program into its machine internal form, the machine code. The machine code is the representation of the program and its data in the main memory, which can be directly interpreted by the microprocessor. Therefore, the mnemonic and symbolic specifications have to be substituted by their equivalent binary representations.

The conversion of the mnemonic op code into machine op code (binary code) is fixed and is the basis for our microprocessor's op code assignment table in Table 1.4. The substitution of the symbolic memory addresses with numerical addresses depends on the position of the program and of its data in the main memory. The numerical addresses of the general purpose and I/O unit data registers cannot be determined in a similar way. For this reason, we had previously bound the symbol Ri to register i. Similarly, we bound the symbol EAREG to address 32768, which is defined by the address decoding of the I/O unit. An assumption for our example is that the program will be in main memory starting from cell 0 and we will therefore use the address mapping in Table 1.5 as a symbol table. The different instruction lengths (one-word, two-word, three-word instructions) are taken into account when defining the values of the symbolic addresses.

Table 1.4. Op code assignment table

mnemonical op code	binary code
MOVE	00000001
SUB	00000010
CMP	00100001
BNE	00001100
JMP	00000101

Table 1.5. Symbol table for the pulse generator program

symbol	numerical address		
	binary	decimal	hexadec.
LABEL1	0000000000001000	8	0008
LABEL2	0000000000001010	10	000A
TIMEC	0000000000010111	23	0017
ZERO	0000000000011000	24	0018
ONE	0000000000011001	25	0019
EAREG	1000000000000000	32768	8000

```
          address              machine code           symbol
         /      \           /            \              |
     dec.   binary    binary            hexadec.
        0   00000    0000000100000000    0100    MOVE
        1   00001    1000000000000000    8000    EAREG
        2   00010    0000000000010111    0017    TIMEC
        3   00011    0000000100000000    0100    MOVE
        4   00100    0000000000011000    0018    ZERO
        5   00101    1000000000000000    8000    EAREG
        6   00110    0000000110010000    0190    MOVE
        7   00111    0000000000011000    0018    ZERO
        8   01000    0000000110100000    01A0    MOVE
        9   01001    0000000000010111    0017    TIMEC
       10   01010    0000001010100000    02A0    SUB
       11   01011    0000000000011001    0019    ONE
       12   01100    0010000110101001    21A9    CMP
       13   01101    0000110000000000    0C00    BNE
       14   01110    0000000000001010    000A    LABEL2
       15   01111    0000000100000000    0100    MOVE
       16   10000    0000000000011001    0019    ONE
       17   10001    1000000000000000    8000    EAREG
       18   10010    0000000100000000    0100    MOVE
       19   10011    0000000000011000    0018    ZERO
       20   10100    1000000000000000    8000    EAREG
       21   10101    0000010100000000    0500    JMP
       22   10110    0000000000001000    0008    LABEL1
       23   10111    ----------------    ----
       24   11000    0000000000000000    0000
       25   11001    0000000000000001    0001
```

Fig. 1.17. Pulse generator program in machine code representation

Finally we will determine the two R/$\overline{M}$ bits for each instruction, whether the address definitions, that are listed on the right of the op code, are register addresses (R/$\overline{M}$=1) or memory addresses (R/$\overline{M}$=0). Thus, all address symbols, that do not concern the register memory, are considered memory symbols (or better: symbols for a processor external data access).

Figure 1.17 shows the final machine code together with the memory addresses of the single machine code words, where the binary number representation of the memory addresses was reduced from 16 to 5 bits. The program code uses cells 0 through 22 and the data area cells 23 through 25. Both operands ZERO and ONE are coded as binary numbers; the content of the memory word TIMEC is not yet defined before the execution of the program, which is indicated by the broken line. The mnemonic or the processor external address symbol is given for each instruction word as an orientation aid.

1.3.2 Program Translation (Assembling)

A comparison of the two program representations in Figures 1.16 and 1.17 shows that the symbolic representation is more understandable to humans than the machine code representation, which the microprocessor needs for interpretation. Thus, a program is first written in symbolic form; it is then translated into machine code and stored in main memory. As shown above, the translation can be

24

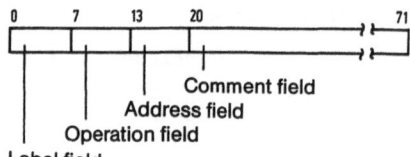

Fig. 1.18. Format of a program statement

done by hand. The mapping table and the memory address of the first machine instruction are needed to generate the symbol table with the address mappings. In the case of large programs, manual translation is very time consuming and above all subject to errors. Moreover, small changes in the assembly program can cause big changes in the machine code. For example, when an instruction is either erased or inserted, all labels referring to memory cells following that instruction have to be changed.

Since the translation process follows specific rules, it can be executed by the microprocessor itself. Thus, the symbolic language has to be defined unambiguously, and a program is needed, that transforms the symbolic program to be translated (input data) into machine code (output data). Such a translation program is called assembler. The rules for symbolic programming result from the definition of an assembly language. Programs, that are written in assembly language, are called assembler programs.

Assembly Language. The assembly language determines the format of a program statement. A statement is divided into fields with specific functions. Depending on the assembly language, the field positions within a statement are either fixed or variable. Figure 1.18 shows a fixed format, in which each field begins in a fixed position. In the case of variable formats, the field position has to be indicated by a specific character, for instance a space.

The label field is used for the symbolic addressing of a program statement, and it may contain a symbol. The operation field contains the mnemonical op code, the address field specifies one or more symbolic addresses divided by commas. The comment field is used for commenting the corresponding program statement. Program statements may consist of comments only; if so, they have to be marked by a special character, for instance '*'. Comments are disregarded during the program translation and do not influence the generation of the machine code.

The assembly language provides the alphabet that can be used to formulate a program statement (capital letters, digits, special characters). Furthermore, it determines which character strings are allowed for the definition of symbolic addresses. For instance, the first character of a symbolic address has to be a letter, it cannot exceed six characters and cannot contain special characters.

Furthermore, the assembly language defines the mnemonical op codes and special symbolic addresses, like R0 through R7 for the register file.

In assembly languages, one symbolic instruction always corresponds to one machine code instruction (1-to-1 translation), which is not the case in higher level programming languages. Thus, an assembly language program is closer to the processor hardware than a FORTRAN or ALGOL program.

Pseudo-Ops. In addition to instructions, our program example also includes the definition of operands which are assigned to memory cells. These operands can even be given a value before the beginning of the execution. For these or similar situations, the assembly language contains pseudo-ops (pseudo instructions) that can be inserted in the symbolic program as program statements. Contrary to machine instructions, pseudo-ops do not always generate binary code; they are used to control the translation process and to produce constants.

The most important pseudo-ops are listed below. As was the case for the program statements mentioned above, they also have to be in a fixed format and accordingly consist of a mnemonical code and an address part. The use of label fields is either optional, which is indicated by a square parenthesis, or required, as is the case of EQU op.

[Symbol] ORG c   Origin of program or data: number c indicates the start address of the following program section or data area; a symbol in the label field is regarded as a symbolic start address.

   END   End of program: it indicates to the assembler where the end of the program is that has to be assembled.

[Symbol] DS c   Define storage: number c indicates how many memory cells are to be reserved; a symbol in the label field defines a symbolic address for the first reserved memory cell.

[Symbol] DC c   Define constant: it stores the value of number c in a memory cell; a symbol in the label field defines a symbolic address of the memory cell.

Symbol EQU c   Equate: it assigns the value of number c to a label in the label field.

With these pseudo-ops our program example can be written entirely in assembly language (Figure 1.19). The ORG op implies that memory is used from cell 0 onwards; the END op specifies to the assembler which is the last program line to be processed. The assignment of an address to the data register EAREG, which was impossible in the former representation, is now feasible by means of the EQU op. The two DC ops create binary numbers for the operands ZERO and ONE; the DS op reserves a memory word for the value of TIMEC, which is still unknown at the beginning of the

```
label   opc    address field   comment

*
* PULSE GENERATOR PROGRAM
*
        ORG    0                ORIGIN OF PROGRAM AT ADDRESS 0
EAREG   EQU    32768
        MOVE   TIMEC,EAREG      READ IN TIME CONSTANT
        MOVE   EAREG,ZERO
        MOVE   R1,ZERO
LABEL1  MOVE   R2,TIMEC         INITIALIZE TIME LOOP
LABEL2  SUB    R2,ONE
        CMP    R2,R1            TEST TIME CONDITION
        BNE    LABEL2
        MOVE   EAREG,ONE        POSITIVE EDGE
        MOVE   EAREG,ZERO       NEGATIVE EDGE
        JMP    LABEL1
*                               BEGINNING OF THE DATA AREA
TIMEC   DS     1
ZERO    DC     0
ONE     DC     1
        END
```

Fig. 1.19. Pulse generator program in assembler language

program execution. The translation of the program by the assembler leads to the machine code, that is illustrated in Figure 1.17.

Assembling. The translation (assembling) of an assembly language program by an assembler generally occurs in two phases, i.e. in two passes through the program to be assembled. In the first pass, the address mappings are produced and an error list is prepared. In the second pass, the machine code is produced and the program is listed in symbolic and binary or hexadecimal representation. In the two passes, the assembly language program is read and processed line by line. The assemblers, that work according to this principle, are also called two-pass assemblers (for additional information on assembler behavior, see for example [10]).

As already mentioned, the address mappings are obtained through the preparation of a symbol table. The address computation begins with the starting address given in the ORG definition and is carried out by a so-called virtual program counter in the assembler. The virtual program counter is started with the beginning address and, after the processing of each program line, is incremented by as many memory words as are used by this statement in the machine code. A symbol in the label field of the program line is entered in the symbol table with the temporary value of a virtual program counter and is indicated as "defined". An external symbol in the address field is also reported in the symbol table, and its attribute is "used". Symbols in the label field of EQU definitions are an exception; their address values automatically result from the number indication in the address field.

Table 1.6. State of the symbol table after processing of the BNE line

symbol	address value	used	defined
EAREG	32768	x	x
TIMEC	–	x	
ZERO	–	x	
LABEL1	8		x
LABEL2	10	x	x
ONE	–	x	

If a program contains several ORG specifications, then the virtual program counter is repeatedly loaded with the value given in the address field at each ORG definition. Thus, for example, the program and the data areas in the memory can be stored separately. When the END definition is reached, all symbols have to be defined. Open address references and words within the program statements that are not allowed by the assembly language are recorded in an error list.

Table 1.6 shows a snapshot of the preparation of a symbol table for our program example after processing the BNE program statement. Until this point, the symbols TIMEC, ZERO and ONE have been used, but no address value could be attached to them, since the program lines, in whose label fields they are defined, were not processed yet. Such forward jump addresses are the reason for the delay in the creation of the machine code, which does not happen at the first pass for each program statement.

In the second pass, the program statements are translated to machine code one after the other, whereby the op code assignment table and the symbol table are utilized. The numerical addresses of the register file are obtained through the strictly agreed upon register symbols R0 through R7. They allow the differentiation between processor internal and external addresses and cannot be employed for the symbolic definition of memory addresses. We thus obtain the R/M bits coding for our example, and therefore the number of machine code words per instruction. Together with the code creation, a program list is produced, which contains, along with the symbolic program (source program), the machine code (usually in hexadecimal representation), the memory addresses of the machine code, a statement numbering and error messages (Figure 1.20).

Depending on the structure of the assembler, the machine code obtained is directly produced in those sections of the memory that were defined by the ORG specifications. Or else, it is first put by the assembler onto an external memory media, then - at a later time if need be - it is loaded by a loading program (loader) into main memory. The loader loads the program either at the memory addresses, that were given by the ORG specifications of the program (absolute loader), or it relocates the program by a loading offset to be set (relocating loader). During the loading process, the address definitions in the address parts of instructions, that were obtained through a virtual

```
Nr. addr. content  label   opc   address field   comment

 1                   *
 2                   * PULSE GENERATOR PROGRAM
 3                   *
 4                           ORG   0                ORIGIN OF PROGRAM AT ADDRESS 0
 5                   EAREG   EQU   32768
 6   0000   0100             MOVE  TIMEC,EAREG      READ IN TIME CONSTANT
            8000
            0017
 7   0003   0100             MOVE  EAREG,ZERO
            0018
            8000
 8   0006   0190             MOVE  R1,ZERO
            0018
 9   0008   01A0    LABEL1  MOVE  R2,TIMEC         INITIALIZE TIME LOOP
            0017
10   000A   02A0    LABEL2  SUB   R2,ONE
            0019
11   000C   21A9            CMP   R2,R1            TEST TIME CONDITION
12   000D   0C00            BNE   LABEL2
            000A
13   000F   0100            MOVE  EAREG,ONE        POSITIVE EDGE
            0019
            8000
14   0012   0100            MOVE  EAREG,ZERO       NEGATIVE EDGE
            0018
            8000
15   0015   0500            JMP   LABEL1
            0008
16                   *
17   0017           TIMEC   DS    1
18   0018   0000    ZERO    DC    0
19   0019   0001    ONE     DC    1
20                           END
```

Fig. 1.20. Program listing of the pulse generator program

program counter, have to be increased by a loading offset. These addresses are called relative or relocatable addresses. Those addresses that are defined as absolute by the EQU's, remain unchanged. They can also be called absolute addresses. In order to allow the relocating loader this distinction, the assembler has to supply additional information to the machine code.

As described in Chapter 3, a program can be made up of several modules, that are assembled separately. In order to resolve the address cross references that occur between the program modules, these have to be linked together either before or during the loading. A linker or a linking loader take care of this. The assembler likewise supplies the information that is necessary to the creation of address cross references.

The development of a program often does not occur on the microprocessor system that has to be programmed, but on so-called development systems or on conventional general purpose computers. Development systems are microprocessor systems that are equipped with translation and test programs for a particular kind of microprocessor. In general, they work with the same kind of processor, so that the developed machine code can be used on both the development system and the

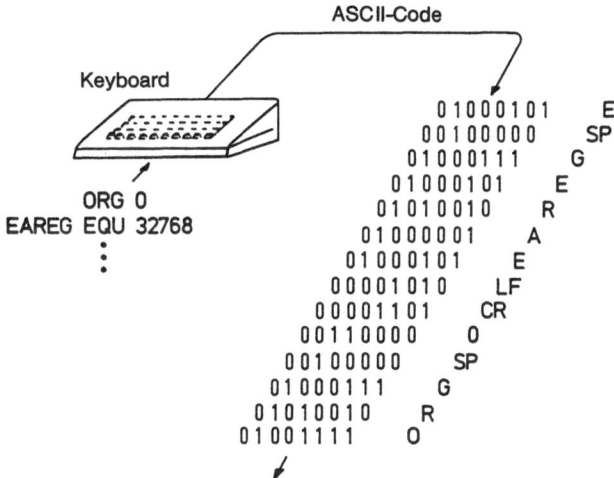

Fig. 1.21. Character input in ASCII code

system to be programmed. If they work with another kind of processor, special translation programs are needed that create machine code for the microprocessor to be programmed. Generally, this is also true for program development with general purpose computers. Translators, that do not produce machine code for the processor on which they run but for other processors, are called cross assemblers and cross compilers, or in general cross software.

1.3.3 Program Input and Text Output

The symbolic program has to be converted to a sequence of ASCII characters (byte string) for input, so that the microprocessor will be able to process it. This happens by means of an input device, for instance an electric typewriter. The corresponding ASCII character is created and transferred to the microprocessor system at the touch of a key. Figure 1.21 illustrates this process on our program example. Empty spaces are defined by Space (SP). The end of a statement is indicated by Carriage Return (CR), the transfer to the next statement by the control character Line Feed (LF). In any case, two ASCII characters (two bytes) can be stored in a 16-bit memory cell or on a 16-bit register. A symbolic program, that is loaded by the assembler as an ASCII character string in the memory, thus uses considerably more memory cells than the machine program it generates.

When outputting a text, for instance a program list on a printer, the processor sends a string of ASCII characters to the peripheral. This character string contains, along with the text, control characters, like carriage return, line feed and tabulation characters as well.

2 The 16-Bit Microprocessor

In Chapter 1 we described 16-bit microprocessors in a very simplified way, so as to illustrate their basic behavior. The processors that are available on the market show a more complex structure and a higher performance when compared to our model. This is also true for 8-bit microprocessors. Some of the features that allow distinction between 16-bit and 8-bit microprocessors are listed below:

- longer word length of 16 bits and therefore 16-bit data paths,

- larger number of data formats (bit, half byte, byte, word, double word, byte string and word string),

- general purpose register set,

- longer address with up to 24 bits,

- larger number of addressing modes,

- two-address instructions,

- more powerful instruction set (multiplication and division instructions, instructions for memory management, string and block processing instructions)

- universal trap and interrupt system,

- different modes (system mode, user mode),

- easy change of status,

- privileged instructions,

- support for multiprocessor configurations.

A 16-bit microprocessor can basically be in one of two processing states: user mode for normal processing, or system mode for exception processing. User programs are run in user mode, which allows only limited access to all functions. Thus for instance, privileged instructions cannot be carried out in user mode. The system mode does not have this restriction; it is used to run system programs that are necessary for the housekeeping of the microprocessor.

The switching from user mode to system mode occurs with an interruption of the running program and thus the execution of an interrupt program. The interruption is caused by either processor internal or external conditions that are called either traps or interrupts. The interruption of a program starts the switching of processor status (context switching). The processor information that will be needed later for the continuation of the interrupted program is saved, and the processor is loaded with the information needed for the execution of the interrupt program.

In this chapter, we will realistically describe the functional and structural features of a 16-bit microprocessor. In order to avoid too close a connection with one of the marketed microprocessors, we will describe a processor structure by using a model that is very similar to the existing microprocessors. First, we will start with a kind of microprocessor that has a limited address length of 16 bits and that is offered by some manufacturers as the most cost effective version.

In particular, Section 2.1 will deal with the principal structural characteristics of the microprocessor: register set, data types, data formats and addressing modes. Section 2.2 will illustrate the instruction set of the microprocessor, and Section 2.3 will discuss the structural characteristics that are important for exception handling, i.e. the trap and interrupt system as well as the two operating modes, user and system mode.

2.1 Microprocessor Structure

Anticipations on the material included in later sections is unavoidable for the discussions in Section 2.1. Thus, in this section, we will introduce some instructions needed to describe general processor features. The MOVE instruction will be the example for the instruction representation:

MOVE d,s

The source s and the destination d are specified in detail by the addressing modes.

As opposed to what we saw in our simplified microprocessor structure in the first Chapter, the byte is the smallest unit that can be addressed. This means that a memory address, written by the processor to the address bus, is always a byte address. Due to the 16-bit data bus, the memory itself is organized in words, i.e. a memory cell contains 16 bits. The access to the memory occurs at byte or word boundaries. The processor defines the word/byte distinction by means of a control signal that is examined by the memory unit for the byte and word selection.

2.1.1 Programming Model

The structure and functionality of processor registers, that can be directly addressed by the program, are referred to as "programming model". This includes the register file with two stack pointer registers, the program counter and the status register (Figure 2.1).

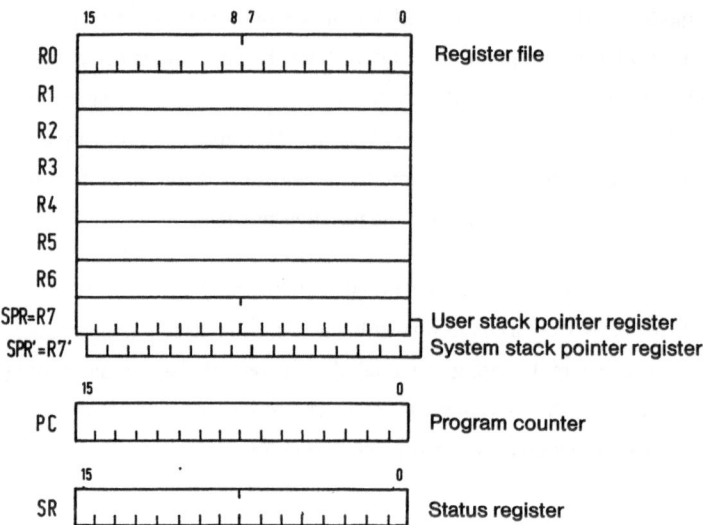

Fig. 2.1. Programmable microprocessor register (programming model)

Register File. The register file includes eight general purpose 16-bit registers named R0 through R7. They are directly addressed in the address part of the instructions, and they can all be used as working registers for operand storage (accumulators). The registers can also store addresses (address registers) and indexes (index registers) for the addressing of memory cells (see Subsection 2.1.4).

Stack Pointer Registers. Some instructions use registers R7 and R7' as Stack Pointer Registers (SPR); this also happens during trap and interrupt handling. Their content, the Stack Pointer (SP), points to a memory area, which is organized as a stack (stack memory). The access organization of such a memory is so that stack elements can be added or deleted only at the top. Thus in a stack, successive incoming data are stored in sequential memory addresses and are read out backwards. The stack pointer indicates the memory place that was used last. During a write operation, the stack pointer is first moved ahead, so that it indicates the first free memory cell of the stack; then a datum is stored at this address. During a read operation, the cell that is addressed by the stack pointer is read first, then the stack pointer is moved backward, so that it indicates the next to last entry (LIFO principle: Last-In-First-Out). Usually, the stack is filled by decreasing the address, and it is emptied by incrementing the address.

The stack's operation mode is illustrated by the two stack instructions PUSH s and POP d. PUSH writes the source operand s in the stack, POP reads the last stack entry and sends it to the destination d. If the transferred data have word lengths, the stack pointer register is incremented or decremented by 2 for the generation of word addresses (Figure 2.2).

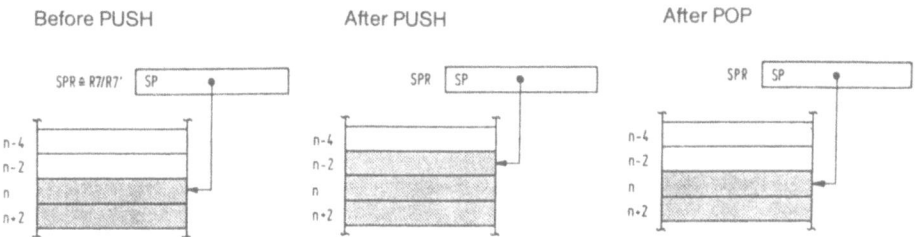

Fig. 2.2. Reading and writing on the stack with the instructions PUSH and POP

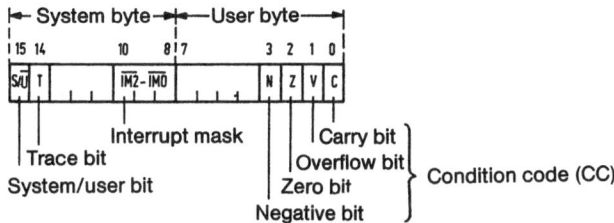

Fig. 2.3. Status register

Both stack pointer registers R7 and R7' have the same register address and are differentiated from each other by the user mode (R7) and the system mode (R7'). Accordingly, the two stack pointers are called User Stack Pointer (USP) and System Stack Pointer (SSP), and their stacks are called user stack or system stack. Both stacks are not only used by the PUSH and POP instructions for data storage, but also by the Jump to Subroutine (JSR) and Return from Subroutine (RTS) instructions for the management of program addresses for subprogram calls. Moreover, the system stack is used for status storage during trap and interrupt handling. The instruction Return from Exception processing (RTE) restores the status.

Program Counter. The 16-bit Program Counter (PC) contains the address of the next instruction word. It is incremented by 2 after each instruction word access. Furthermore, the program counter content can be changed through jump instructions.

Status Register. The 16-bit Status Register (SR) indicates both the current microprocessor state, after each completed instruction execution, and the temporary operation mode of the processor. For this reason it is divided into two bytes, the user byte and the system byte (Figure 2.3).

The user byte contains the information on the processor's state in the condition bits N, Z, V and C (condition code CC). Their value depends on the execution of specific instructions by the ALU, and they contain information regarding the results of arithmetic, logical or other operations. The jump instructions use the condition bits as jump conditions. In particular, condition bits have the following functions:

- Carry bit C indicates with C=1 range transgression for a binary number (see also Subsection 1.1.1).

- Overflow bit V indicates with V=1 range transgression for a two's complement number overflow.

- Zero bit Z indicates with Z=1 that the result of an operation is equal to zero.

- Negative bit N indicates with N=1 that the result of an operation, when regarded as a two's complement number, is negative. In other words, the N bit is equal to the most significant bit of the result.

The condition bits CC can also be changed by using the instruction Move Condition Code (MOVCC).

The system byte of the status register indicates the processor mode by means of mode bits, that generally remain unchanged throughout the execution of the program. They can only be altered in system mode, through the privileged instruction MOVSR (Move Status), or during trap and interrupt handling. Mode bits have the following function:

- The System/User bit (S/$\overline{\text{U}}$) indicates with S/$\overline{\text{U}}$=0 that the processor is in user mode, and with S/$\overline{\text{U}}$=1 that it is in the privileged system mode. System mode allows more processing capabilities when compared to the user mode, like for instance the execution of privileged instructions.

- The Trace bit (T), with T=1 (trace mode), causes a program interruption (trap) at the end of the instruction execution and branches into a trace program. The trace program can be used, for example, to indicate the processor status and then to resume the interrupted program, which will be interrupted again at the next instruction execution (program test).

- The Interrupt Mask ($\overline{\text{IM2}}$ through $\overline{\text{IM0}}$) indicates the processor's priority level and thus the priority of the running program. The priority diminishes when the mask value increases, i.e. level 0 has highest and level 7 lowest priority. External interrupt requests to special Interrupt Lines of the microprocessor ($\overline{\text{IL2}}$ through $\overline{\text{IL0}}$) can only interrupt the running program, if the interrupt level of the request has higher priority than the level of the processor. A request at level 0 is an exception, because it will always be granted.

Processor Status. The basic status of the processor is described by the program counter and by the status register. These two registers contain the minimal information needed to continue a program, that was interrupted between two instruction executions. This information is automatically stored in the system stack by traps and interrupts. The contents of the general purpose register file, that was used by the program, also belong to the complete status. These are not automatically stored, thus. if needed, they have to be saved by the interrupt program with the special transfer instruction MOVEM d,R,n (Move Multiple). With this instruction n successive register contents, beginning with the content of register R, are stored starting from destination address d in consecutive memory cells. The inverse restoring of the register status, occurs with the instruction MOVEM R,n,s.

2.1.2 Data Types, Data Formats and Data Access

Data Types and Formats. Data types are the different kinds of information that can be processed at the hardware level, i.e. by means of the microprocessor instruction set. They are characterized by a definite number of bits - the data format - and their interpretation. Here is a list of the most common data types of a 16-bit microprocessor, according to their format (Figure 2.4):

- status flag (1 bit),

- binary coded decimal digit (1 half byte = 4 bits),

- binary number, two's complement number, logic vector and ASCII character (1 byte = 8 bits),

- binary number, two's complement number, logic vector and memory address (1 word = 16 bits, 1 double word = 32 bits).

In addition we have byte strings (= up to n bytes) and word strings (= up to n words) with the data types mentioned above.

Data Access. Bytes, words and double words are directly addressable from the point of view of memory access. The differentiation of these three data formats, as far as addressing is concerned, is indicated in the op code. Operations with byte operands are defined by the suffix B (e.g. MOVEB) and operations with double word operands by the suffix D (e.g. MOVED) in the instruction symbols. Operations with word operands are not defined by any special suffix (e.g. MOVE).

The distinction between byte and word access in the memory is made through the lowest address bit A0 and the Word/Byte control signal (W/$\overline{\text{B}}$) according to Table 2.1. When a byte is accessed, the other byte of the word, that was not addressed, remains unchanged. As represented in Figure 2.5, word and double word accesses are possible at word boundaries only (A0=0).

As opposed to byte access in main memory, byte access in the register file is limited to the lowest byte, since no distinction for the two register halves is given in the register address; the highest byte remains unchanged (Figure 2.5). A byte transfer by the memory or by an I/O unit occurs either in the higher or in the lower data bus section, depending on whether the memory address is even (A0 = 0) or odd (A0 = 1). (Some microprocessors, e.g. Z8000, also allow the addressing of the higher byte in a register.) Due to internal organization, double word access in the register file is only

Data format Number of bits

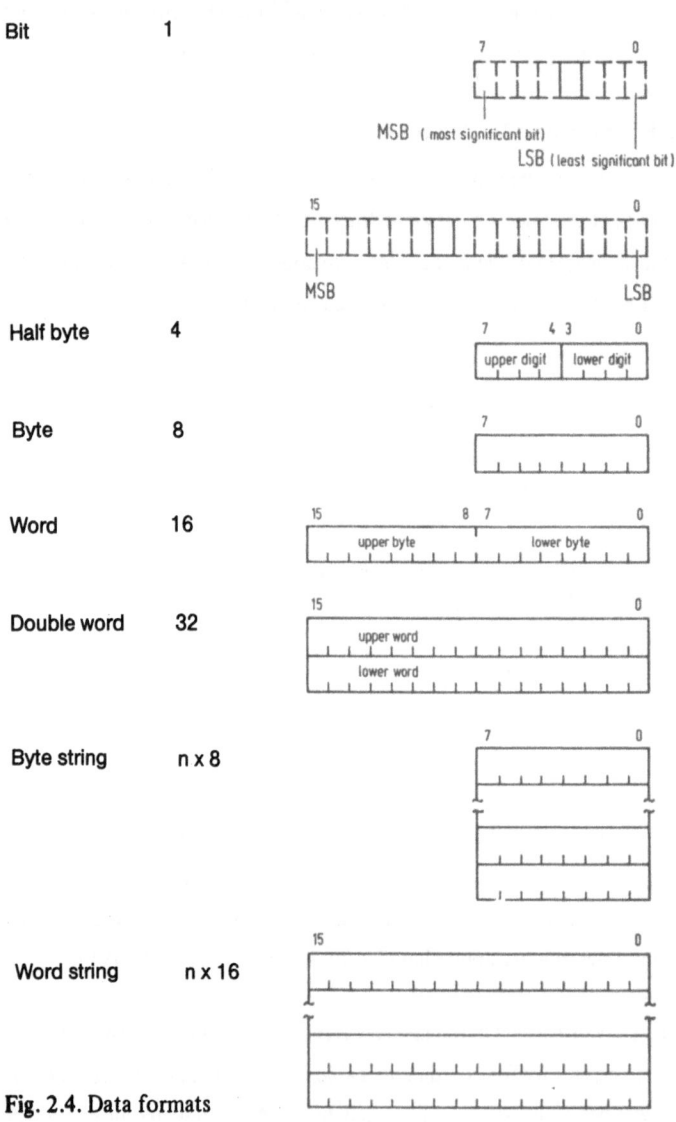

Bit   1

Half byte   4

Byte   8

Word   16

Double word 32

Byte string n x 8

Word string n x 16

Fig. 2.4. Data formats

Table 2.1. Byte and word memory addressing

W/B̄ A0	Memory selection
0 0	Byte 0
0 1	Byte 1
1 0	Word
1 1	Address error trap

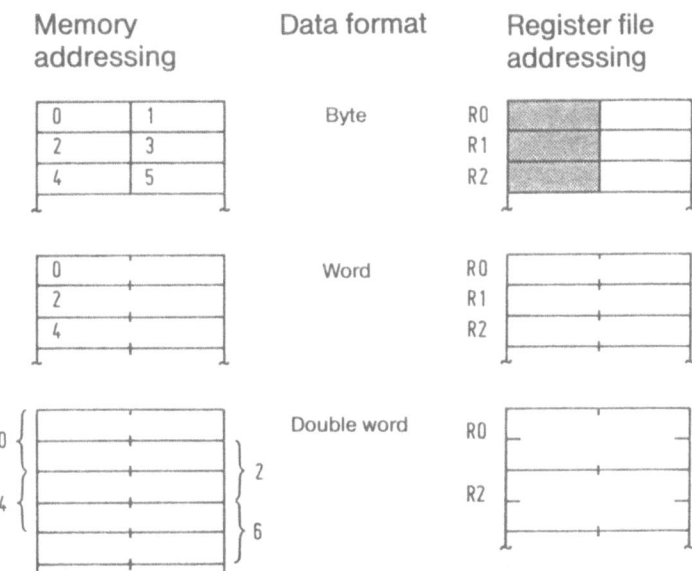

Fig. 2.5. Byte, word and double word allocation in working memory and register file with indication of memory and register addresses

possible when the word boundaries are even. The transfer of a double word on the 16-bit data bus occurs through two successive word transfers.

Bit processing instructions address bit operands in the memory as bytes or words; the access to individual bits occurs through a mask specified in the instruction. BCD digits are combined in pairs, are addressed as bytes and are processed by means of special BCD instructions. Byte and word strings in the memory are addressed by specifying the byte or word address of the first or last element in the string. The number of bytes or words is determined by specifying the length of the string or by testing a condition.

Example 2.1. Three program examples illustrate the word, byte and double word access: a) Transfer the word operand of memory cell LOC to R1. b) Transfer the ASCII control characters Carriage Return CR ($0D, $ indicates hexadecimal constants in assembly language) and Line Feed LF ($0A) to the 8-bit data register OUTR of an I/O unit. The data register is connected with the lower data bus section (odd byte address $FF03). c) Transfer a double word, that is stored in the memory cells LOC and LOC + 2, to registers R2 and R3. LOC has to be an even byte address; the register address in the MOVED instruction is also supposed to be even.

In order to be able to define constants in byte, word and double word formats, we have three specifications DCB, DCW and DCD instead of the assembler specification DC we used in Chapter 1. A similar expansion will be later applied to the DS specification.

```
        LOC     DCW     325
                 .
                 .
        MOVE    R1,LOC
a


        OUTR    EQU     $FF03
        CR      DCB     $0D
        LF      DCB     $0A
                 .
                 .
        MOVEB   OUTR,CR
        MOVEB   OUTR,LF
b



        LOC     DCD     $F050A7C1
                 .
                 .
        MOVED   R2,LOC
c
```

2.1.3 Extended Address Space

An address length of 16 bits, corresponding to the processor's word length, results in an address space of 64 K bytes or 32 K words. However, standard 16-bit microprocessors are equipped with an address space of several M bytes (M means one million: $1\,M\,=\,2^{20}$), so that systems with larger memory needs or with simpler addressing of the system bus components can be designed. To this purpose they need long addresses and a larger address bus.

The easiest solution is the extension of the processor internal address representation to 24 bits, for example, which allows a 16 M byte addressing. This results in the need to extend all processor registers that store addresses to 24 bits, e.g. the program counter and the registers of the register file. Unfortunately, if an operand address extends over two words in the instruction, one additional memory access will be necessary to read the instruction. In order to reduce this disadvantage, additional instruction formats with conventional 16-bit addresses are used. They allow a condensed instruction representation when the operands are in the lower address space. The MC68000 by Motorola is an example of this. In this processor, the internal register contains 32 bits, the 24 lower bits are used for address representation. The 23 higher address bits are used for memory addressing (word address A23 through A1) on the address bus. The lowest bit A0 (byte selection) is given to the control bus as 2-bit code together with the specification for the word/ byte distinction. Zilog Z8001 also works with an extended address representation; its address bus is designed for 23-bit byte addresses. When 23-bit addresses are stored in the register file, two consecutive 16-bit registers are used.

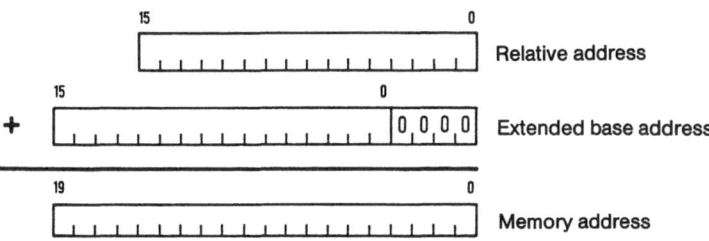

Fig. 2.6. One possible base addressing

Another possibility is the use of base address registers with a 20-bit register for instance, so that 1 M byte addressing is possible. All program addresses are represented as 16-bit relative addresses. The actual memory address results from the addition of the base address to the relative address. If the base address is used as a 16-bit address as well, and if it is extended by four lower zero bits in the processor, then the address storage and transfer can be uniformly executed in the 16-bit format (Figure 2.6). Intel's 8086 microprocessor is an example for this kind of addressing. It is equipped with four 16-bit base address registers, each extended by four zero bits. According to what is accessed, be it program code, data or stack data, one of the four base registers is automatically chosen.

2.1.4 Instruction Formats and Addressing Modes

In the simplified microprocessor structure presented in Chapter 1, the memory address of an operand was indicated directly in the instruction word. Actual microprocessors can rely on different possibilities for address modification. The address of a memory cell (effective address) is computed only during the execution of the instruction (dynamic address computation). This results in a considerable improvement in performance through programming techniques, that will be discussed further in Chapter 3.

Instruction Formats. At the level of assembly language, different addressing modes are characterized by different ways of using the address field. In order to allow distinction between them at the machine level, we have to extend our former address modification bit R/$\overline{\text{M}}$ to an address modification field. Figure 2.7 shows the standard instruction format, that was altered for two-operand operations.

For each of the source and destination specifications s and d, the first instruction word contains one 3-bit Modification field (MOD) to distinguish between eight addressing modes, and a 3-bit Register address field (REG) to address the general purpose registers that participate in the address modification. In the instruction words that follow there can be supplementary specifications for the operand access, like the effective address (Direct Address,DA) itself, a Relative Address (RA) or the

15	12	9	6	3	0
OPC	MOD$_d$	REG$_d$	MOD$_s$	REG$_s$	
DA$_s$, RA$_s$, IM$_s$					
DA$_d$, RA$_d$					

Fig. 2.7. Standard instruction format

operand itself (Immediate operand IM). The op code of the standard instruction formats is reduced to four bits after the extension of the address specifications. Naturally, these are not sufficient for the representation of the whole instruction set. On the other hand, most of the instructions do not need all of the addressing possibilities indicated by the standard instruction format, they might even need only one or no address specification at all. Additional instruction formats, in which the op code field includes more than four bits, exist for these instructions.

Addressing Modes. The following description of eight possible addressing modes will be completed by illustrations, that show the computation of the effective addresses. Address creation is shown by using the example of data transfer through MOVE instructions. Only the modification of the source address is indicated, while the destination address is always R1. The addressing modes could be used the same way for destination addresses. The direct operand addressing is the exception, since direct operands can only be data sources. When addressing words and double words, it is important for the effective address to be an even number.

In the illustrations, single arrows indicate the operand transfer, and arrows with a dot indicate data addressing.

1. Register addressing (R): The effective address is in the REG field; the operand is in the register file. The addressing mode is defined in assembly language by the symbol Ri (i=0 through 7), e.g. MOVE R1,R5.

2. Direct Addressing (DA): The effective address is contained in the second or third instruction word; the operand is in the memory. The address is indicated by an address symbol or by a numeric address; e.g. MOVE R1,LOC1 or MOVE R1,$A004.

3. Immediate operand addressing (IM): The operand is contained in the second instruction word (immediate operand); it can only be the source. The addressing mode is defined by a symbol, a number or a bit pattern preceded by #; e.g. MOVE R1, #325 or MOVE R1, #LOC2. The symbol, which is LOC2 here, has to be defined by a value.

4. Register Indirect addressing (RI): The effective address is in the register; the operand is in the memory. The addressing mode is defined by the register symbol in parentheses; e.g. MOVE R1,(R0).

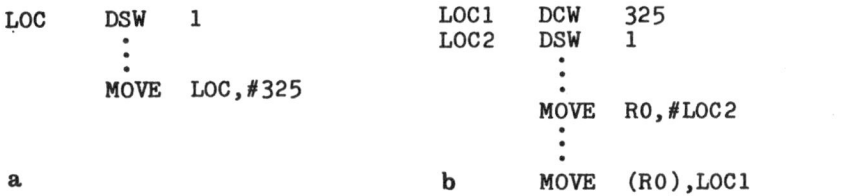

Example 2.2. a) Load the memory cell LOC with the direct operand 325. b) Transfer the content of LOC1 to a memory cell LOC2 whose address was stored in R0 before.

```
LOC     DSW    1              LOC1    DCW    325
  .                           LOC2    DSW    1
  .                             .
  .                             .
MOVE    LOC,#325                .
                              MOVE    R0,#LOC2
                                .
                                .
a                       b     MOVE    (R0),LOC1
```

5. Autoincrement addressing (IN): The effective address is in the register; the operand is in the memory. After memory access, the address is incremented by one during byte addressing, by two during word addressing, and by four during double word addressing. The addressing mode is indicated by a register symbol in parentheses followed by a plus sign; e.g. MOVE R1,(R0)+.

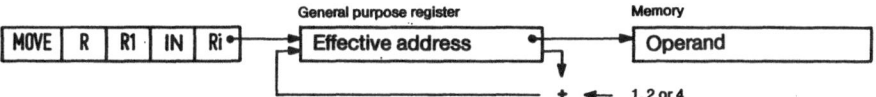

6. Autodecrement addressing (DC): The effective address is in the register; the operand is in the memory. Before the memory access, the register content is decremented by one during byte addressing, by two during word addressing and by four during double word addressing. The addressing mode is indicated by a register symbol in parentheses preceded by a minus sign; e.g. MOVE R1, −(R0).

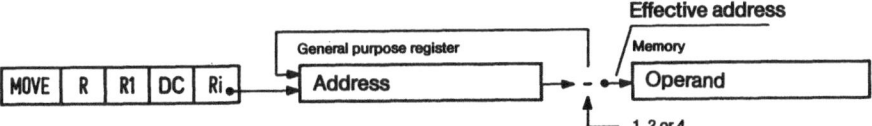

Examples 2.3. a) Transfer the contents of the contiguous memory cells LOC1, LOC2 and LOC3 in a memory area, whose first element is addressed by FIELD. b) Complete the program so that the contents of the area FIELD are then moved in R1, R2 and R3.

```
LOC1    DCW    325
LOC2    DCW    $000F
LOC3    DCW    17
FIELD   DSW    3
          .
          .
          .
        MOVE   R0,#FIELD
        MOVE   (R0)+,LOC1
        MOVE   (R0)+,LOC2
        MOVE   (R0),LOC3
a         .
          .
          .
        MOVE   R3,(R0)
        MOVE   R2,-(R0)
b       MOVE   R1,-(R0)
```

7. Indexed addressing (X): The effective address is formed by adding the 16-bit address, contained in the second or third instruction word, to the content of the index registers (general purpose registers). The 16-bit address indicates the beginning of the area to be addressed (base address), the index (content of the index register) is interpreted as positive 16-bit offset. The operand is in memory. The addressing mode is indicated by an address symbol or a numeric address followed by the index register symbol (R0 through R7) in parentheses; e.g. MOVE R1,FIELD (R0).

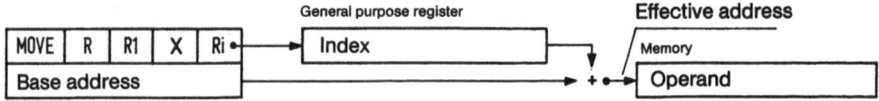

Example 2.4. Transfer the LOC content to the fifth word of a data area FIELD. Use R0 as index register.

```
LOC     DCW    325
FIELD   DSW    100
          .
          .
          .
        MOVE   R0,#4
        MOVE   FIELD(R0),LOC
```

8. Relative Addressing (RA): The effective address is produced by adding the contents of the program counter and the 16-bit byte offset (relative address) contained in the second or third instruction word. The program counter points to the instruction word that follows the relative address. The relative address is considered a two's complement number that allows forward and backward jump addresses. The operand is in the memory. This addressing mode is also called relative to the program counter addressing.

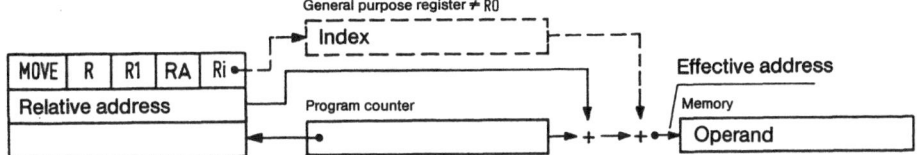

Relative addressing can be expanded by additional indexing. When computing the effective address, the content of an index register, indicated in the register address field, is added to the effective address determined above (broken line in the illustration). Contrary to normal indexed addressing, only the registers R1 through R7 can be used as index registers. The value zero in the register address field shows that no indexing is taking place and allows a distinction between the two addressing modes.

The relative to the program addressing of operands assumes that these operands are a direct (immediate) part of the program block. Such operands are usually constants.

Besides addressing operands, the relative addressing (without index) is often used for specifying the jump destination in the case of jump instructions. Depending on the jump offset, either 16-bit relative addresses (two-word instructions) or 8-bit relative addresses (one-word instructions) are used. The advantage lies in the possibility of moving program blocks in the memory without having to change the jump address within the blocks. This is also true for constants addressed in a relative way. This is called dynamically relocatable program code (see Subsections 3.1.3 and 3.1.4).

Relative addressing and relative index addressing are automatically employed by the assembler in program blocks that begin with a RORG instruction and contain the address relative to the program counter in the RORG pseudo-op as an option. Thus, they substitute the direct or the index addressing, as long as the address symbols used are defined as relocatable in the same block. Relative addressing can also be indicated explicitly by means of a positive or negative value preceded by an asterisk; for instance BNE *−10. The '*' refers to the address of the first instruction word of the current instruction; i.e., the reference points for the programmer and for the processor are different. The assembler takes this into account when creating the relative address.

Example 2.5. The jump offset for the conditional jump instruction BNE must be indicated in such a way that, if the jump condition is satisfied, the preceding comparison instruction CMPB is carried out. The BNE is one word long, the CMPB instruction three words long. Case a) shows the addressing of the jump destination with the value −6 as jump offset, relative to the instruction word of the BNE instruction (backward jump address). The actual jump offset used by the assembler is −8. Case b) shows the symbolic addressing of the jump destination, which is also translated into the addressing with offset −8 by the assembler. (In the case of conditional jump instructions, additional addressing modes are not provided by the processor.)

```
  CMPB    EAREG,#$80
a BNE     *−6


b WAIT    CMPB    EAREG,#$80
          BNE     WAIT
```

2.2 Instruction Set

16-bit microprocessor instruction sets contain between 60 and 120 instructions, and processors with small instruction sets prevail. Small instruction sets are easy to understand and thus facilitate programming. On the other hand, bigger instruction sets support specific applications, which leads to more efficient programming.

As to number of instructions, 16-bit microprocessors are comparable to 8-bit microprocessors, although their instruction sets are substantially more effective. The operations are more complex, dyadic operations can be carried out with one instruction, there are many instructions for byte, word and double word processing and a comprehensive set of addressing modes. When an instruction set is defined, one would like to accept such modifications for all instructions. However, this is not always possible, because the instruction word length and the number of words per instruction are limited. In this respect, the instruction set is always a compromise between the requirements of the application and the technical possibilities.

Instruction sets are easier to overview when divided in groups, according to the similarity of their functions. Typical groups are:

- data transfer instructions

- arithmetic instructions

- logic instructions

- bit processing instructions

- shift and rotate instructions

- jump instructions

- string instructions

- system instructions.

In the following we will describe the instruction set of the microprocessor we introduced in Section 2.1. Each instruction is briefly described in a table, that will be completed by explanations and examples. Regarding the applications that result from the combination of several instructions, we refer to the program examples for programming techniques in Chapter 3.

In the table representation, instructions for byte and double word operations in symbolical (mnemonic) op code are distinguished from standard instructions for word operations by the accompanying letters B or D. If this distinction does not appear in the symbol, the data format is indicated in the column for Operand Length (OL) with B, W or D.

Source and destination specifications in the address part are defined by s (source) and d (destination); if nothing is entered in the comment column, they can use any of the addressing modes. As an exception, immediate addressing of the destination is not allowed. Addressing modes are defined according to the symbols from Subsection 2.1.4 (register R, direct DA, immediate IM, register indirect RI, autoincrement IN, autodecrement DC, indexed X, relative RA). If only one addressing mode is given, for instance R, then it is given directly in the table instead of s or d.

In the formal description of the instructions we employ the above symbols, including the assignment operator : =, the operator that indicates the four basic operations +, −, · and / and the logic operators *and, or, exor* (exclusive or) and *not*. Angle brackets indicate a word's specific bit position, for instance SR ⟨7 - 0⟩ refers to the eight lower bits of the status register. The CC column indicates the effect of the instructions on the single condition bits. The following means that:

v: the bit is changed, i.e. it depends on the result of the operation;

0: the bit is set to zero;

1: the bit is set to one;

-: the bit is not influenced by the result;

u: the bit status is undefined.

2.2.1 Data Transfer Instructions

MOVE (Table 2.2) executes the general purpose data transfer between the source s and the destination d, the source and the destination can be in both the register file and the main memory. All addressing modes described in Subsection 2.1.4 except $d =$ IM are acceptable for s and d. The

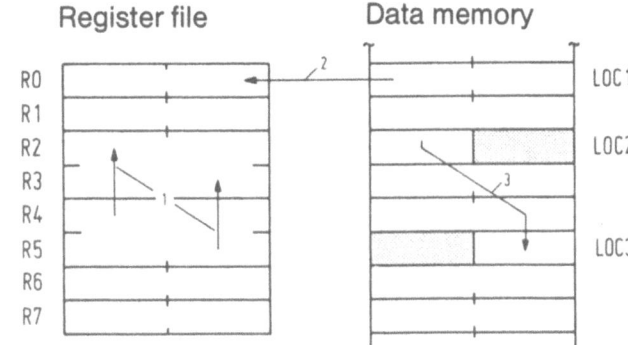

1	MOVED R2,R4
2	MOVE R0,LOC1
3	MOVEB LOC3,LOC2

Table 2.2. Data transfer instructions from MOVE to SWAP

Instruction	Function	Comment	OL	NZVC
MOVE d,s MOVEB MOVED	move d:=s			v v 0 0
MOVEM d,R,n R,n,s	move multiple d:=R or R:=s for n consecutive words (n ≦ 8)	d=s=DA, RI, X RA or d=DC and s=IN		v v 0 0
CLR d CLRB CLRD	clear d :=0			0 1 0 0
EXC R,s EXCB EXCD	exchange TEMP:=s s:=R R:= TEMP	TEMP: buffer register in the processor		- - - -
SWAP R	swap register halves TEMP⟨7-0⟩:=R⟨15-8⟩ R⟨15-8⟩:=R⟨7-0⟩ R⟨7-0⟩:= TEMP⟨7-0⟩	TEMP: buffer register in the processor		v v 0 0

data transfer is executed with bytes, words and double words. Three examples follow, in which LOC3 is odd, whereas LOC1 and LOC2 are even byte addresses (see also example 2.1).

MOVEM allows the storage or loading of several register contents on n consecutive general purpose registers, starting with register R. The base address of the memory can be specified by the addressing modes DA, RI, X and RA. It is automatically increased by two each time data are transferred by the processor. (The content of the register that was used for indirect register addressing or for indexing is not influenced by this.) In order to allow the data transfer to occur with stack memory areas as well, the addressing mode DC for addressing the destination and IN for the addressing the source are accepted. (The content of the stack pointer register defined in the instruction is obviously modified.) During DC addressing, the content of the stack pointer register, as it existed before the MOVEM instruction, is sent to the memory. During DA, RI, X, RA and DC addressing, register accesses start with R0, during IN they start with R7. - MOVEM can be used to save and restore the register status in case of procedure calls (see Subsection 3.3.1) and of program interrupts. MOVEM can be interrupted after each data word transport so as to ensure quick response of the processor to interrupt requests. The following example shows the storage of register contents R2, R3 and R4; here LOC is an even byte address.

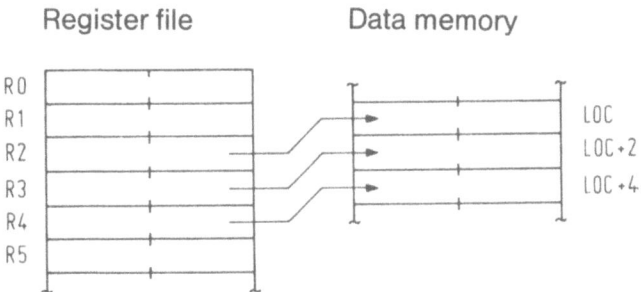

MOVEM LOC,R2,3

CLR, EXC and SWAP represent special cases of data transfer. CLR loads a register or a memory cell with zero. EXC exchanges two operands, whereby one operand has to be in the register file. SWAP exchanges the two bytes of the addressed register and thus allows the access to the higher register byte during byte operations. Three examples follow, in which LOC is an even byte address.

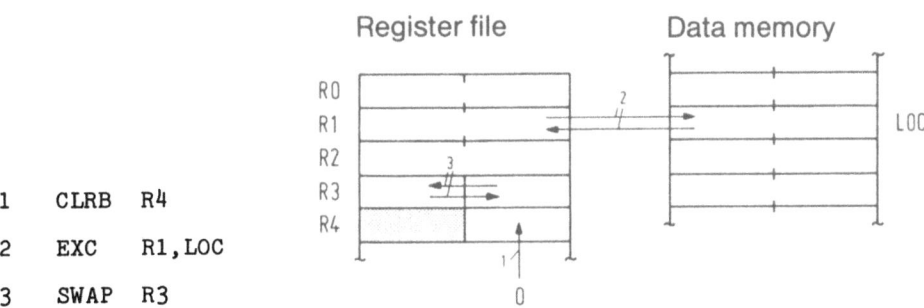

1   CLRB   R4

2   EXC   R1,LOC

3   SWAP   R3

PUSH (Table 2.3) executes a write access and POP executes a read access on the user or the system stack. The accesses occur as words or double words. R7 is used as Stack Pointer Register (SPR) in user mode and R7' is used in system mode. Both stacks are filled towards lower addresses. The Stack Pointer (SP) always points to the last input. In the following example, LOC is an even byte address.

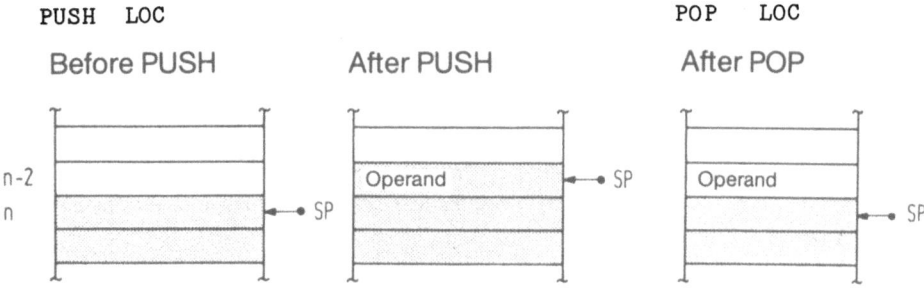

Table 2.3. Data transfer instructions from PUSH to LEA

Instruction	Function	Comment	OL	N Z V C
PUSH s PUSHD	push on the stack SPR:=SPR-2 (SPR):=s	SPR=R7 or SPR=R7'		- - - -
POP d POPD	pop from the stack d:=(SPR) SPR:=SPR+2	SPR=R7 or SPR=R7'		v v 0 0
PEA s	push effective address SPR:=SPR-2 (SPR):= effective s address	SPR=R7 or SPR=R7' s≠R,IM	W	- - - -
LEA d,s	load effective address d:= effective s address	s≠R,IM	W	- - - -

Additional stacks with R0 through R6 as stack pointer registers can be generated with the MOVE instruction and the addressing modes autodecrement and autoincrement. Depending on the addressing mode, the stacks are filled towards lower or higher addresses. In the first case, the stack pointer points to the last input (which corresponds to the effect of the PUSH and POP instructions); in the second case, it points to the first free cell. The following example illustrates the direction of the filling and the actual stack pointer.

```
write:      MOVE  -(R0),s              MOVE  (R1)+,s

read:       MOVE  d,(R0)+              MOVE  d,-(R1)
```

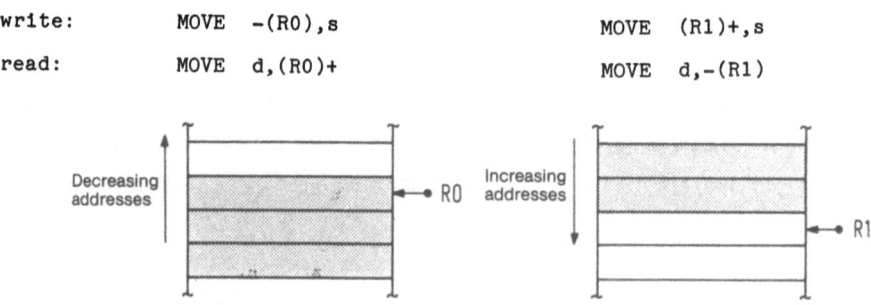

PEA computes the effective address *s* and writes it on the stack; LEA loads the effective address *s* into a register or a memory cell. The address, for example, can be used for indirect register addressing of an operand. Both instructions are employed for parameter passing during procedure calls (see Subsection 3.3.2). In the following example, the effective address is created by means of indexed addressing.

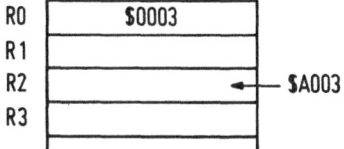

Register file

R0	$0003
R1	
R2	← —— $A003
R3	

LEA   R2,$A000(R0)

Table 2.4. Arithmetical instructions from ADD to SBCD

Instruction	Function	Comment	OL	NZVC
ADD(C) d,s ADDB(C) ADDD(C)	add binary (with carry) d:=d+s(+C) ·	C= Carry bit		v v v v
SUB(C) d,s SUBB(C) SUBD(C)	subtract binary (with carry) d:=d-s(-C)	C= Carry bit		v v v v
MULU Rn,s MULS	multiply unsigned multiply signed Rn_Rn+1:=Rn+1×s	n = even	W W	v v 0 0
DIVU Rn,s DIVS	divide unsigned divide signed Rn+1:=Rn_Rn+1/s Rn:= rest	n = even	D,W D,W	v v v 0
ABCD(C) d,s	add BCD (with carry) d:=d+s(+C)	2 BCD digits per operand	B	u v u v
SBCD(C) d,s	subtract BCD (with carry) d:=d-s(-C)	2 BCD digits per operand	B	u v u v

2.2.2 Arithmetic Instructions

ADD, SUB, MUL and DIV (Table 2.4) describe the four basic operations. ADD and SUB can be used on binary numbers (unsigned numbers) and on two's complement numbers (signed numbers). Since it is possible to include the Carry bit (C) in the operation with ADDC and SUBC, it is simple to program arithmetic operations with multiple word length operands. MULU and DIVU deal with binary numbers, whereas MULS and DIVS process two's complement numbers. MULU and MULS imply that the multiplier and the multiplicand have single word length and the product double word length. Product and dividend are stored in a double register, with the most significant portion in a register with even address Rn (n=0,2,4,6) and the least significant portion stored in the next register Rn+1. In a division, the quotient is stored in Rn+1 and the rest in Rn. The following example refers to DIVU, LOC is an even byte address.

```
DIVU   R2,LOC
```

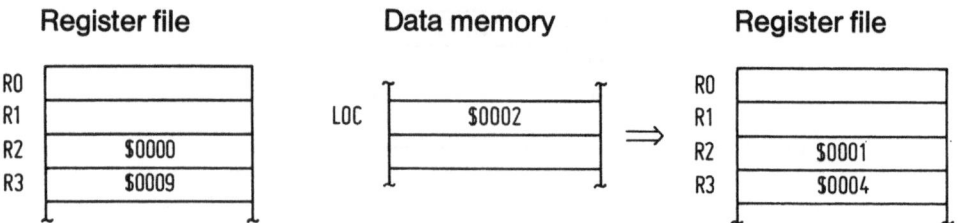

Register file   Data memory   Register file

Table 2.5. Arithmetical instructions from EXTS to DEC

Instruction		Function	Comment	OL	NZVC
EXTS EXTSD	R	extend sign of the lower data half to the upper data half	upper- lower half		v v 0 0
NEG(C) NEGB(C) NEGD(C)	d	negate (with carry) d:=0–d(–C)			v v v v
INC INCB	d,n	increment by n d:=d+n	n=1,2,···,16		v v v v
DEC DECB	d,n	decrement by n d:=d–n	n=1,2,···,16		v v v v

ABCD and SBCD permit the addition or subtraction of Binary Coded Decimal numbers (BCD numbers). Two decimal digits are always combined together in a byte. If the Carry bit (C) is included, operands with more than two decimal digits can be processed in this case as well.

EXTS and EXTSD (Table 2.5) double the length of byte or word operands, without changing the two's complement value. For this purpose, the sign bit of the original operand is extended to the higher half of the resulting operand. NEG, INC and DEC are special instructions for arithmetic operations. NEG creates the two's complement of a number (multiplication by −1), INC and DEC are short instructions for adding and subtracting an unsigned number from 1 to 16; they can be used to implement counters. The following example shows the effect of EXTS.

EXTS   RO   1 1 0 1 0 1 0 0   RO

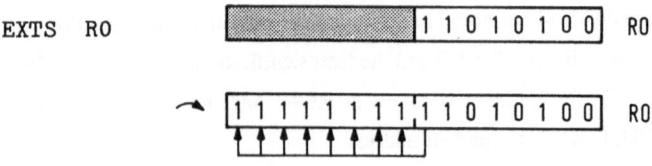

1 1 1 1 1 1 1 1 1 1 0 1 0 1 0 0   RO

Table 2.6. Compare instructions CMP and TAS

Instruction		Function	Comment	OL	NZVC
CMP CMPB CMPD	d,s	compare d-s ⌐ CC			v v v v
TAS	d	test operand and set sign d-0 ⌐ CC d⟨7⟩:=1		B	v v 0 0

CMP and TAS (Table 2.6) are comparison instructions, whose results affect the condition bits. CMP compares two operands d and s by subtracting them without changing the operands. TAS compares a byte operand with zero, it then influences the condition bits and finally sets the operand sign bit to 1. Branches can be programmed with both instructions by examining the condition bits with a conditional jump instruction after the comparison (see Subsection 3.2.2). In particular, the TAS instruction is used to implement semaphores (see Subsection 6.2.2). The following example illustrates the effect of CMPB.

CMPB RO,#$05 | $04 | RO

⌐ N=1, Z=0, V=0, C=1

2.2.3 Logic Instructions

AND, OR and EXOR (Table 2.7) generate the logic *and, or* and *exor* with the corresponding bits of the two operands. NOT complements the bits of an operand (creation of the one's complement, logic operation *not*). The following examples contain instructions ANDB and OR.

Table 2.7. Logical instructions from AND to NOT

Instruction		Function	Comment	OL	NZVC
AND ANDB	d,s	and d:=d and s			v v 0 0
OR ORB	d,s	or d:=d or s			v v 0 0
EXOR EXORB	d,s	exclusive or d:=d exor s			v v 0 0
NOT NOTB	d	not d:=not d			v v 0 0

```
ANDB  RO,#$0F  MASKING OF A HALF BYTE IN RO
```

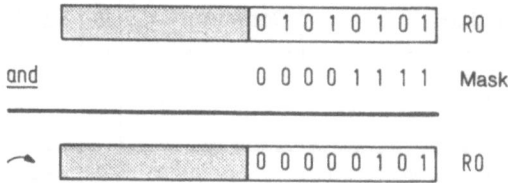

```
                    | 0 1 0 1 0 1 0 1 |  RO

     and              0 0 0 0 1 1 1 1     Mask
     _____

                    | 0 0 0 0 0 1 0 1 |  RO
```

```
OR    RO,#$004A  MERGING OF TWO BYTES INTO ONE WORD
```

```
           | 1 0 1 0 1 0 1 0 0 0 0 0 0 0 0 0 |  RO

     or      0 0 0 0 0 0 0 0 1 0 0 1 0 1 0      = $4A
     _____

           | 1 0 1 0 1 0 1 0 0 1 0 0 1 0 1 0 |  RO
```

2.2.4 Bit Processing Instructions

When bit processing instructions are used (Table 2.8), the operand bits involved in the operation are indicated by the bits of value 1 in a mask. The mask can be defined either as direct operand (constant) or as register content (variable). BTST is a comparison instruction, that tests the masked operand bits for value 0 or 1 and sets the condition bit Z according to the result of the comparison. In addition, BSET and BCLR set the masked operand bits to 1 or 0. The following example illustrates the effect of BCLRB.

Table 2.8. Bit processing instructions from BTST to BCLR

Instruction	Function	Comment	OL	NZVC
BTST d,mask BTSTB	test masked bits d and mask ⟶ CC	mask=R, IM		- v - -
BSET d,mask BSETB	test and set masked bits d and mask ⟶ CC d::=d or mask	mask=R, IM		- v - -
BCLR d,mask BCLRB	test and clear masked bits d and mask ⟶ CC d::=d and not mask	mask=R,IM		- v - -

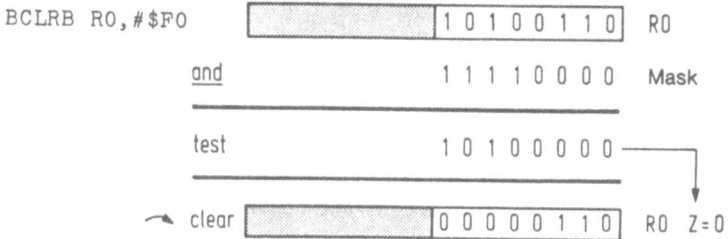

BCLRB RO,#$FO

1 0 1 0 0 1 1 0	RO

and   1 1 1 1 0 0 0 0   Mask

test   1 0 1 0 0 0 0 0

clear | 0 0 0 0 0 1 1 0 | RO   Z = 0

Table 2.9. Shift and rotate instructions from ASL to RORC

Instruction	Function	Comment	OL	N Z V C
ASL d,n ASLB ASLD	arithmetic shift left	Shift constant n=1,2, . . . ,16		v v v v
ASR d,n ASRB ASRD	arithmetic shift right	Shift constant n=1,2, . . . ,16		v v 0 v
LSL d,n LSLB LSLD	logical shift left	Shift constant n=1,2, . . . ,16		v v 0 v
LSR d,n LSRB LSRD	logical shift right	Shift constant n=1,2, . . . ,16		v v 0 v
ROL d,n ROLB ROLD	rotate left	Shift constant n=1,2, . . . ,16		v v 0 v
ROR d,n RORB RORD	rotate right	Shift constant n=1,2, . . . ,16		v v 0 v
ROLC d,n ROLCB ROLCD	rotate left with carry	Shift constant n=1,2, . . . ,16		v v 0 v
RORC d,n RORCB RORCD	rotate right with carry	Shift constant n=1,2, . . . ,16		v v 0 v

2.2.5 Shift and Rotate Instructions

Shift instructions (Table 2.9) shift an operand by n bit positions, where n is defined in the instruction ($n=1,2...16$). We distinguish between three kinds of shift instructions, depending on the kind of insertion or replication of bits on data format boundaries. These are: the arithmetic and logical shift instructions as well as the rotate instructions. In the arithmetic shift instructions ASL and ASR, the shift left by n digits corresponds to a multiplication by 2^n (insertion of zeroes), and the shift right corresponds to a division by 2^n (replication of the sign bit). In the logical shift instructions LSL and LSR, zeroes are inserted every time. In the rotate instructions ROL, ROR, ROLC and RORC, the bits that are pushed out at one end are inserted at the other end, so that no bit is lost. Moreover, in ROLC and RORC the Carry bit (C) is included in the rotation. In all shift and rotate instructions, the last bit that is pushed out is stored as C bit. Here is an example with the ASLB instruction.

ASLB   RO,4

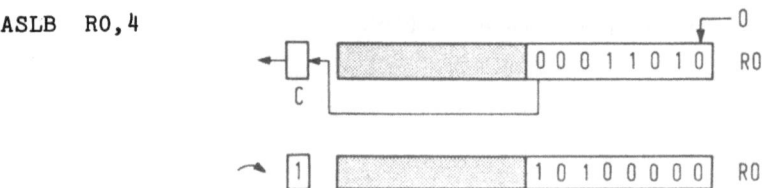

2.2.6 Jump Instructions

The unconditional jump instruction JMP (Table 2.10) loads the program counter with the effective address d stored in the instruction; i.e., the program is continued with the instruction stored at this address (unconditional jump). With the conditional jump instructions Bcond, a jump is only executed if the jump condition (cond), indicated in the instruction, is satisfied. If it is not, the

Table 2.10. Jump instructions JMP and Bcond

Instruction.	Function	Comment	OL	NZVC
JMP d	jump PC::= effective address taken from d	d+R,IM		- - - -
Bcond dist	branch conditionally if test=true then PC:=PC+dist else next instruction	dist=8-bit or 16-bit byte offset as two's complement number		- - - -
	cond	test		
BGT	GT greater (signed)	Z=0 and N=V		
BGE	GE greater or equal (signed)	N=V		
BLE	LE less or equal (signed)	Z=1 or N≠V		
BLT	LT less (signed)	N≠V		
BHI	nI higher (unsigned)	Z=0 and C=0		
BLS	LS lower or same (unsigned)	Z=1 or C=1		
BPL	PL plus	N=0		
BMI	MI minus	N=1		
BEQ	EQ equal	Z=1		
BNE	NE not equal	Z=0		
BVC	VC overflow clear	V=0		
BVS	VS overflow set	V=1		
BCC	CC carry clear	C=0		
BCS	CS carry set	C=1		

program is continued with the instruction following Bcond (conditional jump, branch). The jump conditions refer to the condition bits CC in the status register, as shown in Table 2.10. Program branches are programmed so that an instruction preceding the conditional jump instruction (generally the Compare instruction CMP) influences the CC bits, then the result of its operation can be examined. The mnemonic symbols for the jump conditions are also explained in connection with the compare instruction.

The BGT, BGE, BLE and BLT instructions are designed for comparing two's complement numbers (Overflow bit V!), BHI and BLS for comparing unsigned numbers (Carry bit C!). BPL, BMI, BEQ and BNE are independent from the number representation. BPL and BMI refer to the most significant bit of the result, BEQ and BNE to the result value zero or not equal zero. BVC, BVS, BCC and BCS are employed to test the overflow or the carry bit.

The following example regards conditional jump instructions: Two program branches. that result from the comparison between two register contents (subtraction). interpret the register contents a) as two's complement numbers and b) as unsigned numbers. The following Table shows the result of the two branches for two different data pairs a and b.

			a	7	0		Jump condition
1)							
	CMPB	RO,R1		0 0 0 0 0 1 0 1	RO	1a	Satisfied
	BGT	DEST1		0 0 0 0 0 0 1 1	R1	1b	Not satisfied
2)						2a	Satisfied
	CMPB	RO,R1	b			2b	Satisfied
	BHI	DEST2		1 0 0 0 0 1 0 1	RO		
				0 0 0 0 0 0 1 1	R1		

The conditional jump instructions are only designed for relative to the program counter addressing, whereas this addressing mode is only one of the 6 possibilities for unconditional jump instructions. If all jump instructions within one program are equipped with relative to the program counter addresses, then the program can be relocated, without requiring a change in the jump addresses of the jump instructions (dynamically relocatable program code; see also Subsections 3.1.3 and 3.1.4). The relative address (jump offset) is determined by the assembler either as an 8-bit two's complement number (one-word instruction, offset : − 128 to + 127 bytes) or, if this offset is not enough, as a 16-bit two's complement number (two-word instruction, offset : − 32768 to + 32767). The program counter is the reference point; it points to the instruction word following the relative address.

Table 2.11. Jump instructions from JSR to RTE

Instruction	Function	Comment	OL	NZVC
JSR d	jump to subroutine SPR:=SPR−2 (SPR):=PC PC:= effective address taken from d	d≠R, IM		− − − −
RTS	return from subroutine PC:=(SPR) SPR:=SPR+2			− − − −
RTE	return from exception processing SR:=(SPR) SPR:=SPR+2 PC:=(SPR) SPR:=SPR+2	privileged instruction		v v v v

JSR (Table 2.11) works as subprogram call. As with JMP, the jump is unconditional, although the actual program counter value (address of the next instruction) is loaded beforehand as return address in the user or system stack. The return from the subprogram to the instruction following JSR occurs with RTS, which loads the last stack input to the program counter. Accordingly, RTS serves to terminate a subprogram (see Subsection 3.3.1). The following example shows the calling of a subprogram, whose first instruction has the symbolic address UP.

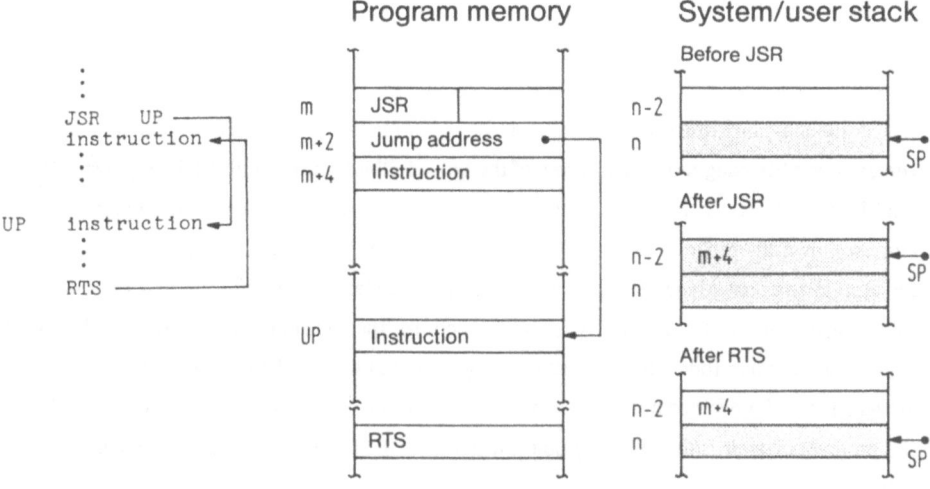

Trap and interrupt programs are terminated with the return instruction RTE. RTE loads the last two values input to the system stack in the status register and in the program counter. Thus, it restores the processor status to what it was before the program interruption. RTE is a privileged instruction and can therefore only be executed in system mode. RTS and RTE carry out the return correctly only when, during the instruction execution, the stack pointer (USP or SSP) points to the same address it had when it entered the subprogram, or the trap or interrupt program.

2.2.7 String Instructions

MOVES (Table 2.12) transfers a contiguous data block (byte string, word string) with the beginning address s to a contiguous memory field with beginning address d. The block length is indicated in a general purpose register Ri and is automatically decremented by one for each data transfer. When the register content reaches zero, the data transfer is stopped. One single operand can also be the source of the transfer, e.g. zero as memory operand to clear a memory field. CMPS compares the corresponding pairs of operands in two fields and influences the condition bits with each comparison result. The termination condition is the value zero in register Ri or the satisfaction of the condition *cond* indicated in the address field. The possible conditions are identical to those of the conditional jump instructions. Like MOVEM, MOVES and CMPS can be interrupted between two single operations.

The following example relates to CMPS: In the memory there is a string of ASCII characters, whose beginning address is indicated in R0 and whose byte number is indicated in R1. Find the first space character ($20, space) in the string. When this character is found, a program branch has to be started after FOUND.

Table 2.12. String instructions MOVES and CMPS

Instruction	Function	Comment	OL	NZVC

MOVES d,s,R
MOVESB
	move string
	while R≠0
	do modify DC address(es)
	  d::=s ⌢ CC-Bits
	  R::=R-1
	  modify IN address(es)
		d=IN,DC		v v 0 0

CMPS d,s,cond,R
CMPSB
	compare string
	while R≠0
	do modify DC address(es)
	  d-s ⌢ CC-Bits
	  modify IN address(es)
	  if test=true
	  then next instruction
	  else R::=R-1
		d=IN,DC
		cond = conditions of
		the conditional jump
		instructions
				v v v v

Data memory

RO ► $4D	$41
$52	$4B
$45	$31
$20	$4D
$4F	$56
$45	$20

```
CMPSB (R0)+,#$20,EQ,R1
BEQ   FOUND
```

2.2.8 System Instructions

System instructions are designed for the control of the system's state. In view of their operation, they can be divided into privileged instructions, that can only be executed in system mode, and trap instructions, that allow the controlled transfer from user to system mode.

MOVSR (Table 2.13) is a privileged instruction. It allows read and write access to the status register, so that the processor status can be changed. MOVCC permits the same but only for condition bits, so that it can be also used in user mode. MOVUSP allows access to the user stack pointer register R7 in system mode.

Table 2.13. System instructions from MOVSR to MOVUSP

Instruction	Function	Comment	OL	NZVC
MOVSR d,SR SR,s	move status d::=SR or SR::=s	privileged instruction	W	v v v v
MOVCC d,CC CC,s	move condition code d::=SR⟨7-0⟩ or SR⟨7-0⟩::=s		B	v v v v
MOVUSP d,USP USP,s	move user stack pointer d::=USP or USP::=s	privileged instruction	W	- - - -

Table 2.14. System instructions from NOP to RESET

Instruction	Function	Comment	OL	NZVC
NOP	no operation			- - - -
STOP	stop processing	privileged instruction		- - - -
RESET	reset external devices set RESET output signal for a few cycles	privileged instruction		- - - -

Table 2.15. System instructions TRAPV and TRAP

Instruction	Function	Comment	OL	N Z V C
TRAPV	trap on overflow if V=1 then R7':=R7'-2 (R7'):=PC R7':=R7'-2 (R7'):=SR PC:= trap vector N.8 else next instruction			- - - -
TRAP n	trap unconditionally R7':=R7'-2 (R7'):=PC R7':=R7'-2 (R7'):=SR PC:= trap vector N.32 + n	n= 0,1, . . . ,15		- - - -

NOP (Table 2.14) does not execute any operation; it only needs time for instruction fetch and interpretation. Gaps in the program can be filled or time conditions in time loops can be determined with NOP for instance. STOP is a privileged instruction that stops the program execution, which will only be resumed by means of an external interrupt request (reset signal or interrupt signal). RESET is a privileged instruction. It sets the $\overline{\text{RESET}}$ output to zero in some machine cycles, so that system components, like interface units for example, can be initialized by means of their $\overline{\text{RESET}}$ inputs.

TRAPV and TRAP (Table 2.15) cause a program interruption and branch to the corresponding trap programs, whose start addresses are listed in the vector table in the memory (see Subsection 2.3.1). With TRAPV, the interruption depends on the status of the overflow bit, with TRAP it is unconditional. The TRAP instruction specifies n and thus permits a choice between 16 trap programs; n is used by the processor to generate the trap vector number.

2.3 Exception Processing

Exception processing refers to the reaction of the microprocessor to interrupt requests like traps and interrupts. Since this reaction is supposed to occur very quickly, 16-bit microprocessors support it with an effective interrupt system as part of the processor hardware. User and system modes are tied to exception processing, since interrupt situations always cause a switching to the system mode.

2.3.1 Trap and Interrupt Management

Traps are program interruptions that are triggered synchronously to the processing by conditions internal to the processor. Conversely, interrupts are caused by processor external conditions, e.g. by

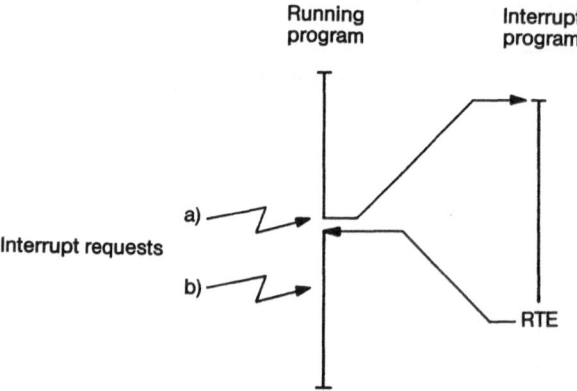

Fig. 2.8. Program interrupt. a) interrupt request is accepted, b) it is not accepted

peripheral devices; thus they are asynchronous to the processing. What they have in common is the interrupt handling by the processor hardware, which we will discuss in this section. Section 4.4 will describe the signal flow during interrupts, and examples for interrupt programming will be found in Chapter 5.

Program Interruption. An interrupt request, if allowed by the processor, causes an interruption of the running program. Thus, the processor executes a fixed procedure in order to handle the interruption. In simple terms, it first stores the current processor status, consisting of the contents of the program counter and of the status register, in the system stack. Then it branches to one of the interrupt programs associated with the interrupt request and executes it. The interrupt program is terminated by the RTE instruction, which loads the original processor status so that the interrupted program can resume processing after the interruption. Figure 2.8 is a schematic representation of the program flow during a program interrupt.

Interrupt and Trap Vectors. The addresses of all interrupt programs are stored in a vector table in the memory starting with address 0; they are called interrupt vectors or trap vectors. Each vector represents a 16-bit address and uses one memory word in this memory area. The addresses of these memory words are called vector addresses. They are formed from vector numbers that are closely linked with interrupt requests. Depending on the kind of interrupt request, the vector number is either produced by the processor itself, or it is taken from the outside and input to the processor through the lower half data bus (see Subsection 4.4.1). Figure 2.9 shows the necessary addressing operations for the selection of an interrupt program.

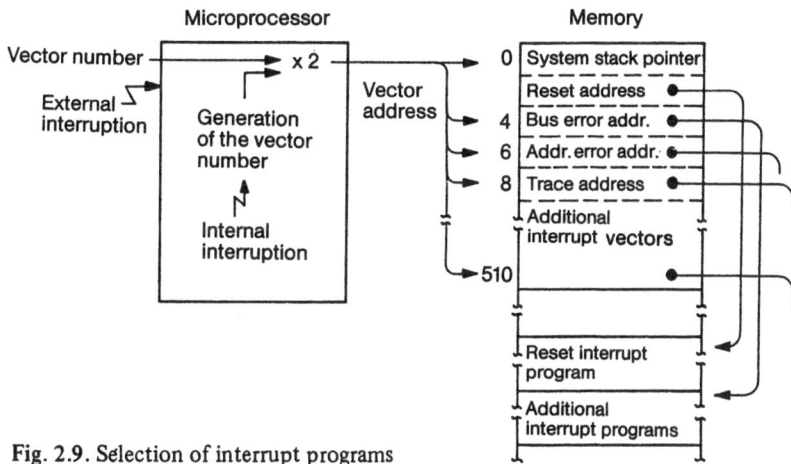

Fig. 2.9. Selection of interrupt programs

Table 2.16. Interrupt conditions

vector number	vector address	interrupt condition	internal/ external	priority
0	0	reset	e	0.0
2	4	bus error	e	0.1
3	6	address error	i	0.2
4	8	trace	i	1.0
5	10	illegal instruction	i	1.2
6	12	privilege violation	i	1.3
7	14	zero divide	i	2.0
8	16	TRAPV instruction	i	2.0
9	18	OPC emulation 1	i	2.0
10	20	OPC emulation 2	i	2.0
11–24	22 48	not used		
25	50	level 0 autovector interrupt	e	1.1
26	52	level 1 " "	e	1.1
27	54	level 2 " "	e	1.1
28	56	level 3 " "	e	1.1
29	58	level 4 " "	e	1.1
30	60	level 5 " "	e	1.1
31	62	level 6 " "	e	1.1
32–47	64 94	TRAP instructions (16)	i	2.0
48–63	96 126	not used		
64–255	128 510	vector interrupts (192)	e	1.1

Interrupt conditions are listed in Table 2.16 according to vector numbers and vector addresses. In the vector table, the corresponding memory words contain the starting addresses of interrupt programs. The internal/external column indicates the source of an interrupt request by i or e. Furthermore, priorities (g, i) are assigned to the conditions; we distinguish between group priority g and group internal priority i. 0 refers to the highest and 3 to the lowest priority. A running interrupt program can only be interrupted by a higher priority interrupt program. In the following explanation of Table 2.16, we distinguish between special condition traps and interrupts and general purpose traps and interrupts.

Special Traps and Interrupts. Special traps and interrupts are caused by conditions, that are mainly useful for initialization, system test and debugging. Their vector numbers range from 0 to 10 and they are listed in decreasing priority in the Table.

- Reset interrupt: It is generated through the $\overline{\text{RESET}}$ control input, for example manually by a system reset button. It causes the system initialization and has thus highest priority. It is the exception among the interrupt processing, because it loads the instruction counter with the start address of the interrupt program as well as the system stack pointer register with the starting value out of the vector table. Furthermore, it sets the general purpose processor registers to zero. The reset interrupt program is used to initialize the units that are connected to the system bus and makes system programs accessible.

- Bus error interrupt: It is generated by the $\overline{\text{BERR}}$ signal input, after discovery of a bus error by a unit in the system. This could be the failure of an acknowledgement signal ($\overline{\text{DTACK}}$) to the processor.

- Address error trap: It is generated by a word or double word access with odd address.

In all three cases, the interrupt handling occurs immediately after recognition of the condition, i.e. in the next machine cycle.

- Trace trap: The Trace bit (T) in the status register is set (trace mode). The interruption occurs after processing of the instruction. The trace program is used for system test, for instance to display the processor status.

- Illegal instruction trap: The processor interprets an op code that is not defined. The interruption occurs immediately in conjunction with the interpretation stage.

- Privilege violation trap: The processor is in user mode and interprets the op code of a privileged instruction. The interruption occurs immediately in conjunction with the interpretation stage.

- Zero divide trap: The processor finds a denominator with value zero during the execution of the division instruction. The interruption occurs during the processing of the instruction.

- TRAPV instruction trap: An interruption occurs during the execution of the TRAPV instruction, if the overflow bit V is set by a previous operation (overflow trap).

- OPC emulation traps: The processor interprets specific op codes of instructions that were not implemented. The interruption occurs directly in conjunction with the interpretation stage; the instruction is simulated in the trap program.

General Purpose Traps and Interrupts. General purpose traps and interrupts can be divided into TRAP instructions (vector numbers 32 through 47) and autovector and vector interrupts (vector numbers 25 through 31 or 64 through 255). Both groups can be used for many different functions.

TRAP instruction interruptions occur during the execution of a TRAP instruction. 16 trap programs are available, because of the 4-bit additional field in the instruction. They are used to control the switching from user mode (user programs) to system mode (system programs).

General purpose interrupts are generated by external units and transmitted to the processor by a 3-bit interrupt code over interrupt inputs $\overline{IL2}$ through $\overline{IL0}$. The processor uses the code to distinguish between 7 interrupt levels with different priorities. Interrupt code 0 has the highest, interrupt code 6 the lowest priority. Code 7 means that there is no interrupt request. Program interruptions occur when an interrupt is requested, which has higher priority than the running program, with the exception of level 0. The priority of a program is determined by the 3-bit interrupt mask ($\overline{IM2}$ through $\overline{IM0}$) in the status register; it is immediately updated to the interrupt code when a program is interrupted.

Highest priority interrupts (level 0) are generated by signal transitions (edges). These will always be granted, hence the name of non-maskable interrupts. The other interrupts (level 1 through 6) operate with signal levels; their granting will depend on the interrupt mask. Therefore, they are called maskable interrupts.

In the case of autovector interrupts, each one of the seven interrupt levels is associated with a vector number (25 through 31); i.e., the selection of interrupt vectors depends on the interrupt code. On the contrary, in the case of vector interrupts, the interrupt source delivers an 8-bit vector number (64 through 255) on the data bus of the processor. Thus, the processor can choose one out of 192 possible interrupt vectors. The processor distinguishes between autovector and vector interrupts by means of an input signal $\overline{AVEC}$. It is defined by interrupt sources as 0 (autovector interrupts) or as 1 (vector interrupts).

Table 2.16 defines some vector locations as "unused". They can be utilized for additional tasks in case the microprocessor were expanded.

Example 2.6. A real time clock generates program interruptions at regular intervals, that are used to increment a memory cell COUNT. To this purpose, the clock has a 3-bit register CODE, that is loaded with the binary code 001 at each clock pulse, and whose outputs as interrupt code affect the interrupt inputs $\overline{IL2}$ through $\overline{IL0}$. The $\overline{AVEC}$ input of the processor is set to 1, so that the processor is able to recognize an interrupt request as vector interrupt. If it accepts a request, it confirms this by means of an acknowledgement signal $\overline{IACK}$ (Interrupt Acknowledge; see also Subsection 4.4.1). At this point, the clock delivers the vector number 64 on the data bus of the microprocessor. Then the processor loads the program counter with the interrupt vector that is stored at the vector address 128. This is the starting address of the interrupt program TIMER.

Microprocessor

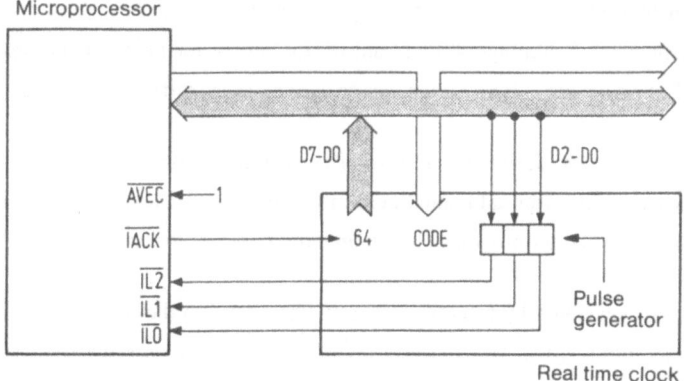

Fig. 2.10. Connection of a real time clock

The interrupt program TIMER increments the content of the memory cell COUNT by 1, then loads the register CODE with the value 7 and terminates the interrupt request. During the execution of the interrupt program, an additional request of level 1, as well as requests of levels 2 through 6, are blocked by the interrupt mask in the status register.

```
TIMER   INC    COUNT,1
        MOVEB  CODE,#7
        RTE
```

Interrupt Cycle. Interrupt handling is carried out in four steps; this procedure is called interrupt cycle.

1. The status register content is first copied in a processor internal buffer register. Then the status is changed, by setting the S/$\overline{\text{U}}$ bit (switching to system mode) and by clearing the T bit (suppression of the trace function). In the case of general purpose interrupt request, the interrupt mask is also set equal to the interrupt code; in the case of reset interrupt, it is set to zero (highest priority). With the exception of level 0, all interruptions of equal or lower priority, are impossible after this step.

2. The vector number is determined and is multiplied by 2 to create the vector address.

3. The processor status is saved; i.e., the program counter content and the status register content in the buffer are written on the system stack. (This step is not performed in the case of reset interrupt.)

4. The instruction counter is loaded with the interrupt vector, and the fetching of the first instruction of the interrupt program is started.

2.3.2 System and User Mode

As already mentioned, the microprocessor works in two modes, either in system mode or in user mode; the mode depends on the S/$\overline{\text{U}}$ bit in the status register. When compared to the user mode, the system mode is privileged as far as the access to the hardware and software components of the general system. It allows the execution of privileged instructions that would lead to a program interruption in user mode (privilege violation trap). These instructions are:

- the STOP instruction, that stops the processor during processing (this situation can only be terminated by an external interrupt request),

- the $\overline{\text{RESET}}$ instruction, that initializes the units of the system bus by means of the $\overline{\text{RESET}}$ signal,

- the MOVSR instruction (Move Status), that can read and alter the content of the status register,

- the MOVUSP instruction (Move User Stack Pointer), that can read and alter the content of the user stack pointer register, and

- the RTE instruction, that is used to return from the trap or interrupt program.

Traps and interrupts that occur in user mode always lead to a switching to system mode. The only possibility for user mode programs to reach system mode is through traps and interrupts (controlled switching). The switching from system mode to user mode is either caused by an RTE instruction, if the interrupted program was executed in user mode, or it occurs by explicit clearing the $S/\overline{U}$ bit through the privileged instruction MOVSR that changes the status.

In user mode, accesses to the stack occur with the User Stack Pointer (USP) in R7; in system mode, they occur with the System Stack Pointer (SSP) in R7'. Moreover, since all operational devices are reachable in system mode, an access to the user stack pointer is possible with the privileged instruction MOVUSP. The processor status is usually saved in the system stack during interrupt handling.

The introduction of two modes of operation is particularly useful when dealing with large systems, in which the operational components, i.e. the system's hardware and software components, are shared for several applications. This task is duty of the operating system, which is in charge of several high ranking tasks: translating and loading programs, providing aids for debugging programs, implementing data traffic with peripheral devices, providing trap and interrupt vectors, and so on. In order to protect the operating system from the program activities of single applications, the operating system is associated with the system mode, whereas the user programs are associated with the user mode. Thus, the two modes of operation substantially contribute to the system's safety. For additional information on structure and behavior of operational systems for microprocessors see for example [11, 12].

3 Programming Techniques

As is the case with conventional digital computers, to efficiently program a microprocessor system we need basic programming techniques; i.e., we should know how to handle programs. First, programming techniques can be described independently from the instruction set of a processor. When programming techniques are converted into instruction sequences though, some differences that depend on the processor come to the surface. These concern the need of program memory space, program execution time and support from the processor's instruction set.

In Section 3.1. we will first describe some of the basic ways to represent programs, and we will choose the flow chart representation as a means for the generation of assembly programs. An additional means of representation will be the assembler language, which was defined in Chapter 1 and was completed in Chapter 2. It will be adapted to the current assembly languages of 16-bit microprocessors. Section 3.2 describes different possibilities of program flow control by means of jumps, branches and program loops. This will be completed in Section 3.3 by subprogram techniques, where different data accesses during parameter passing are described.

3.1 Assembler Programming

3.1.1 Flow Charts

Algorithm and Program. A processing specification, according to which input data has to be converted into output data through intermediate results, is called an algorithm. A program is the description of an algorithm that is tailored to the microprocessor. If the program is written in machine code, the microprocessor can interpret it directly; if it is written in symbolic language, for example as an assembly language program or in a higher programming language, it first has to undergo a preparation stage in which it is converted into machine code by a translation program (assembler or compiler).

In order to facilitate program representation, the algorithm is first written in a processor-independent way that is easy for humans to understand. This is useful especially when programming at a relatively low level, like the assembler level, and it is absolutely necessary when dealing with larger problems. The description can be either language oriented, with passages in natural language (see Knuth [13]) or in a higher programming language (e.g. PASCAL), or it can

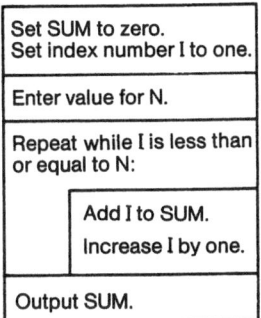 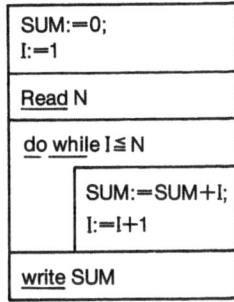

Fig. 3.1. Structured flow chart representation

be graphic, through structured flow charts (see Nassi and Shneiderman [14]) or conventional flow charts (e.g. according to DIN 66001 [15]).

Structured Flow Charts. Structured flow charts are based on the language constructs of higher programming languages, in particular on their control structures. Thus, the description level is higher than that of the assembly language and is suitable for a condensed representation of complex procedures. Furthermore, structured flow charts support structured descriptions of problems and thus simplify the writing of structured programs [16].

Example 3.1. The algorithm in a structured flow chart representation. Natural numbers 1 through N have to be added. Value N will be read as input data and the result SUM will be the output data.

The two representations in Figure 3.1 are different in the sense that one is in natural language, the other is in programming language. The flow is described by consecutive blocks and by the sequence of operations within the blocks. The while loop is used as an example of control structure. As long as the loop condition $I \leq N$ is valid, the operations $SUM := SUM + I$ and $I := I + 1$ are executed repeatedly. ∎

Conventional Flow Charts. If compared with structured flow charts, conventional flow charts (in short, flow charts) are more related to program representation at the assembler level. Control structures like the while loop appear in expanded form. Thus, flow charts reflect the actual program flow with all its branches.

Flow charts are also represented by geometrical symbols that are connected by flow lines or arrows and are labelled like structured flow charts. Thus, the problem introduced in Example 3.1 can be described as in Figure 3.2a. The while loop from Example 3.1 is created by increasing a variable, by testing a condition and by resuming the program flow after completion. The steps immediately following each other can be combined in one symbol (Figure 3.2b). They are read from top to bottom, independently from the direction of the flow arrows; i.e., Figures 3.2b and 3.2c convey the same meaning. Figure 3.2d shows another representation of the condition test, that is, how it is used to represent three-way branches.

68

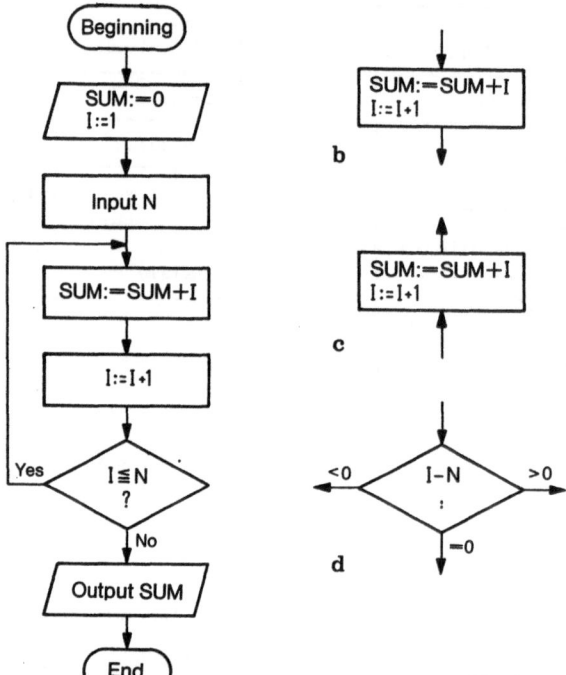

Fig. 3.2. Conventional flow chart representation

The assignment symbol := indicates the assignment of the value of the expression on the right to the variable on the left, e.g. I:=1. The variable on the left can also appear in the expression on the right; for example in I:=I+1 the current value I (right) is increased by 1 and the result is assigned to I (left) again. If I corresponds to a symbolic address, the content of the addressed memory location is increased by one.

On the contrary, the character = indicates the equivalence of two quantities and will not be used for value assignment in this book. It is used to express conditions, together with the characters > (greater than), < (less than) and ≠ (not equal), for instance if I≤N, then..., else....

3.1.2 Assembly Language

Chapter 1 introduces a simple assembly language that was adapted to the simple processor described there. We would like to extend this language by considering the processor functions described in Chapter 2. A first attempt in this direction was already made in Section 2.1, where the different addressing modes of the processor (dynamic address computation) were discussed. Furthermore, we will add functions to the language, that will facilitate programming. Thus, additional tasks will be given to the assembler, e.g. address computation at translation time (static address computation).

Format of a Program Statement. We will retain the format of a program statement with label, operation, address and comment field. Symbols (labels or names) can be used in the label field, and mnemonical instructions from Section 2.2., as well as those of the subsequently described pseudo-ops, can be used in the operation field. Constants, symbols and arithmetic expressions are allowed in the address field. Comments have to be separated from the address field by at least one empty space or have to be indicated by an asterisk (•) in the first column.

Constants. A constant for the assembler is a value fixed at the translation time, that is given as a number in decimal, hexadecimal or binary form or as an ASCII character string. Decimal constants are represented without special characterization, hexadecimal constants are preceded by a $ sign and binary constants by a % sign; for instance

decimal: 1234, + 527, -12

hexadecimal: $04, $FF03

binary: %00000100, %1111000010100101.

One or more ASCII characters, that are enclosed by quotation marks (' '), create an ASCII character string. When a quotation mark is part of a character string, it is represented by two consecutive quotation marks, e.g.

'TEXT' or 'IT''S ALL RIGHT'.

The representation of non-printable ASCII characters (e.g. control characters) is hexadecimal, e.g. $0A as the control character for line feed.

Symbols. We assume that symbols can contain a maximum of six letters or digits, and the first character has to be a letter. A symbol is relative when its value is related to the beginning of a relocatable program block. It is absolute when its value is fixed. The value assignment occurs either in relation to the assembler pseudo-ops RORG and AORG, or directly by means of the EQU and SET specifications. The symbol type is important when creating expressions.

The asterisk (∗) is used both as an indication of a comment statement and as a symbol for the program counter during relative addressing. Its assigned value is the address of the first instruction word in the address section it is used in; this address and therefore the symbol can be absolute or relative. Symbols R0 through R7 and SPR are register symbols; SPR (Stack Pointer Register) can be used instead of symbol R7. The program counter symbol • and the register symbols can only be used in the address field.

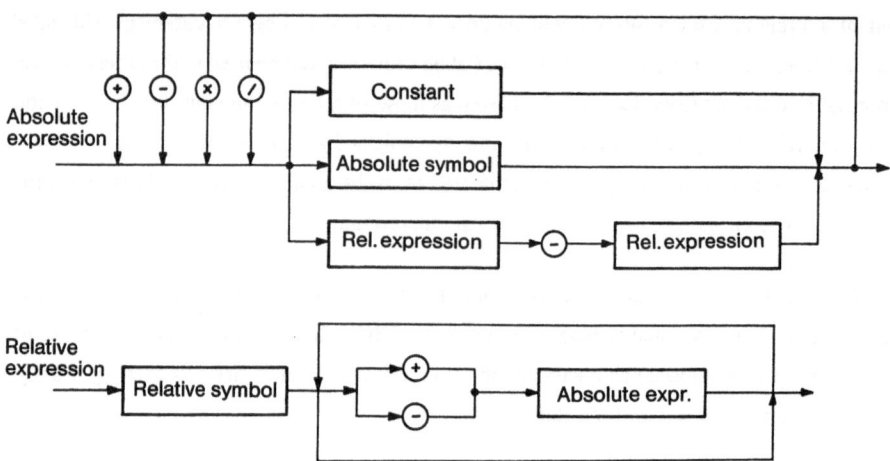

Fig. 3.3. Creation of absolute and relative expressions

Table 3.1. Addressing modes

Adressing mode	Assembler representation	Address/operand
R (register)	Ri with R7 = SPR	register address = i with i = 0 to 7
DA (direct)	expression	address = expression value
IM (immediate)	# expression	operand = expression value
RI (register indirect)	(Ri)	address = Ri content
IN (autoincrement)	(Ri)+	address = Ri content; the content of Ri is increased by 1, 2 or 4 after memory access.
DC (autodecrement)	−(Ri)	the content of Ri is decreased by 1, 2 or 4 before the memory access; address = Ri content
X (indexed)	expression (Ri)	address = expression value + content of Ri
RA (relative)	* ± constant * ± absolute symbol	address = instruction address ± value of the constant or symbol

Expressions. Expressions are created from constants and symbols that are joined by the arithmetic operators +, -, · and /. As with symbols, they can be either relative or absolute according to their values. Figure 3.3 shows a schematic representation of the possibilities when creating expressions.

The value of an expression is determined by the assembler at translation time (static address computation), with operators · and / having priority over operators + and -. Equivalent operators are processed from left to right. The result is represented as a whole number; i.e., the remainder is not taken into account when dividing. The division by zero is "not defined".

Expressions are a general form of representation for numerical and symbolic address and operand specifications including the following addressing modes: Direct (DA), Immediate (IM), Relative (RA) and Index (X). They are also used to define program constants in DC pseudo-ops. Table 3.1 shows a summary of the processor's addressing modes, described in Subsection 2.1.4 (dynamic address computation), in relation to the use of constants, symbols and expressions.

Some examples will show the possibilities of address and operand representation by means of expressions and will illustrate the effect of addressing modes.

MOVE	R1,FIELD+2	loads R1 with the memory word following FIELD (direct addressing); the FIELD value has to be even.
MOVEB	R1,M+2·3	loads R1 with the sixth memory byte following M (direct addressing).
MOVE	R1,=#N+5/2	loads R1 with the value of N that was increased by $5/2=2$ (immediate operand addressing).
MOVE	R1,•+6	loads R1 with the third memory word following the MOVE instruction (relative addressing).
JMP	•-2	loads the program counter with the address of the memory word preceding the JMP instruction (relative addressing).
MOVE	R1,A+4(R2)	loads R1 with the memory word, whose address corresponds to the value of A increased by four plus the content of register R2 (indexed addressing).

Usually, assemblers accept both arithmetic as well as logic expressions; to this purpose, reference should be made to the assembler descriptions by microprocessor vendors.

3.1.3 Pseudo-ops

The set of pseudo-ops, that was defined in Subsection 1.3.2 and that was tailored to the simplified processor described in Chapter 1, is adapted to the processor structure that was discussed in Chapter 2 and is expanded with some specifications. The specifications in square parentheses are optional, i.e. they can be either used or ignored.

        NAME   symbol   assign program label

NAME is the first specification of a program and assigns the symbol as program label. The program label can be used by the system software as program identifier for the management of program libraries.

END   end assembling stage

END indicates the last source code statement to be translated. The source code following this statement is ignored.

AORG expression   start an absolute program or data block

AORG (Absolute Origin) indicates the beginning of an absolute program or data block that cannot be relocated in memory. It also loads the program counter with the value of the expression. Absolute addresses, starting with this value, are assigned to the machine code created afterwards. The expression has to be defined; i.e., it cannot contain forward jump addresses or undefined external addresses (e.g. symbolic addresses, contained in the REF specifications). A program or data block starting with AORG finishes with the next AORG, RORG or END specification.

RORG symbol,[PCR] start a relocatable program or data
               block

RORG (Relative Origin) indicates the beginning of a relocatable program or data block and labels it with a symbol. If the label appears for the first time in a RORG specification, the virtual program counter is loaded with zero. If the label appears again afterwards, the virtual program counter is loaded with the value of the virtual program counter that was reached last under this label. Relative addresses are then assigned to the machine code produced afterwards, starting with the value of the virtual program counter. The block ends with the next AORG, RORG or END specification. If the block has to be relocated in the memory, the relative addresses in machine code have to be increased by the loading address before the program's execution, e.g. by means of a relocating loader. Such a block is called a statically relocatable block.

The PCR (Program Counter Relative) option directs the assembler to replace the direct and the indexed addressing in the machine instructions with the relative addressing or the relative indexed addressing, as long as the address specifications within the block or in another RORG block with the same name are defined as relative addresses. Thus, the changes of the address references because of a program relocation in memory occur during program execution by means of the relative to the program counter addressing. Such a block is called dynamically relocatable block (see also Subsection 3.1.4).

symbol EQU   expression equate

EQU (equate) equals the symbol in the label field to the value of the expression in the address field. The value assignment cannot be altered by subsequent EQU or SET specifications. The symbols appearing in the expression have to be defined before the EQU specification.

symbol   SET   expression   assign

SET assigns the value of the expression in the address field to the symbol in the label field. Contrary to EQU, a second SET specification can re-define the symbol; and the symbol, that was already defined, can be used in the expression.

[symbol]	DCB	operand(s)	define byte constant(s)
[symbol]	DCW	operand(s)	define word constant(s)
[symbol]	DCD	operand(s)	define double word constant(s)

DC specifications (Define Constant) allocate constants in byte, word and double word format in the memory. They are defined by one or more operands in the address field, that are separated by commas. Constants can be in hexadecimal, decimal and binary representation as well as in the ASCII format; moreover, symbols and expressions can be used.

DCB allocates byte operands that start with the higher byte (byte 0) of the next free memory word. If a DCB specification follows immediately after, it continues memory allocation with the first free byte. The DCW instruction allocates word operands at the first free memory cell. If in the previous word only the higher byte is defined, the lower byte will be set to zero. The same is true for the allocation of double word operands by means of the DCD specification. If a symbol is in the label field of a DC specification, then it defines the first memory byte that is used by the specification. Every time, the virtual program counter is increased by the amount of the allocated bytes. Here are some examples:

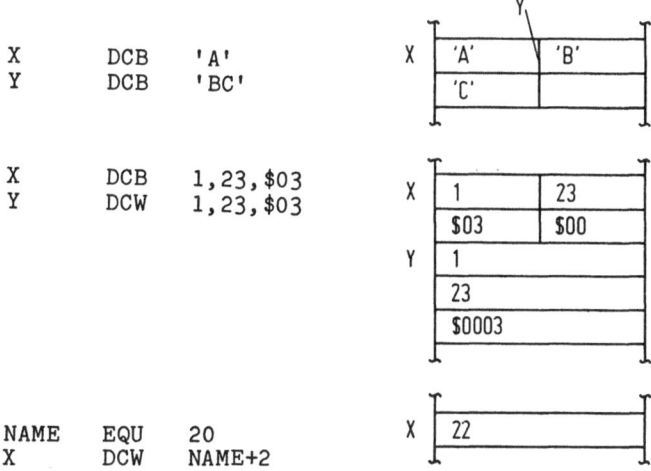

```
X       DCB     'A'
Y       DCB     'BC'


X       DCB     1,23,$03
Y       DCW     1,23,$03




NAME    EQU     20
X       DCW     NAME+2
```

DC specifications are used to create constants, i.e. operands, whose values are not altered by the program. When used to initialize variables, one should take into account that the program has to be translated again before each start, since the values of the variables can be changed during the running of a program.

[symbol]	DSB	operand	reserve byte memory space
[symbol]	DSW	operand	reserve word memory space
[symbol]	DSD	operand	reserve double word memory space

DS (Define Storage) reserves memory space in byte, word and double word format without using the space with values. The amount of bytes, words or double words is indicated in the address field by means of an operand. With the exception of ASCII characters, the same representations used in DC specifications are allowed. If there is a symbol in the label field, it defines the first memory byte of the reserved area. The virtual program counter is incremented by the amount of the reserved bytes. Here are some examples:

STRING DSB 11	reserves 11 subsequent bytes; the first byte has the symbolic address STRING.
FIELD DSW $10	reserves 16 subsequent words, starting with the first even byte address; the first word has the symbolic address FIELD.
BLOCK DSD N·2	reserves 2N subsequent double words, starting with the first even byte address; the first word has the symbolic address BLOCK. The value for N has to be defined previously.

EVEN   make virtual program counter even

EVEN makes the virtual program counter point to the first available even memory address (word address). An odd counting is increased by one, an even value remains unchanged.

ODD   make virtual program counter odd

ODD makes the virtual program counter point to the first available odd memory address. An even value is increased by one, an odd value remains unchanged.

DEF   symbol list   label symbols as "defined"

DEF (Defined) lists the symbols that are defined in the program section and that are used in other program sections translated separately. The assembler generates the linkage information for the subsequent linking of the program sections that were translated separately. The symbols in the symbol list are separated by commas.

REF   symbol list   label symbols as "used"

REF (referenced) is the counterpart to DEF, it lists the symbols used in the program section, that were defined in other program sections translated separately.

Apart from the described specifications, there is a sequence of additional pseudo-ops that for example output particular information at the end of the translating procedure.

OPT   keyword list

OPT (option) causes the generation of the following information contained in the key word list:

LIST   program list

SYMB   symbol table

XREF   cross-reference list (expanded symbol table specifying where the symbols will be used.)

PAGE   start new page

PAGE makes the assembler begin a new page when printing the list of statements.

TITLE   text   create heading

TITLE makes the assembler print the text given in the address field at the heading of each page of the program list.

3.1.4 Absolute and Relocatable Program Blocks

One of the goals in microprocessor techniques is to write programs so that they can be easily relocated within the address space of the memory. This is particularly true for programs and constants that are stored in ROM's or EPROM's and whose address relations are either impossible or very hard to change during a relocation. Whether a program can be relocated or not depends on the generation of absolute or relative addresses during the translation and on the use of relative addressing by the processor. Pseudo-ops AORG and RORG play a determinant role in this matter.

Example 3.2. Absolute and relocatable program blocks. Some excerpts from a program example illustrate three possibilities for the creation of absolute and relative addresses by using three different ORG specifications.

```
1.    AORG  $200
2.    RORG  BLOCK1
3.    RORG  BLOCK1,PCR,
```

They have to precede the following program block:

```
N         DSW   1
FIELD     DSW   100
LOC       DSW   1
            .
            .
            .
AGAIN     MOVE  R0,N
            .
            .
            .
          MOVE  R1,FIELD(R2)
            .
            .
            .
          LEA   R3,LOC
          MOVE  R2,(R3)
          JMP   AGAIN
            .
            .
          END
```

1. AORG $200. With the AORG specification, all addresses, that are related to the AORG specification, i.e. N, FIELD, LOC and AGAIN, are defined as absolute addresses at translation time. A subsequent program relocation is impossible. This is also true for address references which lead from other blocks to this block (absolute block).

2. RORG BLOCK1. All addresses that are related to the RORG specification, i.e. N, FIELD, LOC and AGAIN, are defined as relative addresses with the RORG specification. The point of reference for the assembler is the value of the virtual program counter when entering this block. This is zero for the first block with the label BLOCK1. When linking or loading the program, the relocation or load address is added to the address values of the block. This means that the block is relocatable either to the linking time or to the loading time (static relocatable block). The addresses are absolute during execution time.

3. RORG BLOCK1,PCR. The PCR option in the RORG specification requires the assembler to substitute the direct and the index addressing with relative to the program counter addressing and relative to the program counter addressing with index. All addresses related to the RORG specifications are involved: N, LOC and AGAIN as direct address specifications, and FIELD as indexed address specification. The instruction word (program counter) following the corresponding relative address is the point of reference for the creation of relative addresses. Thus, the block is relocatable during execution time (dynamically relocatable block). ■

A symbolic program consist of several consecutive AORG and RORG blocks. The absolute code obtained with AORG blocks is mainly used for small microprocessor systems, where the memory areas - e.g. a ROM area for program and a RAM area for data - are initially limited in their size by an incomplete address decoding and are pre-assigned in the address space (see also Subsection 4.2.2). In the case of larger systems working with relocatable code AORG blocks are mainly used to create non-relocatable tables, or for instance to fill a vector table or to define stack areas. In these systems, several independent relocatable program and data areas can be defined by using labels in RORG blocks. The relative to the program counter addressing caused by the option PCR refers to RORG blocks with the same label. Address references to other areas are produced either as absolute addresses by the assembler or as relative addresses by the linker or the linking loader.

A program or data block with relative to the program counter addressing within the block and with exclusive absolute address references for surrounding blocks is - as already mentioned - dynamically relocatable in the memory. If the program section is stored in a ROM, its location can be arbitrarily determined without requiring a change in memory content. A relocation in the address space occurs for instance through a change of address decoding on the memory board (see also Subsection 4.2.2). The drawback is that the data in the RAM area are to be relocated as well.

Dynamic data relocation, independent from program code relocation, occurs by means of base relative addressing. The effective address of a datum is created by adding the starting address of the data area (base address) to an offset in the instruction (relative address). The register, e.g. a general purpose register, containing the base address is called base address register. This register has to be loaded before the execution of the program.

Base relative addressing can be modelled with index addressing. The index register assumes the role of a base address register and is initialized with the data base address at the beginning of the program execution. Values, which were addresses when indexed addressing was used, are now relative data addresses; they have to be relative to the zero of the data base during the assembly. An additional indexing within the dynamic relocatable data area is not possible with our somehow simple processor version. In order to combine base relative addressing with index addressing, some microprocessors accept base addressing with index. Thus they allow the processing of data fields within a dynamically relocatable data area.

3.1.5 Structured Assembler Programming

Today's microprocessor systems contain assemblers that can translate not only one statement into machine code, but pieces of assembler programs containing several statements as a unit. 1-to-1 mapping of assembler instruction statements to machine instruction words is not used. Also machine-related program representation is abandoned in favor of machine-independent program representation. This technique is used in particular to clarify the control structure of assembler programs. Thus, the clarity of the program can be improved without losing efficiency in relation to space and time needs.

Similar to what happens with higher-level programming languages, the language elements that are used allow many possibilities of goto-less programming of program branches and of program loops. Such higher pseudo-ops are for instance:

- IF together with THEN and ELSE,

- FOR together with STEP, TO and DO or

- WHILE together with DO.

In order to be able to combine several statements into larger compound statements within such specifications, additional assembler keywords are necessary, e.g. BEGIN, END or keywords FI or OD together with IF and DO.

Instead of defining single specifications and of considering details of their application, we will describe this programming technique by means of a simple example containing the structured assembler program as well as the machine program that was translated by the assembler into symbolic representation.

Example 3.3. The structured assembler program. The algorithm for the addition of natural numbers 1 through N, represented as a structured flow chart in example 3.1, has to be programmed with the WHILE statement. - In the WHILE statement, the keyword WHILE is followed by a condition which depends on two operands. The keyword LS (lower or same) is used in the example to represent the comparison relation ≤. The instructions, that will be executed if the comparison is successful, are surrounded by the keywords DO and OD. For the input of number N and the output of the result SUM, there is a peripheral device whose interface register is addressed by the numerical address $FFFF or its symbolic equivalent EAREG. The program ends by calling the operative system by means of a TRAP instruction.

```
*
*  SUM OF NUMBERS FROM 1 THROUGH N
*
           RORG   NSUM
EAREG      EQU    $FFFF
N          DSW    1
I          DSW    1
SUM        DSW    1
*
START      MOVE   N,EAREG        START      MOVE   N,EAREG
           MOVE   I,#1                      MOVE   I,#1
           MOVE   SUM,#0                    MOVE   SUM,#0
           WHILE  I LS N         LBL1       CMP    I,N
           DO                               BHI    LBL2
           ADD    SUM,I                      ADD    SUM,I
           INC    I,1                       INC    I,1
           OD                               JMP    LBL1
           MOVE   EAREG,SUM      LBL2       MOVE   EAREG,SUM
           TRAP   0                         TRAP   0
           END
```

The assembler program was not designed for fast execution time, but for the best possible clarity. An overflow of the numeric variables, which could possibly occur during the addition if too large a number is input, is not considered in the program. On the right, next to the structured assembler program and at the same level, there is the assembler-created machine program, that is represented symbolically. This program contains an additional instruction that is not necessary. Without utilizing the structured programming, the test CMP/BHI (branch if higher) at the beginning of the block would be substituted by the complementary test CMP/BLS (branch if lower or same) at the end of the block. Thus, the JMP instruction could be omitted. ∎

3.1.6 Macroinstructions and Conditional Assembling

Assembler languages in current microprocessor systems permit, besides the 1-to-1 conversion from assembler into machine instructions, also the 1-to-n translation of so-called macroinstructions into a larger number of machine instructions. This expansion of an assembly code statement to n machine code statements during translation time is called macroexpansion.

Macroinstructions have the same structure as symbolic machine instructions. The name of the macro corresponds to the code of the machine instruction, and the parameters of the macroinstruction correspond to the addresses. Although the machine instructions' format and number depend on the processor hardware, macroinstructions can be defined by the programmer within the assembly language itself. Similarly, the number of parameters and their importance can be determined by the user to a large extent. Even the number of macroinstructions and their effect are independent from the processor hardware.

Macroinstructions allow an expansion of the processor's instruction set at the assembler level, and thus largely contribute to the clear encoding of assembler programs. The user of a microprocessor system can define a problem-oriented higher-level assembly language that is tailored to his problem by defining suitable and compatible macroinstructions. If the software of the microprocessor system allows the storage of such a user-defined programming language in a macrolibrary or the integration of the language in the operating system of the machine, in an extreme case the microprocessor system can be programmed without using one single machine instruction.

In order to produce the most efficient machine programs while using this programming technique, that is so strongly influenced by the task and the style of the user, conditional assembling has to be used. Depending on the kind and number of parameters in an assembler program macroinstruction, a different machine code is produced during the macroexpansion. Given the limitations of the assembly language, the achievement of the goal heavily depends on the ability of the programmer to define and to program the macroinstruction. The goal is maximum clarity in the assembler program and minimum memory space and execution time.

In order to define macroinstructions and to use conditional assembling, the assembly language is expanded with additional language elements. Such macroassembler pseudo-ops are for instance:

- MACRO (Macro begin) in connection with ENDM (End Macro) for the definition of a macroinstruction,

- NUMB (Number) for determining the number of the parameters when a macroinstruction is used,

- IFEQ (If Equal), IFGR (If Greater) and so on, in connection with ENDC (End Condition) for the test of conditions known at the time of assembly, and

- REPT (Repetition) in connection with ENDR (End Repetition) for the repeated assembling of a certain number of assembler statements.

The last two pseudo-op groups are substantially different from all other assembler pseudo-ops, since the traditional translation line by line of the source program is temporarily discontinued.

Depending on a test, program statement assembling can be avoided or, depending on a counter, it can be repeated several times.

During the translation of an assembler program, the parameter symbols of a macroinstruction (in short, actual parameters) are substituted, in the sense of a text substitution, to their formal correspondents (in short, formal parameters) that were used during the macrodefinition. By conditional assembly, different machine instruction sequences will be produced when expanding a macroinstruction.

The following example provides an idea of the programming possibilities of macroinstructions as well as of the stages during macroexpansion. It contains the definition of a macroinstruction together with three macrocalls and their different expanded forms as symbolic machine programs, produced by the macroassembler.

Example 3.4. Macroinstruction with several macroexpansions. Write a macroinstruction SAVR that loads the contents of the registers starting from the second parameter on the stack if the first parameter is "STACK", or that saves the register contents in an area, whose starting address is indicated by the first parameter. - The MACRO specification contains the name in the label field and a special character - here / - indicating the formal parameter of the macroinstruction. A decimal number immediately following this character points to the position of the actual parameter in the macroinstruction call. The NUMB expression generates the number of elements in the list given in its address field - here the number of the actual parameters - and assigns it to the symbol in the label field. If the text is the same in the label and in the address field, the IFEQ specification causes the assembly of the program statements between IFEQ and ENDC. According to the expression appearing in the address field, the REPT specification repeats the assembly of the statements between REPT and ENDR, and the value of the label is increased by 1 every time.

If the first actual parameter is called STACK, as many PUSH instructions will be produced during the expansion of the macroinstruction, as there are register contents which have to be loaded on the stack. Otherwise, a MOVE instruction will be generated, which loads the content of the register indicated as the second actual parameter into the field starting at the address indicated by the first actual parameter. If more than one register content has to be saved, then the following instructions are added: LEA instruction, that loads the field starting address in the register emptied by the preceding MOVE instruction; INC instruction, increasing this address by 2; and as many MOVE instructions as there are register contents with the autoincrement of the memory address.

The macroexpansions given along with the macrocalls illustrate how three machine instruction sequences, that strongly differ from each other as far as memory space requirements and execution times, are created by using different parameter specifications.

```
*
* SAVING SPECIFIC REGISTER CONTENTS
*
SAVR    MACRO  /
N       NUMB   /
I       SET    2
/1      IFEQ   STACK
I       REPT   N-1
        PUSH   /I
        ENDR
        ENDM
        ENDC
        MOVE   /1,/2
N       IFEQ   2
        ENDM
        ENDC
        LEA    /2,/1
        INC    /2,2
I       SET    I+1
I       REPT   N-2
        MOVE   (/2)+,/I
        ENDR
        ENDM


        3 SAVR MACROCALLS

        SAVR   STACK,R0,R1,R7      PUSH   R0
                                   PUSH   R1
                                   PUSH   R7

        SAVR   FIELD,R7            MOVE   FIELD,R7

        SAVR   (R6),R6,R7          MOVE   (R6),R6
                                   LEA    R6,(R6)
                                   INC    R6,2
                                   MOVE   (R6)+,R7
```

3.2 Program Flow Control

When a program is processed, each time an instruction is read from the memory for execution in the microprocessor, the program counter is incremented so that it will address the next instruction in memory. This sequential processing of instruction sequences can be interrupted by jump instructions, that load the program counter with a jump address given in the instruction and thus permit the continuation of the program in another place. Depending on whether the jump is combined with a condition or not, we have either a conditional or and unconditional jump.

3.2.1 Unconditional Jump

Figure 3.4 shows a schematic representation of three program sections with unconditional jumps. Cases a) and b) respectively show three instruction sequences that are stored in the same way, but that are processed in a different order. There are jumps, whose jump addresses are bigger than the address of the jump instruction (forward jumps), and jumps, whose jump addresses are smaller than the address of the jump instruction (backward jumps). Case c) contains a backward jump in an already executed instruction sequence, through which a program loop is created. The program

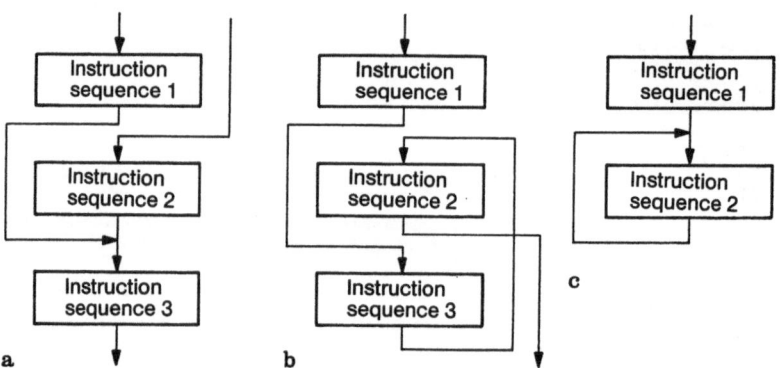

Fig. 3.4. Instruction sequences connected by unconditional jumps

cannot leave the loop because an unconditional jump was used. Such an infinite loop can only be exited with a program interrupt.

Example 3.5. Infinite loop. The values 0 and 1 have to be written repeatedly and in the shortest time into an external data register EAREG (compare program example in Subsection 1.3.1). - The repeated output is generated by an infinite loop with the JMP instruction. In order to have the shortest time intervals possible between the single outputs, values 0 and 1 are previously stored in the register file. Otherwise, they could be also defined as immediate operands in the MOVE instructions of the infinite loop.

```
        AORG  $200
EAREG   EQU   $FFFF       INITIALIZATION
START   MOVE  R0,#0
        MOVE  R1,#1
LOOP    MOVE  EAREG,R0    OUTPUT 0
        MOVE  EAREG,R1    OUTPUT 1
        JMP   LOOP
        END
```

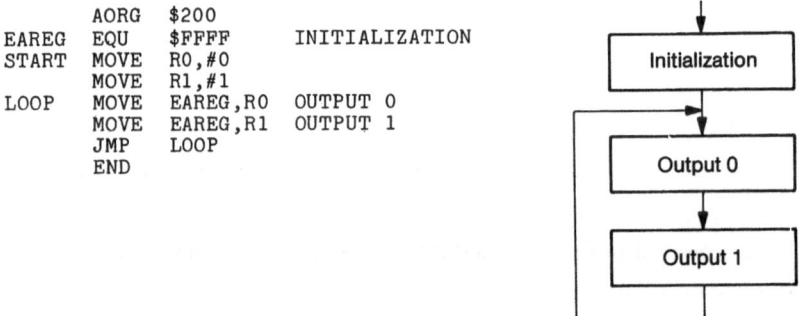

3.2.2 Conditional Jump and Simple Branch

In general, program loops are not programmed to be infinite, but rather in such a way that they can be exited depending on a condition, e.g. after a specific number of loop executions. For this purpose, there are the conditional jump instructions Bcond, with which the jump occurs depending on a condition indicated in the instruction (condition satisfied), or with which the program is continued with the instruction following the jump instruction (condition not satisfied). Thus we obtain a branch of the program towards one of the two possible program paths.

In order to check the jump condition, the conditional jump instructions evaluate the status of the condition bits CC in the status register. These bits can be influenced by the execution of most instructions, so that most of the instructions can be used to prepare a program branch. Especially, the compare instructions CMP and BTST are used, for which the result of the compare operation only affects the condition bits. In order to obtain understandable and safe programming, the condition bits should always be influenced by an instruction immediately preceding the jump instruction. Interfering instructions influence the condition bits again and thus lead to wrong branches.

In the flow chart, program branches are represented as a rhomb indicating the jump condition (Figure 3.5a). A hexagon indicates if the branch is preceded by a compare instruction (Figure 3.5b).

Figure 3.6 shows three important cases of branching in flow chart representation. In case a), an instruction sequence is skipped if the condition is satisfied. In case b), one of two instruction sequences will be executed depending on the condition; an additional unconditional jump is necessary for the final join of the two paths. In case c), the preceding instruction sequence is run again if the condition is satisfied (program loop).

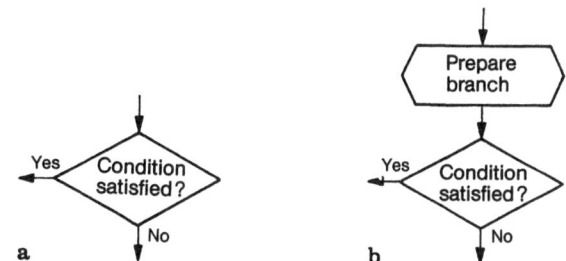

Fig. 3.5. Flow chart representation of branches

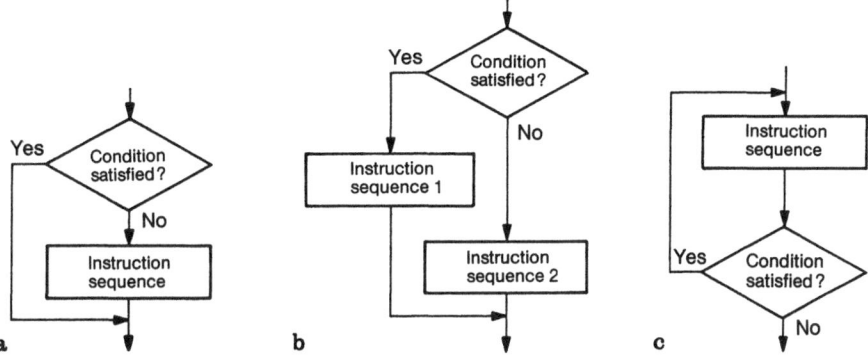

Fig. 3.6. Examples of simple branches

In order to construct a branch, we have to consider the preparation of the branch, the jump instruction and the data types of its operands. In the following, we will discuss some possibilities for the construction of simple branches by distinguishing three kinds of data types:

- two's complement number,

- unsigned number, and

- logic vector.

Arithmetic Conditional Values. Program branches, in which numbers represent the conditional values, are preferably prepared with the CMP instruction. CMP compares two values by subtraction and influences all condition bits with the result. The distinction between two's complement numbers and unsigned numbers is only obtained through the choice of the conditional jump instruction. All jump instructions checking bits N, Z or V are suitable for a test with two's complement numbers. All jump instructions checking bits Z or C are suitable for a test with unsigned numbers. Note: the V bit indicates arithmetic overflow in two's complement number operations, the C bit indicates arithmetic overflow in unsigned number operations.

Example 3.6. Compare two's complement numbers. A 16-bit two's complement number is in the memory and has the address NUMBER. Check whether it lies in the value range of $0 \leq NUMBER \leq 1000$. - The

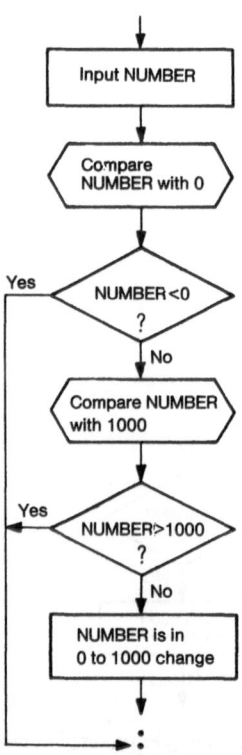

```
NUMBER DSW    1
        :
*  INPUT NUMBER
*
        CMP    NUMBER,#0
        BMI    OUT
        CMP    NUMBER,#1000
        BGT    OUT
*  NUMBER IS IN 0 TO 1000 RANGE
        :
OUT     :
```

comparison with the range limits is carried out through the CMP instruction, whose effect on the condition bits is evaluated with the conditional jump instructions BMI and BGT. BMI and BGT refer to bits N or N and V that are used when handling two's complement numbers. ▪

Example 3.7. Compare unsigned numbers. An 8-bit unsigned number is in the memory and has the address BIN. Check whether it lies within the value range of $0 \le BIN \le 9$. - The test of range limit 0 can be avoided, since the number has no sign in the case of a BIN value. The test of the higher range limit is carried out by the compare instruction CMPB and the conditional jump instruction BHI. BHI refers to bits Z and C that are used when dealing with unsigned numbers.

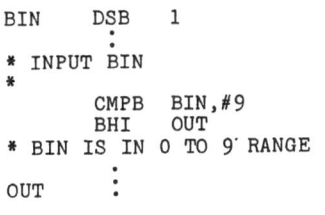

```
BIN     DSB    1
        :
* INPUT BIN
*
        CMPB   BIN,#9
        BHI    OUT
* BIN IS IN 0 TO 9 RANGE
        :
OUT     :
```

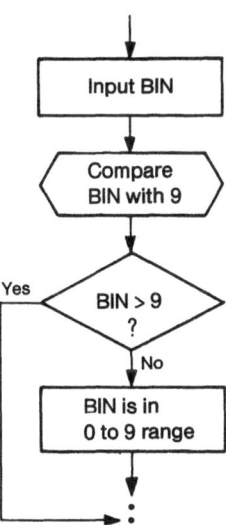

Logic Conditional Values. In control applications there are often binary data that are combined as logic vectors (bit strings) in byte, word or double word format. Thus for instance, the conditions of external switches are represented by means of the values of the single bits within a byte (binary-value condition). The BTST instruction is used for testing one or more bits of such a vector. This contains a bit mask - either as immediate operand (constant mask) or as register operand (variable mask) - with the bit positions to be tested set to 1. The test is carried out by a comparison with zero, so that condition bit Z is influenced. Then the branching can take place with one of the jump instructions BEQ or BNE.

Example 3.8. Test of single-bit signals with the same status. Eight single-bit signals are connected to the eight lower data lines of the data bus by means of the external data register EASIG. A program has to wait in a specific section in a waiting loop until the signals in bit positions 0, 1 and 3 have value 1, independently from the other signals. - Since the BTSTB instruction is comparing the masked bit positions with 0, but the problem needs to test ones, the signal values have to be inverted beforehand. Thus, they are first loaded in register R0.

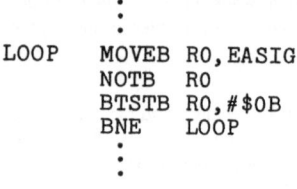

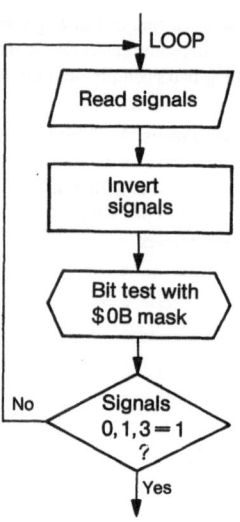

If the test of the masked bits cannot be carried out uniformly on 0 or on 1 after the inversion, the CMP instruction has to be used instead of the BTST instruction. Each bit pattern can be used as a compare value in CMP; however, the masking has to be programmed additionally by using the AND instruction.

Example 3.9. Test of single-bit signals with different status. As a variation of the problem presented in Example 3.8, the program has to wait in a waiting loop until signal 3 has value 0 and signal 0 and 1 have value 1. - The masking occurs in R0 with mask $0B. The values of the three signal bits in question remain unchanged, the remaining bits of the lower register byte are set to zero. This 0/1 combination in R0 is compared with the bit pattern $03 by means of the CMPB instruction.

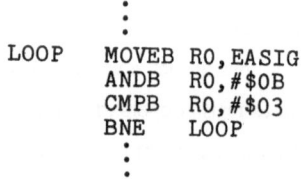

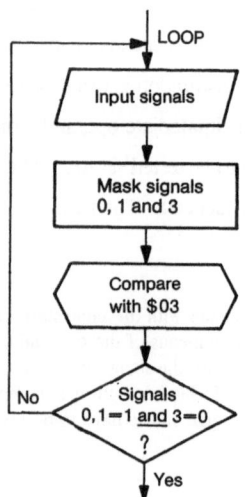

If the program flow has to be controlled by a string of single bits, and if these bits are combined in one operand, there is the possibility of using shift instructions to prepare a program branch. By shifting the bits into the most significant bit place (affecting the N bit) or in the carry flip flop (affecting the C bit), branches can be performed with jump instructions BPL and BMI or BCC and BCS. The bit string is not changed if a rotate instruction is used for shifting.

Example 3.10. Control of the program flow by means of a bit string. A program has to branch depending on the eight consecutive bits of the 0/1 combination $5A to the program paths ZERO or ONE. Starting from the lowest bit, the bit string has to be evaluated in an infinite loop. - The preparation of the test is done with rotate instruction RORB, where the lowest bit of the bit string in R0 is transferred to the carry flip flop and, at the same time, to the most significant bit position of R0. The state of the C bit is to be tested by using the conditional jump instruction BCS.

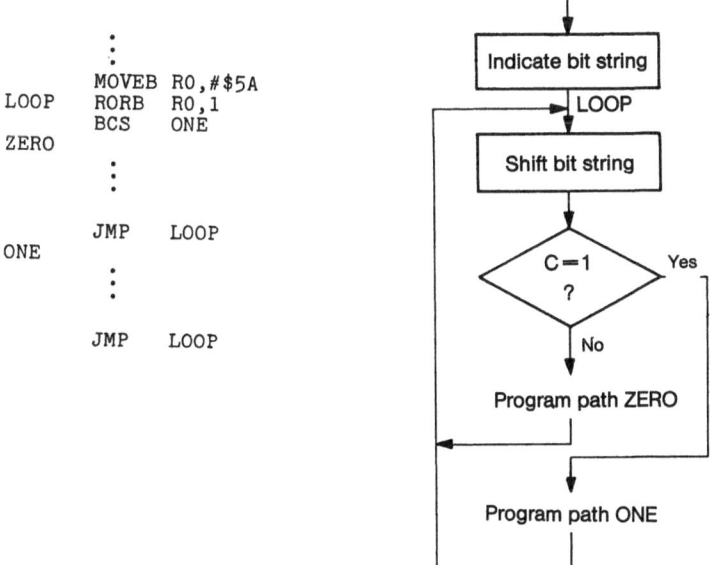

3.2.3 Multiple-Way Branch

Sequence of Binary Conditions. Often a separate program path is needed for each condition specification, and a multiple-way branch determines which path will be executed. Example 3.11 shows a multiple-way branch, in which the bits of a logic vector are successively evaluated as binary conditions like in Example 3.10.

Example 3.11. Sequential test of binary conditions. A data byte (EASIG) reflects the state of eight input signals. When the value of some of the bits is 1, an appropriate branch has to be executed. The processing order of the input signals is given by the sequence of the bits, starting with the highest bit. - The content of EASIG is loaded in register R0 with MOVEB. Testing of the single bits is done sequentially with the conditional jump instruction BMI. This evaluates the sign bit N of the result obtained before. Before the first test, N is determined by the MOVEB instruction, before each of the following tests it is influenced by a 1-bit left shift of R0. Since the logic shift instruction LSLB is used, the bit string contained in R0 is lost. However, it is loaded again with the correct signal conditions with each jump to address LOOP.

88

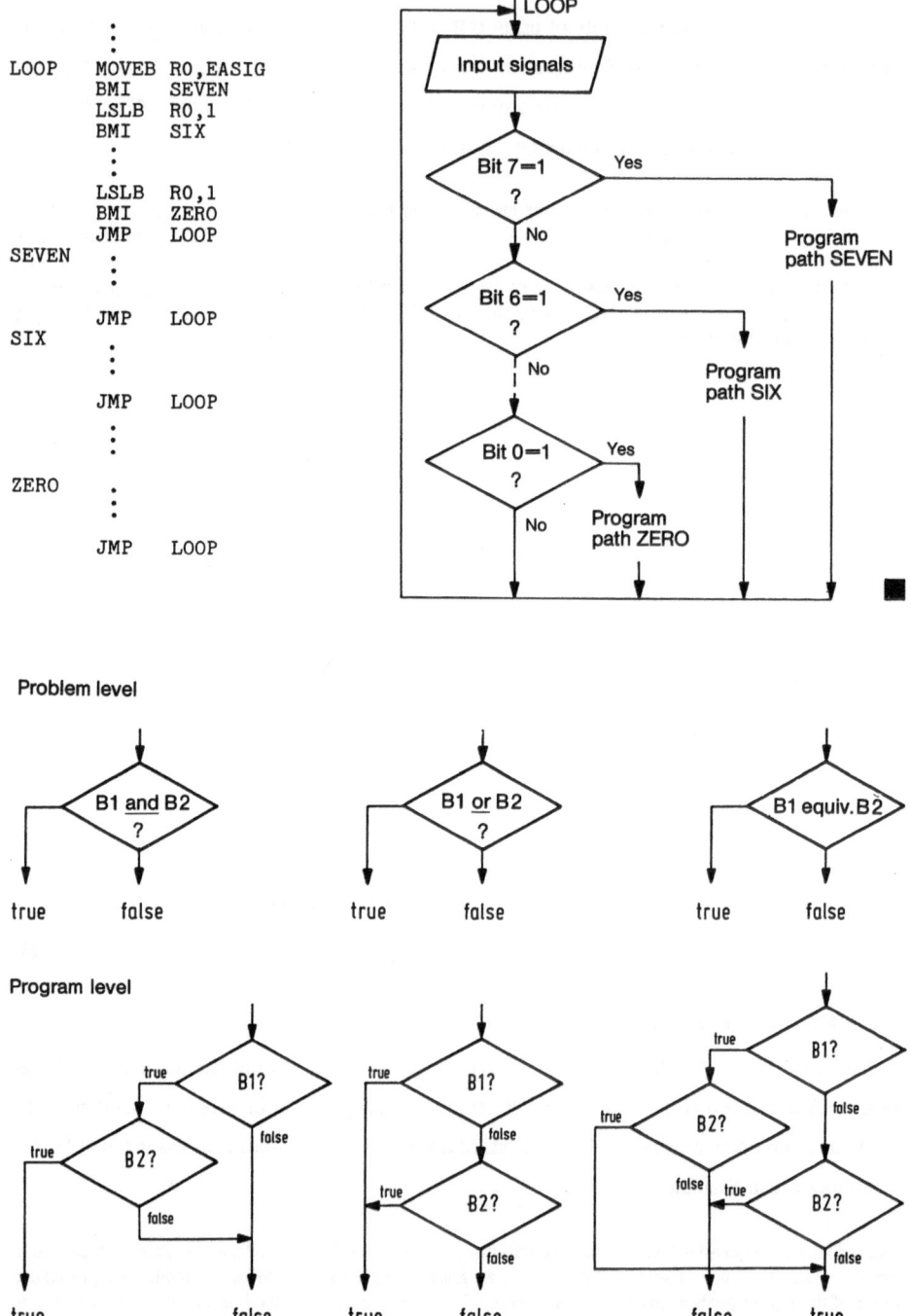

Fig. 3.7. Multiple-way branch through combination of binary conditions

Combination of Binary Conditions. Condition specifications in which several conditions are combined logically, also lead to a multiple-way branch. To this purpose, Figure 3.7 shows three examples in which two binary conditions B1 and B2 are combined by means of the logic operators *and, or* and *equivalence*, and respectively branch to one of two program paths with the labels *true* and *false*. Example 3.12 shows a program in which branching occurs on one of three possible program paths.

Example 3.12. Multiple-way branch through condition combination. Two two's complement numbers have to be compared with each other. Depending on the satisfaction of the conditions A less than, equal or greater than B, the branching has to occur in either one of the three possible program branches. - One single CMP instruction is sufficient to perform the test, since the condition bits it influences are not changed by the BLT instruction.

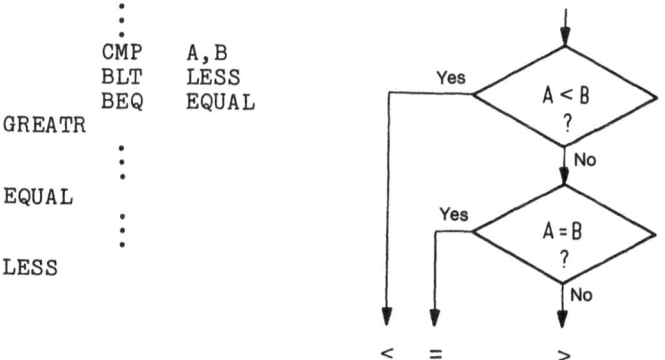

```
        CMP   A,B
        BLT   LESS
        BEQ   EQUAL
GREATR
        .
        .
EQUAL
        .
        .
LESS
```

Multiple-Value Conditions. A multiple-way branching also occurs when a single conditional variable can assume more than two values, and these are evaluated as different branch criteria (multiple-value condition). Usually it is consecutive values of unsigned numbers.

The test of the conditional values can basically occur sequentially, while the single tests are prepared by CMP instructions (sequential branching). This procedure is very time consuming due to the amount of tests, which, in the worst case, is equal to the amount of the possible values. Figure 3.8 shows a more efficient programming technique. The bits of the conditional value are evaluated in a tree fashion, where the number of tests is always equal to the number of bits required for value representation (binary branching). The tests can be prepared with BTST instructions. Compared to the sequential branching, the program is less understandable. Figure 3.8 shows the example of a 2-bit conditional variable which can assume values from 0 to 3.

Another possibility of multiple-way branch programming with a multiple conditional variable consists in the use of the JMP instruction with, for instance, register indirect addressing of the jump destination. First, the address register is loaded with the starting address of a so-called jump table,

90

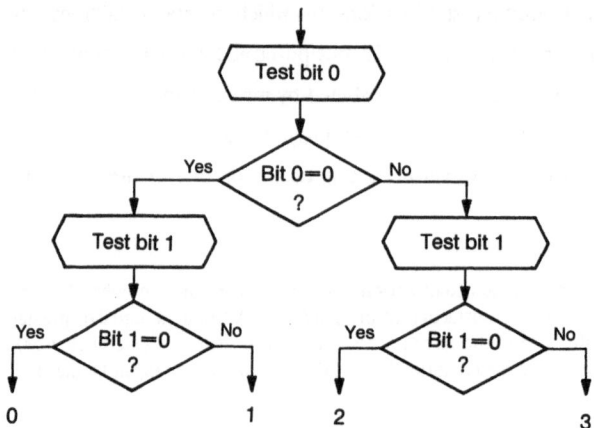

Fig. 3.8. Tree of evaluation of multiple-value conditions

which contains the addresses of the single program paths. Before execution of the jump instruction, the register content is changed by adding the value to be tested, so that it points to the destination address corresponding to the branch in the jump table.

Example 3.13. Multiple-way branch with jump table. Depending on the Conditional value (COND) which can assume values 0, 1, 2 and 3, a multiple-way branch has to jump to one of the four possible program paths with addresses ZERO, ONE, TWO and THREE. - The Jump Table (JMPTAB) with the destination addresses ZERO, ONE, TWO and THREE is indicated by DCW pseudo-ops. The branching occurs by means of register indirect addressing in the JMP instruction with R0 as address register. R0 is first loaded with the starting address of the Jump Table (JMPTAB) and then increased by twice the value of the value to be tested COND. The doubling is necessary, because the address entries in the jump table include two bytes each; this is done by means of an arithmetic 1-bit left shift.

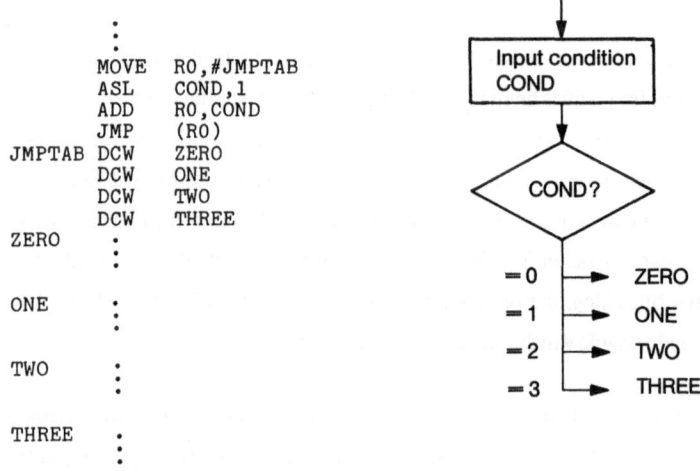

Index addressing can be employed instead of register indirect addressing. In this case, the jump table consists of JMP instructions that lead the jumps to the single program paths. The starting address of the jump table serves as base address for the index; the distance in the index register is obtained from the conditional value. The branch occurs with a two-way jump.

3.2.4 Program Loops

As already mentioned at the beginning of this section, the instruction sequence that is run repeatedly is called program loop. The loop is implemented with a jump instruction at the end of the instruction sequence, that leads back to its beginning. If this instruction sequence only contains one unconditional jump instruction, the loop is infinite and can only be left through a program interrupt. If the instruction sequence contains at least one conditional jump instruction, leaving the loop will depend on the condition. Figure 3.9 shows two basic kinds of loops, in which the conditional jump instruction is a) at the end or b) at the beginning of the instruction sequence. There are complementary condition specifications: The loop is exited in case a) when the condition is not satisfied, and in case b) when the condition is satisfied. In case b) an additional unconditional jump is necessary to create a loop.

A further distinctive characteristic of program loops is the specification of the number of loop iterations. This can either occur inductively or iteratively.

Inductive Loops. In the case of inductive loops, the number of loop iterations is known at the beginning of the loop and is independent from the processing within the loop. An iteration variable is used to count loop iterations. It is initialized before entering the loop, changed at each loop iteration and evaluated as termination criterion in the condition test. Thus we have two different kinds of organization: 1. the iteration variable is initialized with zero or one, is increased by one at each loop iteration and is compared with the number of loop iterations during the testing (upward counting loop). 2. The iteration variable is initialized with the number of loop iterations, is

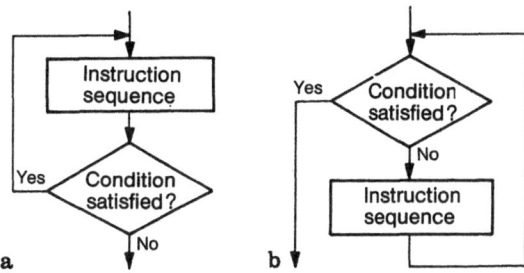

Fig. 3.9. Program loop. a) with condition test at the end, b) with condition test at the beginning

decreased by one at each loop iteration and is compared with zero or one in the test (downward counting loop). Inductive loops are also called *for*-loops.

Example 3.14. Inductive loop with up-counting iteration variable. Add natural numbers 1 through N and assign the result to the variable SUM.

```
EAREG   EQU    $FFFF
SUM     DSD    1
N       DSW    1
I       DSW    1
          .
          .
          .
        CLRD   R0
        MOVE   I,#1
        MOVE   N,EAREG
LOOP    ADD    R1,I
        ADDC   R0,#0
        INC    I,1
        CMP    I,N
        BLS    LOOP
        MOVED  SUM,R0
```

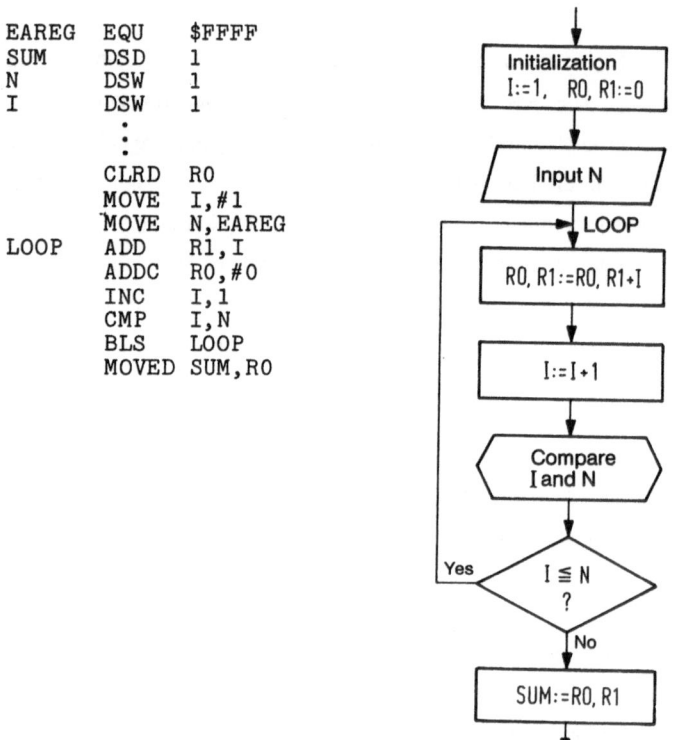

N is indicated by an external 16-bit data register EAREG (see Example 3.1 and Figure 3.2). - Variable I is used to count loop iterations. It is initialized with one and is increased by one at each iteration. Since it indicates the exact value of the sum for each iteration, it is used in the addition. The actual addition occurs in R1; the resulting carry is added to R0, so that the result is a double word. I and N are here in the memory for demonstration purposes; for more efficient programming they would be kept in the register file for quick access. ∎

Example 3.15. Inductive loop with down-counting iteration variable. Add 100 16-bit unsigned numbers, that are in a data block FIELD, assign the result to the variable SUM. - The counting is carried out by an iteration variable stored in R2, that was initialized with value 100 and is decremented by one in each loop iteration. Unlike example 3.14, the CMP instruction is not necessary, because the test for 0 refers to the result of the DEC instruction. In order to address field elements, the field starting address is loaded into R3 with LEA and autoincrement addressing is used.

```
FIELD   DSW    100
SUM     DSD    1
          .
          .
          .
        CLRD   R0
        MOVE   R2,#100
        LEA    R3,FIELD
LOOP    ADD    R1,(R3)+
        ADDC   R0,#0
        DEC    R2,1
        BNE    LOOP
        MOVED  SUM,R0
```

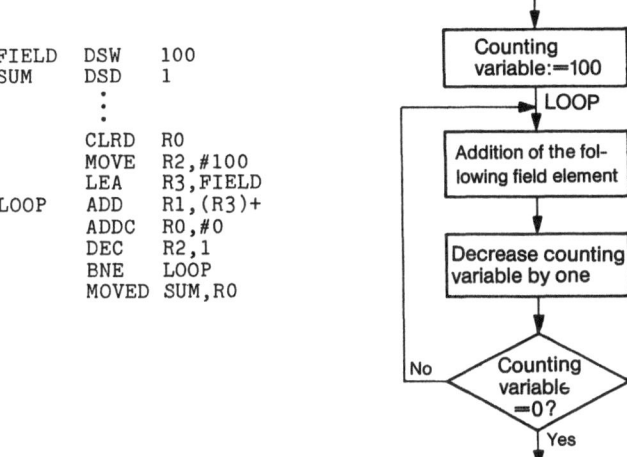

Iterative Loops. In the case of iterative program loops, the number of loop iterations when entering the loop is not known, it depends on the result of the processing in the loop. In order to specify the conditions for the loop termination, an arithmetic value and a compare value are used; the comparison value can be either a constant or a variable. If the test precedes the loop, it is important to remember that the values have to be initialized before entering the loop in order to obtain a given test in the first iteration. Iterative loops are also called while-loops.

Iterative loops do not always end with a loop termination; in particular, this does not occur when the iteration does not converge. If this is the case because of the problem to be solved, it is necessary to complete the iteration condition with an induction condition in order to limit the number of loop runs. Thus, the loop contains two condition tests for loop termination that can be combined either before or afterwards in different ways.

Example 3.16. Iterative loop with additional inductive restriction of the number of iterations. A specific character, that is in memory cell CHAR, has to be found in a buffer area BUFFER with N = 512 ASCII characters. When the character is found, or after a maximum number of search steps indicated by the buffer length N, abandon the search. - The characters are compared in a program loop, which is terminated iteratively if the characters are the same, or which is terminated inductively after N search steps. In order to address the buffer, the highest buffer address, that was increased by one, BUFFER + N is loaded into R3, which is then decremented by one because of the autodecrement addressing in the compare instruction CMPB during each loop iteration. Accordingly, the search process starts with the last character of the buffer area. If the loop termination is iterative, the counting register R0 indicates the position of the found character in the buffer; if the loop termination is inductive, R0 contains value zero.

94

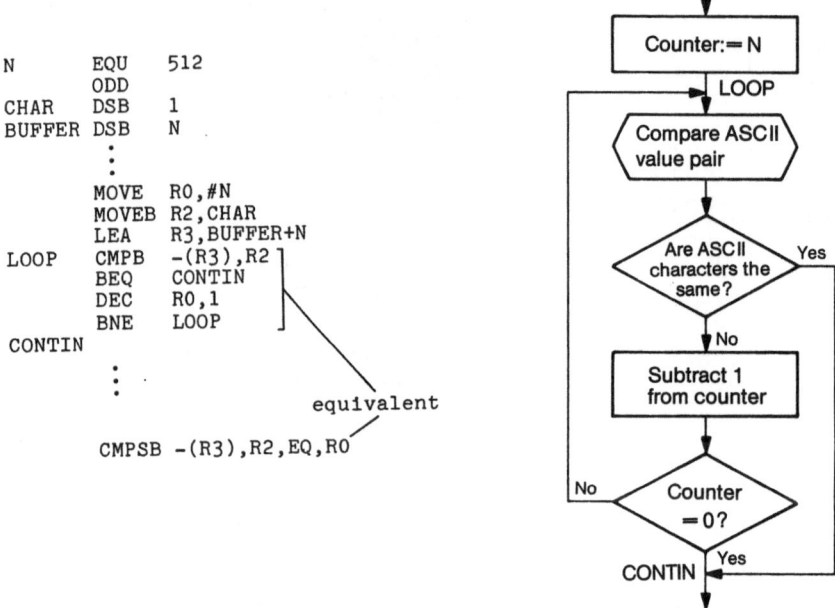

```
N        EQU    512
         ODD
CHAR     DSB    1
BUFFER   DSB    N
           .
           .
           .
         MOVE   R0,#N
         MOVEB  R2,CHAR
         LEA    R3,BUFFER+N
LOOP     CMPB   -(R3),R2
         BEQ    CONTIN
         DEC    R0,1
         BNE    LOOP
CONTIN
           .
           .
           .
                              equivalent

         CMPSB  -(R3),R2,EQ,R0
```

3.3 Subprogram Techniques

Subprograms are self-contained instruction sequences, that can be repeatedly called and executed at random points of a main program. After completion of a subprogram, the main program is resumed past the call point. Figure 3.10 shows the order of execution of two subprogram calls. When called, a subprogram can be provided with variables and it can, on its part, return results to the main program. These variables are called parameters and this operation is known as parameter passing.

The use of subprograms offers the following advantages:

- Instruction sequences that are frequently repeated only need to be programmed and stored once.

- Programs can be build in a modular way; thus, they are more understandable, easier to test and to document.

- A subprogram can be translated independently from the main program and from other subprograms. If an error in the subprogram has to be corrected, only the subprogram needs to be translated again.

- Bigger programs can be divided into subprograms and can be written by several people at the same time.

- Libraries with standard subprograms can be made available to all microprocessor system users.

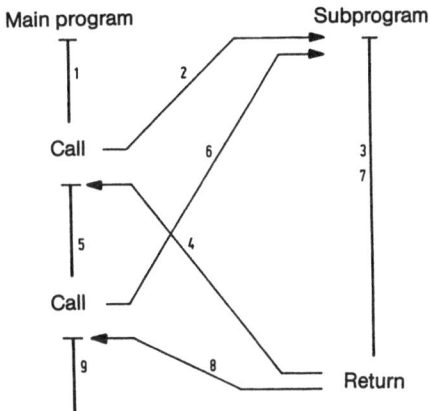

Fig. 3.10. Flow of control when the subprogram
is requested twice

3.3.1 Subprogram Call and Return

Subprogram Call. A subprogram is called by using instruction JSR with the name of the subprogram as address. This address is the symbol in the label field of the first operative instruction in the subprogram. JSR stores the actual program counter content (the address of the instruction following JSR) as return address in the current stack (user or system stack) and loads the program counter with the subprogram address contained in the address section of JSR. Then, the control is in the subprogram. The return into the main program occurs with instruction RTS, which terminates the subprogram. RTS reads the last stack entry - the return address - and loads it into the program counter.

If the subprogram uses the stack for data storage for example through the instructions PUSH and POP, it is important to keep in mind that the RTS instruction needs the stack pointer that is directly after the subprogram jump; otherwise there could be an uncontrolled jump. Thus, return addresses and data are usually put in a program and in a data stack separately.

Saving The Status. If the subprogram and the main program use the processor registers independently from each other, the whole processor status has to be saved when calling a subprogram, and it has to be reloaded when returning into the main program. The processor status includes the program counter content as well as the contents of the general purpose processor registers and the content of the status register. While the program counter is automatically saved and loaded during the execution of instructions JSR and RTS, one has to explicitly program the saving of the other registers. General purpose registers can be saved and loaded with the MOVEM instruction, the status register uses the MOVSR instruction. If the programs are in user mode, MOVCC, which simply moves condition bits, is to be used instead of the MOVSR instruction. This is no limitation though, since in user mode the status bits cannot be changed in the status register.

The place to store status information can be the user or the system stack, which is also used to save the return address.

The processor status can be loaded both in the main and in the subprogram. Which possibility should be chosen is a question of program organization. If the saving operation is performed in the main program and it is unknown which registers are used in the subprogram, then all general purpose processor registers have to be taken into account. On the other hand, if the saving operation occurs in the subprogram, only the registers used by the subprogram are important. Thus, the process of saving the status is accelerated.

Example 3.17. Saving and loading the processor status. When calling a subprogram in user mode, the processor status, consisting of return address, condition bits CC and general purpose registers R0 through R6, has to be saved. - The saving of the return address occurs by means of the JSR instruction. The condition bits and the register contents R0 through R6 are written on the user stack by the subprogram with the MOVCC and MOVEM instructions; R7 is used as stack pointer register. When the subprogram is finished, the loading of the status is performed in reverse order; RTS gives the program control back to the main program with the return address stored in the stack. The corresponding numbers in the program and in the illustration show the effect of the instructions when the stack is used.

System/User stack

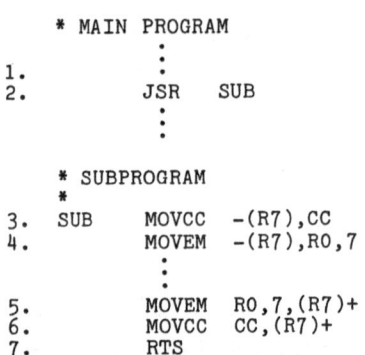

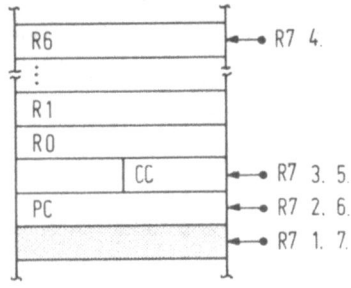

3.3.2 Parameter Passing

Three factors influence the programming technique used when transferring parameters to the subprogram or back to the main program:

1. the type of parameter, e.g. value, address,

2. the area for parameter passing, e.g. general purpose processor registers, stack, data area of the main program, program area of the main program,

3. the number of parameters.

Type of Parameters. In a subprogram call with call-by-value, the value of a variable is copied as a parameter in the data area of the subprogram, where a storage area must be reserved for it. The subprogram has direct access to the value and can change it, without influencing the original value in the main program. In a subprogram call with call-by-reference, the address of a variable is transferred to the subprogram as a parameter; i.e., the operand itself remains in the main program. The access of the operand by the subprogram occurs indirectly through the address parameter. The return of parameters back to the main program occurs either directly as call by value, e.g. in the register file, or indirectly by means of an address parameter.

The parameters, that are used as fictitious elements to write the subprogram, are called formal parameters. Before the execution of the subprogram, these have to be substituted by the parameters known at the time of the call, i.e. the actual parameters.

Whether call by value, call by reference or a combination of the two is used in a subprogram call depends both on the case at hand and on the following criteria:

- time involved in the parameter passing,

- storage space needed for the parameters,

- addressing overhead involved in the access by the subprogram,

- write protection for data in the main program.

Call by value is generally only used for single values; if fields have to be passed, call by reference is preferred because of the time and storage space savings. - Figure 3.11 shows the basic step of

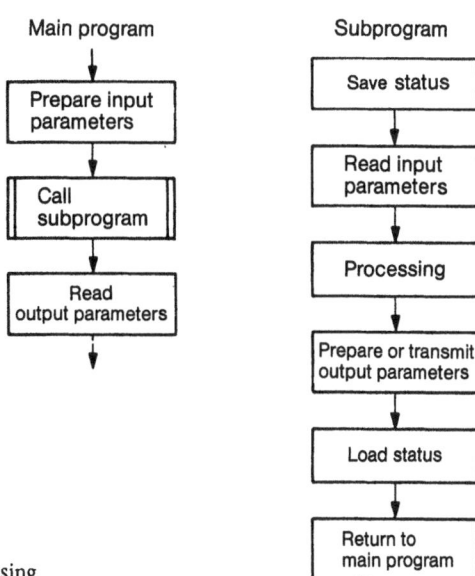

Fig. 3.11. Subprogram call with parameter passing

parameter passing. In the flow chart representation, a subprogram call is characterized by double side lines in a rectangle.

Parameters that are passed to the subprogram and whose values are used there, but are not changed, are called input parameters. Accordingly, parameters, that cannot be assigned values until in the subprogram and can only then be used, are called output parameters. Parameters, whose values are first used in the subprogram and then changed, are called input/output parameters.

Area for Parameter Passing. The area for parameter passing has to be accessible from both the main and the subprogram. If only a few parameters are passed, then the processor register file is to be used. This possibility requires the lowest cost for the preparation and execution of the parameter passing. If the number of the available registers is not sufficient, the parameters have to be passed into a memory area that is controlled by both the main and the subprogram. This requires a greater organizational effort. At this point, there are three possibilities:

1. The parameters are written in a stack area before the subprogram call, and the stack pointer in the register file is transferred to the subprogram; the parameter access occurs through the stack pointer.

2. The parameters in the data area of the main program are combined in a parameter field and its starting address is passed to the subprogram; the call-by-reference can occur by means of a general purpose register or through the user or the system stack; parameter access takes place through this address.

3. The parameters in the program area of the main program are combined in a parameter field that is stored directly after the subprogram jump instruction JSR; parameter access occurs through the return address of the subprogram stored in the user or in the system stack.

In the following, we discuss the different possibilities of parameter passing by means of the problem described in Example 3.16, which is not very representative due to the small size of the program text. So as not to shorten the program any more, we will not use the CMPS instruction. Which alternative will be chosen - including the parameter passing in the register file - depends on the problem at hand, on the data area structure and on the personal style of the programmer.

Example 3.18. Parameter passing in the register file. A subprogram has to carry out a search for a specific character in a buffer area of 512 ASCII characters (compare with Example 3.16). When this character is found, its position in the buffer is to be communicated to the main program; if the character is not in the buffer, the return value is to be set to zero. - The input parameters are transmitted to the subprogram as values (in R0 the buffer length N, in R2 the compare character CHAR) and as an address (in R3 the highest buffer address, increased by one, BUFFER + N). For returning the positions in the buffer to the main program, the subprogram call transmits the address INDEX in R1 as the address of the output parameter.

```
* MAIN PROGRAM                          * SUBPROGRAM
       :                                *
       :                         COMP    CMPB    -(R3),R2
N          EQU    512                    BEQ     RET
INDEX      DSW    1                      DEC     R0,1
           ODD                           BNE     COMP
CHAR       DSB    1                RET    MOVE    (R1),R0
BUFFER     DSB    N                       RTS
       :
       :
           MOVE   R0,#N
           LEA    R1,INDEX
           MOVEB  R2,CHAR
           LEA    R3,BUFFER+N
           JSR    COMP
       :
       :
```

As already mentioned, parameter passing in the register file involves the least organizational effort and is accordingly more efficient. One of the conditions though, is that the number of input parameters cannot exceed the number of available registers.

Example 3.19. Parameter passing in the stack. Example 3.18 has to be changed so that parameters are passed in the user or in the system stack. The stack also has to contain the status of registers R0 through R6 of the

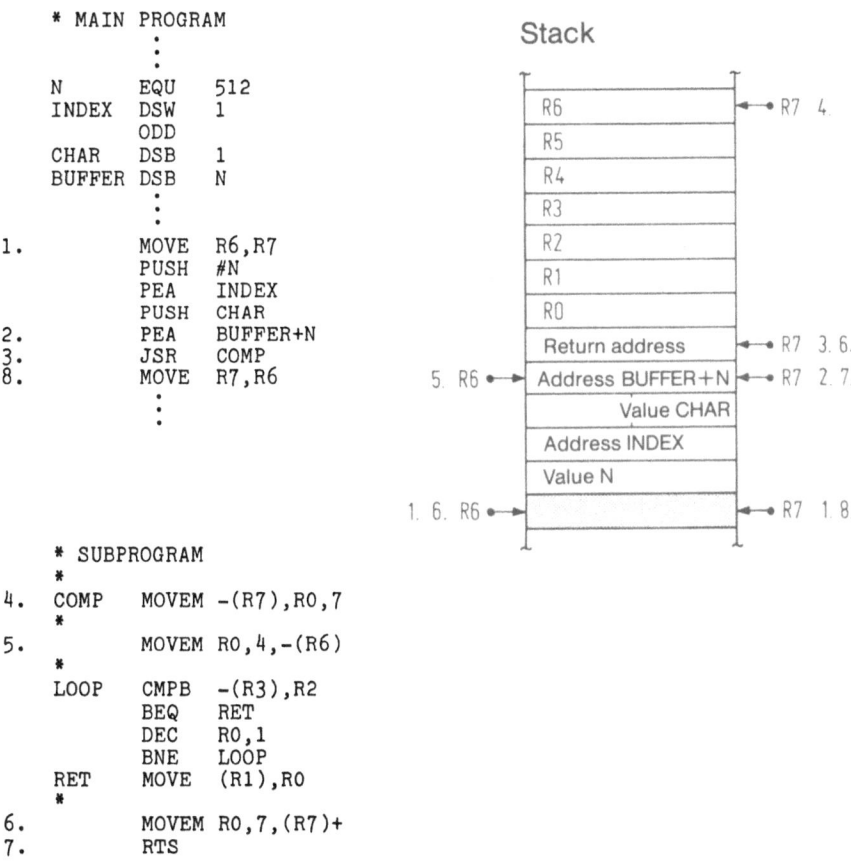

```
    * MAIN PROGRAM
           :
           :
N          EQU    512
INDEX      DSW    1
           ODD
CHAR       DSB    1
BUFFER     DSB    N
           :
           :
1.         MOVE   R6,R7
           PUSH   #N
           PEA    INDEX
           PUSH   CHAR
2.         PEA    BUFFER+N
3.         JSR    COMP
8.         MOVE   R7,R6
           :
           :
```

```
    * SUBPROGRAM
    *
4.  COMP    MOVEM  -(R7),R0,7
    *
5.          MOVEM  R0,4,-(R6)
    *
    LOOP    CMPB   -(R3),R2
            BEQ    RET
            DEC    R0,1
            BNE    LOOP
    RET     MOVE   (R1),R0
    *
6.          MOVEM  R0,7,(R7)+
7.          RTS
```

Stack

```
┌──────────────────┐
│        R6        │ ◄──── R7  4.
├──────────────────┤
│        R5        │
├──────────────────┤
│        R4        │
├──────────────────┤
│        R3        │
├──────────────────┤
│        R2        │
├──────────────────┤
│        R1        │
├──────────────────┤
│        R0        │
├──────────────────┤
│  Return address  │ ◄──── R7  3. 6.
├──────────────────┤
│ Address BUFFER+N │ ◄──── R7  2. 7.
5. R6 ◄──►
├──────────────────┤
│    Value CHAR    │
├──────────────────┤
│   Address INDEX  │
├──────────────────┤
│      Value N     │
├──────────────────┤
1. 6. R6 ◄──►       │ ◄──── R7  1. 8.
└──────────────────┘
```

main program. - The main program writes the input parameters with instructions PUSH and PEA as values or addresses in the stack, while register R7 (or R7') is implicitly used as stack point register. Before writing the parameters, it copies the content of R7 into R6. The subprogram uses R6 to read the parameters, after saving the register status in the stack with the MOVEM instruction. Thus, the subprogram is independent of R7, whose content was changed both by saving the return address as well as by saving the register status. Moreover, the actual stack content is thus indicated by R7, which makes it possible to re-enter the subprogram (see Subsection 3.3.4). When the subprogram is finished, the register status of the main program is re-loaded, so that R6 has the same content it had in the main program before parameter preparation. The main program copies the content of R6 into R7, which releases the parameter area in the stack. The corresponding numbers in the program and in the illustration show the effect of the instructions on the use of the stack. ■

Parameter passing in the stack is preferred in the case of block structured programs, in which the data areas of the subprograms are pushed and popped according to the LIFO principle (dynamic data memory management).

Example 3.20. Parameter passing in the data area of the main program. As a variation of Example 3.18, the parameters have to be combined in a Parameter List (PLIST) in the data area of the main program, and their starting address has to be.transmitted to the subprogram. The status of registers R0 through R3 of the main program has to be stored in the stack. - The main program writes the parameters in the field PLIST and communicates the R6 field starting address to the subprogram. The subprogram reads the parameters in the register file after writing the main program register status on the stack.

```
* MAIN PROGRAM                          * SUBPROGRAM
          .                             *
          .                             COMP    MOVEM  -(R7),R0,4
N        EQU    512                      *
INDEX    DSW    1                                MOVEM  R0,4,(R6)+
         ODD                            *
CHAR     DSB    1                       LOOP    CMPB   -(R3),R2
BUFFER   DSB    N                               BEQ    RET
          .                                     DEC    R0,1
          .                                     BNE    LOOP
PLIST    DSW    4                       RET     MOVE   (R1),R0
          .                             *
          .                                     MOVEM  R0,4,(R7)+
         MOVE   PLIST,#N                         RTS
         LEA    PLIST+2,INDEX
         MOVE   PLIST+4,CHAR
         LEA    PLIST+6,BUFFER+N
         LEA    R6,PLIST
         JSR    COMP
          .
          .
```

When parameters are passed in the data area of the main program, there are several parameter lists for a subprogram, and each time, depending on one condition, one of the lists is given to the subprogram.

Example 3.21. Parameter passing in the program area of the main program. Change Example 3.18 so that the parameters are read by the subprogram in a parameter field, which immediately follows the JSR instruction. - The parameter field in the main program code is determined statically through the DCW specification. Unlike the previous examples, in the case of CHAR the address is transmitted, not the value. In the subprogram, the value is read by the MOVE instruction before the LOOP statement. N, whose value is constant, is passed by call by value. The access of the subprogram to the parameter field occurs by means of

```
* MAIN PROGRAM              * SUBPROGRAM
            :               *
            :               COMP   MOVE   R6,(R7)
N        EQU   512                 MOVEM  -(R7),R0,4
INDEX    DSW   1             *
         ODD                        MOVEM  R0,4,(R6)+
CHAR     DSB   1                    MOVE   R2,(R2)
BUFFER   DSB   N             *
            :               LOOP   CMPB   -(R3),R2
            :                      BEQ    RET
         JSR   COMP                DEC    R0,1
         DCW   N                   BNE    LOOP
         DCW   INDEX        RET    MOVE   (R1),R0
         DCW   CHAR         *
         DCW   BUFFER+N            MOVEM  R0,4,(R7)+
            :                      MOVE   (R7),R6
            :                      RTS
```

the return address in the stack, which is loaded into R6. At the end of the subprogram, the return address, which was increased by eight, is written again in the stack, so that RTS causes the return into the main program to occur with the first instruction after the parameter field. ∎

Parameter passing in the program area of the main program is less flexible than the possibilities described above because of the static parameter field. On the other hand, it is characterized by clear representation, limited storage space requirement and low execution times.

Number of Parameters. The assumption in Examples 3.18 through 3.21 was that the number of parameters was known right away in the case of a subprogram call and at the time of writing of a subprogram. However, there are applications, in which the number of parameters varies from one call to the other. In these instances, the parameter number has to be given to the subprogram as an additional parameter, e.g. with a general purpose register or as the first parameter entry in the stack or in the parameter field.

3.3.3 Global Program and Data Accesses

Main programs and subprograms can be translated as programs independently from each other, provided they always begin with an AORG or a RORG specification and finish with an END specification. Only address references within such a program or module can be directly produced by the assembler, i.e. without the knowledge of the other program modules. This is true for program jumps and branches as well as for accesses on data, for which space is reserved within the module storage space. These data are also called local data.

Beside the program and data accesses within a module (local accesses), there are global accesses between the single modules. These include subprogram jump and access to global data, i.e. data stored in the data areas of other modules, that are accessible to several modules. The corresponding address references have to be known by the time the program module is loaded, so that they can be introduced in the program code as absolute or relative to the program counter addresses.

In order to create address cross references, assembler specifications DEF and REF described in Subsection 3.1.3 are needed. In the DEF specification, the symbolic addresses, that are defined in the module but are used in other modules, are listed. On the contrary, the REF specification lists the symbolic addresses, that are used in the module but are defined in other modules. The assembler evaluates this information and creates additional specifications for each module's machine code. These are used by the linker or by a linking loader to resolve address cross references.

If the common data area includes only a few variables, these can also be stored in the register file. In this case, the creation of address cross references during the linking procedure is not necessary. Thus, the register file represents the simplest form of common data area.

Example 3.22. Common data area in the main program. A main program using several subprograms as modules has to communicate with them over a common data area. The access to this area has to occur globally, so that parameter passing to the modules does not take place. - The program representation shows the main program calling two subprograms by means of global addresses MOD1 and MOD2 (REF specification) and putting its data area C1 through CFIELD (DEF specification) as common area at their disposal. The subprogram MODUL1 with entry address MOD1 (DEF specification) reads the two variables C1 and C3 of the common area (REF specification). To quote a simple example, it adds the value of its local variable X to the value of the global variable C3 and assigns the result to the global variable C1.

```
* MAIN PROGRAM                           * SUBPROGRAM
*                                        * MODULE ONE
        RORG   MAINPR                     *
C1      DSW    1                                   RORG   MODUL1
C2      DSW    1                          X        DSW    1
C3      DSW    1                                   DEF    MOD1
CFIELD  DSW    100                                 REF    C1,C3
        DEF    C1,C2,C3,CFIELD           MOD1      ADD    X,C3
        REF    MOD1,MOD2                           MOVE   C1,X
          .                                        RTS
          .                                        END
          .
        JSR    MOD1
          .
          .
          .
        JSR    MOD2                       * SUBPROGRAM
          .                              * MODULE TWO
          .                              *
        END                                       RORG   MODUL2
                                                    .
                                                    .
                                                   DEF    MOD2
                                                   REF    C1,C2,CFIELD
                                         MOD2
                                                    .
                                                    .
                                                   RTS
                                                   END
```

3.3.4 Nested Subprograms

The call of subprograms is not limited to a single main program as the principal calling program; a subprogram itself can call subprograms and thus assume the function of a main program. The call mechanism, starting from the main program, can thus extend over several subprograms. This is called nesting subprograms. Depending on the place of the call, there are three kinds of nested subprograms:

1. simple subprograms,

2. recursive subprograms, and

3. reentrant subprograms.

Simple Subprograms. Figure 3.12 shows the diagram of simple subprogram nesting. Several programs call each other, starting from a main program, while saving the status and parameter passing occur as described above. The stack used for saving and then loading the status exactly corresponds to the nesting structure of the subprogram calls with its last-in-first-out mechanism. The information entered consecutively in the stack during the subprogram call (in the simplest case, return addresses) is read again in inverted sequence when returning to the main programs.

Recursive Subprograms. Recursive subprograms are subprograms, that are called again before they have concluded their current processing. The new call occurs either directly, if the subprogram calls itself, or indirectly if the new call occurs on a detour over one or more subprograms. Accordingly, these are called direct and indirect recursive subprograms. Unlike what happens in simple subprograms, a new data area for the subprogram has to be prepared at each call in recursive subprograms, so that the last actual data area is not destroyed by the new call. Accordingly, the data area mapping has to occur at running time, i.e. dynamically. In this case, because of the nesting structure of the subprogram calls, the stack can be used as the area for subprogram data and parameters. During the new call and the return, the current subprogram data can be considered an expansion of the processor status.

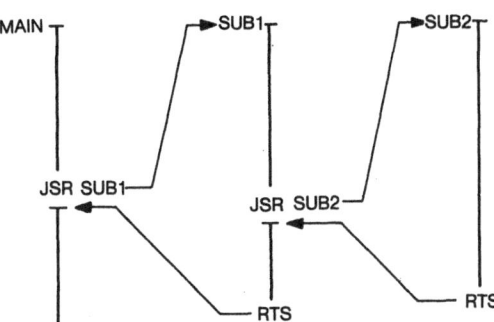

Fig. 3.12. Nesting of subprograms

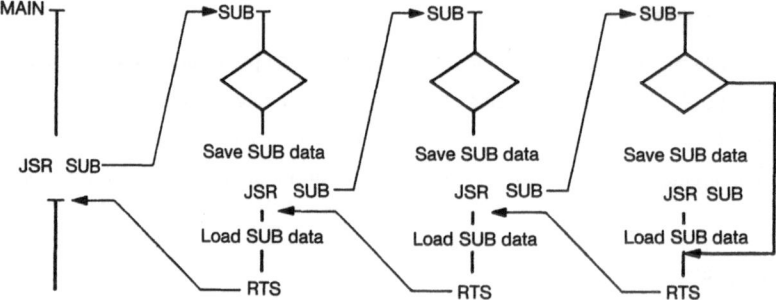

Fig. 3.13. Subprogram nesting by recursion

Figure 3.13 shows the diagram of a recursive subprogram nesting. A main program calls a subprogram that repeatedly calls itself until a program branch jumps this call. The respective current data of the subprogram are saved before the self-call and are re-loaded after the return. If the data are located on the stack, the saving and loading simply mean a change of the stack pointer. On the contrary, if the data are located in a fixed (static) subprogram area, they first have to be moved to the stack and then picked up again from there. Oftentimes, the data stack is used independently from the user or the system stack in order to separate accesses to the subprogram data from accesses to the actual processor status.

Reentrant Subprograms. Reentrant subprograms can be called from different interrupt programs and can accordingly be interrupted by them. The call or interrupt locations are not determined in advance, as is the case in recursive subprograms, because they depend on external interrupt conditions. This means that data saving of an interrupted program has to occur immediately after the call to the subprogram, and subprogram data restoring has to be carried out immediately before returning to the interrupted subprogram. Due to the nesting structure of the subprogram calls, the stack can be used for storage as is the case with recursive subprograms.

Figure 3.14 shows the double call of a reentrant subprogram. The intervention of an interrupt IR1 leads to an interrupt program IP1 (1), which calls a subprogram SUB (2). During the execution of the subprogram (3) on behalf of IP1, an interrupt is granted higher priority IR2. Its interrupt program IP2 newly calls the subprogram SUB (6), executes it (7,8) and finally returns the program control to the interrupt point in the subprogram (11). At this point the subprogram finished its task for the first interrupt program (12). The subprogram itself takes care of the saving and restoring of the subprogram data from the preceding subprogram execution. Data is saved at the time of the first call as well, even if it is not really necessary. This is usually taken into account when additional program branches, that would lead to an increase in running time for each new call, are to be avoided.

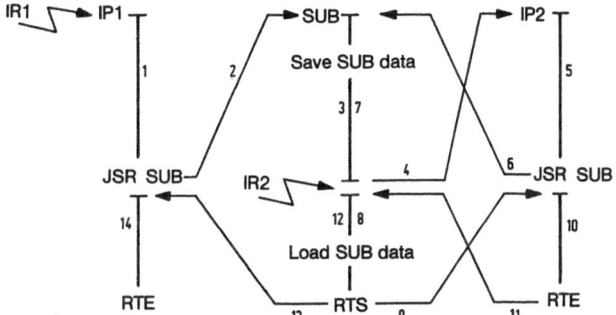

Fig. 3.14. Double call of a reentrant subprogram

4 System Structure

Beside the microprocessor, a microprocessor system includes several additional components, in particular memory and interface modules as well as support modules. Programs and data to be processed are available in the memory modules; the connection with the peripheral of the microprocessor system is implemented by the interface components. Support modules are divided into those that are absolutely necessary for the functioning of a microprocessor system, and those that are required for a more complex system structure. For instance, the first group includes the clock frequency generator and the reset logic that are often already integrated into the microprocessor and that are thus not discussed here. The second group includes simple components, like driver modules (signal amplifiers), address decoders and address comparators. Furthermore, a microprocessor system comprises priority, memory management and timer components which are very complex at times.

In this Chapter, we will discuss the structural aspects of microprocessor systems together with the support modules needed to assemble a system and some basic control structures. Section 4.1 describes the most important types of system structure: the single-chip system, the single-card system and the modular multiple-card system. Furthermore, there is a brief description of microprocessor signals, which make up the system bus in a modular system. Section 4.2 deals with the different possibilities of addressing system components, and Section 4.3 introduces data transfer control. The last two Sections describe processor external handling of exceptions: Section 4.4 deals with interrupt handling and interrupt priority, Section 4.5 discusses bus allocation in the case of several bus masters.

4.1 System Structure

When designing microprocessor systems, different points of view have to be considered, for instance economical concerns, like the minimization of development and production costs, and technical considerations, like high processing speed and large memory capacity. Moreover, the possibilities of peripheral interconnections have to be taken into account, and often high system reliability is required. Technical requirements are generally met by a proportionately higher hardware usage which, in turn, leads to higher system costs. Thus, compromises have to be made when designing a system; these range from the minimization of hardware for single-card systems to the flexible structures of modular multiple-card systems.

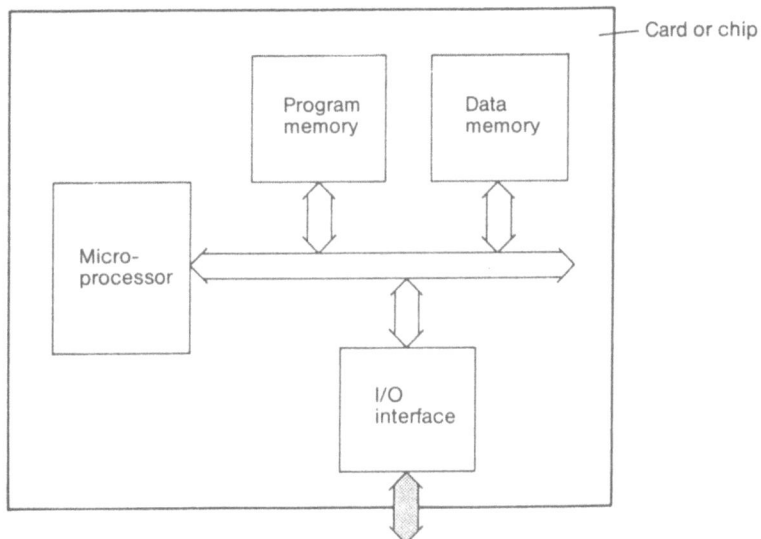

Fig. 4.1. Single-card system or single-chip system

4.1.1 Single-Chip and Single-Card Systems

Microprocessor systems with minimum hardware are usually designed for very specific limited purposes, for example for control problems. The entire hardware is arranged on a single printed circuit card (single-card system, Figure 4.1). On one hand, this has the advantage of having low production costs, on the other hand, it has the disadvantage of being a structure that cannot be altered any more. If in an extreme case all functional units of the system - the processor, the program and data memory and the I/O interface - are combined into one component, the system is called single-chip system. Such a component is also called single-chip computer. In order to be connected to the peripheral it only has to be completed with signal amplifiers at the input and output interfaces.

4.1.2 Bus Oriented Multiple-Card Systems

Microprocessor systems for general purpose applications are usually designed as modular multiple-card systems. These cards in a card-cage make up the microprocessor system, the type and the number of cards depend on the requirements of the system. Figure 4.2 shows a typical configuration including a microprocessor card, a program memory card (ROM), a data memory card (RAM), an interface card and a power supply card.

4.1.3 System Bus

The connection of the single cards in a modular multiple-card system takes place in the card cage, where card signals - address, data and control signals - are connected to the backplane wiring by

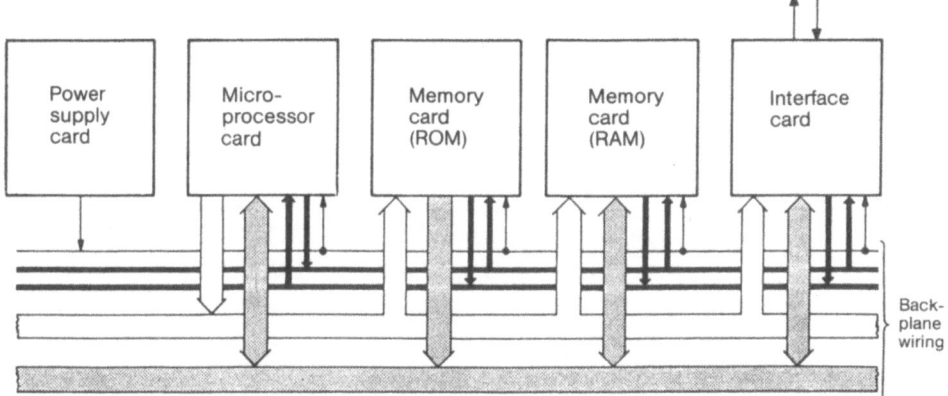

Fig. 4.2. Modular multiple-card system

means of plug connections. This wiring, that is produced either with a printed circuit card (mother board) or with single wires (e.g. in wire wrapping technique), joins the connectors with the same function of each card and thus creates the system bus shared by all cards. At any time, additional cards can be attached to this bus, the position of a card in the card cage is of no importance. (This is true with limitations for signal chains according to the daisy-chain principle; see Sections 4.4 and 4.5). The peripheral specific signals of interface cards are sent to a separate connector, e.g. on the card's front side.

The number of system bus lines basically depends on the number of connection points (pins) of the microprocessor in use. It ranges between 40 and 64 for 16-bit microprocessors. 16 to 24 bits are thus used for the system address bus, 16 bits for the system data bus and up to 24 bits for the system control bus. In addition, there are power supply lines, the clock frequency line and additional control lines that depend on the interrupt, DMA and multiprocessor structure of the system (see Sections 4.4 and 4.5).

Suggestions are made from some of the producers for a standardization of system buses, so that the cards from different makers could be combined. Here are some examples:

- the S100 bus (MITS Inc. Altair Microcomputers) for 8-bit microprocessor systems based on the Intel 8080 processor [17],

- the VERSA bus (Motorola) for 16-bit and 32-bit microprocessor systems based on the Motorola MC68000 processor [18],

- the VME bus (Motorola), a different version of the VERSA bus for 16-bit microprocessor systems in Eurocard format [19],

• the Z bus (Zilog) for 16-bit microprocessor systems based on the Z8000 microprocessor family, and

• the MULTIBUS (Intel) for 8-bit and 16-bit microprocessors based on the 8080 and the 8086 microprocessor families [2].

4.1.4 Microprocessor Signals

Microprocessor signal lines are either unidirectional according to their function, i.e. they are defined either as input or as output lines; or they allow bidirectional operation, i.e. input and output signals are interleaved at different times. The group of unidirectional signal lines includes address lines and part of the control lines. The data bus and the remaining control lines are laid out as bidirectional signal lines.

Figure 4.3 shows the microprocessor described in Chapter 2 with its input and output signals combined in functional groups. Beside the power supply connectors it shows the address and the data bus; the remaining signal groups create the control bus. The signals are defined by acronyms derived from their functions. The arrows indicate the signal flow direction. Most of the signal outputs are equipped with Three-State Logic (TSL). In addition to logic states 0 and 1, they can assume a high impedance state for signal decoupling. This allows the microprocessor to release the system bus to a different bus master, i.e. to a different functional unit with processor capabilities. An additional signal characteristic of the components around the processor is that signal outputs can be open-collector. If combined together, open-collector outputs create an OR connection (wired or). This characteristic is used, for instance, to switch an interrupt input or the $\overline{\text{BREQ}}$ input

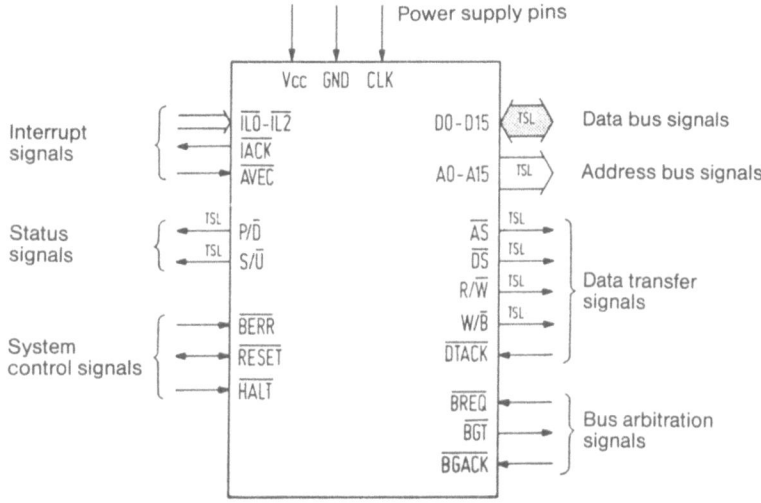

Fig. 4.3. Microprocessor signals

of the microprocessor with request signals by several functional units, without the need for an additional OR module.

When it is not in high impedance state, a control line is either in active state, i.e. its function is performed, or in inactive state, i.e. it has no effect. Active non-negated signals have the logic value 1 (active-high signals); active negated signals have the logic value 0 (active-low signals). In order to achieve a unity in the description of signal states, we will call *signal setting* the activation of both kinds of signals, and we will call their deactivation *signal resetting*. In microprocessor technology, most of the control signals that can be in inactive state are designed as negated signals. Thus, more operational safety in case of voltage variations is acquired. Some control signals, like the $S/\overline{U}$ signal, are in active state with value 1 (system mode) as well as with value 0 (user mode). Thus they have two names, that are divided by a slash. In the case of these signals, value 1 indicates the active state of the non-negated definition and value 0 the active state of the negated definition.

In the following, each microprocessor signal is described. Their use is clarified in the next sections of this chapter in connection with the different control procedures.

Vcc, GND (Voltage, Ground): Inputs for power supply. Vcc = 5 V, GND = 0 V.

CLK (Clock): Input of a constant frequency clock signal from which the necessary internal clock frequency signal is produced.

D0-D15 (Data): bidirectional 16-bit data bus with Three-State Logic. It receives or sends data in word or byte format. During an interrupt cycle, the vector number of the interrupt source is received through data lines D0-D7.

A0-A15 (Address): 16-bit address bus with Three-State Logic. It allows direct addressing of 64K byte or 32K words. During an interrupt cycle, the accepted interrupt code is distributed over address lines A0-A2; in the meantime, the remaining address lines are in state 1.

$\overline{AS}$ (Address Strobe): Three-state output. It indicates that a valid address is on the address bus. For instance, it is used to free the address decoder from the units connected to the system bus.

$\overline{DS}$ (Data Strobe): Three-state output. During a write cycle, it indicates that the datum is on the data bus and it is used as data transfer signal by the data receiver. During a read cycle, $\overline{DS}$ shows that the microprocessor is ready to accept the data, and it is also interpreted as a data transfer signal by the data sender. Moreover, $\overline{DS}$ is used to select data bus drivers and to start processor-external generation of the $\overline{DTACK}$ signal.

R/$\overline{\text{W}}$ (Read/Write): Three-state output. It gives the direction of the data transfer on the data bus (R/$\overline{\text{W}}$ = 0: write cycle, R/$\overline{\text{W}}$ = 1: read cycle). R/$\overline{\text{W}}$ is used to control memory, interface and controller components and to indicate the direction of bidirectional data bus drivers.

W/$\overline{\text{B}}$ (Word/Byte): Three-state output. It signals a word access (W/$\overline{\text{B}}$ = 1) or a byte access (W/$\overline{\text{B}}$ = 0) to the addressed unit. The selection of the high or low byte occurs through A0 (see Subsection 2.1.2).

$\overline{\text{DTACK}}$ (Data Transfer Acknowledge): Input. During a write cycle, it indicates that the data receiver has taken data from the data bus. During a read cycle, $\overline{\text{DTACK}}$ indicates that valid data is on the data bus and can be retrieved by the microprocessor. In both cases, the microprocessor is in waiting state until the arrival of $\overline{\text{DTACK}}$, then it ends the cycle. $\overline{\text{DTACK}}$ allows the connection of receivers and senders with different data transfer speeds.

$\overline{\text{BREQ}}$ (Bus Request): Input. It indicates that another bus master wants to have bus control. First the microprocessor ends the present bus cycle, then it switches its three-state outputs to high impedance state and sets the $\overline{\text{BGT}}$ signal.

$\overline{\text{BGT}}$ (Bus Grant): Output. It indicates that the microprocessor has decoupled itself with its three-state outputs from the system bus as a reaction to a $\overline{\text{BREQ}}$ signal and has thus released the bus.

$\overline{\text{BGACK}}$ (Bus Grant Acknowledge): Input. It indicates that a bus master is in control of the bus. It causes the reset of the $\overline{\text{BGT}}$ signal, so that new requests for bus allocation will be possible.

$\overline{\text{IL0-IL2}}$ (Interrupt Level): Inputs. They signal an interrupt request. The 3-bit code (interrupt code) indicates the interrupt level and thus the priority of the request: level 0 has the highest, level 6 has the lowest priority; Code 7 indicates that there is no request. A request at level 0 is dynamically triggered by a change in code; requests at levels 1 through 6 occur statically with a 3-bit code.

$\overline{\text{IACK}}$ (Interrupt Acknowledge): Output. It acknowledges an accepted interrupt request. The interrupt code has to be smaller than the interrupt mask in the status register. Requests at level 0 are an exception; they are always granted independently from the interrupt mask.

$\overline{\text{AVEC}}$ (Automatic Vectoring): Input. During an interrupt request, it reports to the microprocessor that the addressing of the interrupt program has to occur with the autovector of the corresponding interrupt level.

P/$\overline{\text{D}}$ (Program/Data fetch): Three-state output. It indicates whether there is an instruction access (P/$\overline{\text{D}}$ = 1) or a data access (P/$\overline{\text{D}}$ = 0) in a bus cycle. P/$\overline{\text{D}}$ is valid during $\overline{\text{AS}}$ and can be used as an additional address bit to expand the address space.

S/$\overline{\text{U}}$ (System/User state): Three-state output. It indicates whether an operation is in system mode (S/$\overline{\text{U}}$ = 1) or in user mode (S/$\overline{\text{U}}$ = 0). S/$\overline{\text{U}}$ is valid during $\overline{\text{AS}}$ and can be used to control access rights to memory areas.

$\overline{\text{BERR}}$ (Bus Error): Input. It reports a mistake identified by an external unit and triggers the bus error interrupt.

$\overline{\text{RESET}}$ (Reset): Bidirectional connection. As input it causes the initialization of the microprocessor hardware and generates the reset interrupt for the software initialization of the microprocessor system. As output it is set for a short time by the RESET instruction and can be used to initialize external units.

$\overline{\text{HALT}}$ (Halt): Input. At the end of the present bus cycle it transfers the microprocessor to a halt state. At this point all three-state outputs are high impedance. The halt state is maintained as long as the $\overline{\text{HALT}}$ signal is set.

4.2 Addressing of System Components

The switching of data lines between the microprocessor and one of the system components, for instance a memory unit or an interface unit, is controlled by the addressing mechanism. The address, that was asserted by the microprocessor on the address bus, is evaluated by all units connected to the system bus. One of the units identifies with this address and connects to the data bus. In the following, the different possibilities and techniques for system component addressing are discussed.

4.2.1 Isolated and Memory-Mapped Addressing

Two different techniques are customary for addressing system components used for input/output (interface modules). They are called isolated addressing and memory-mapped addressing or isolated input/output and memory-mapped input/output if related to data transfer.

In the case of isolated input/output, the address space of the memory and of the I/O units are isolated from each other. The data transfer with interface components is carried out with special I/O instructions, like INP (Input) and OUT (Output); the address of the source or destination register of the interface is contained in the address part of the instruction. This address is asserted like a memory address on the address bus. The distinction, whether it is a memory address or an

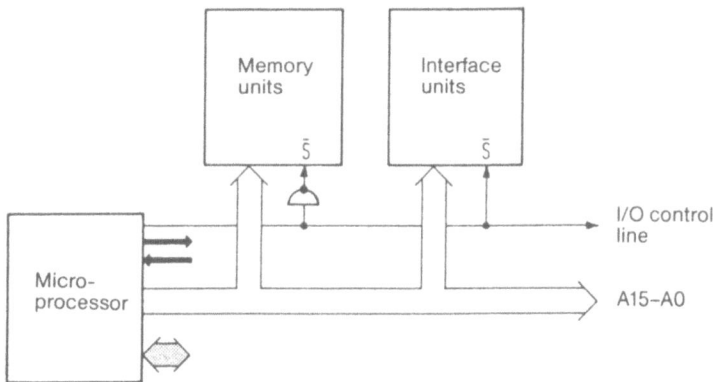

Fig. 4.4. Isolated addressing

interface address, is indicated by an I/O control line. This control line is set or reset depending on the op code, I/O instruction or memory access instruction, and it is evaluated by the system components through their Select inputs $\overline{S}$ (Figure 4.4). For example, if the address length is 16 bits, both address spaces contain 64K addresses each (Figure 4.5a).

No special I/O instructions are needed in the case of memory-mapped input/output. The interface unit registers are addressed like memory cells; thus the control line and the inverter disappear in Figure 4.4. Accordingly, there is only one shared address space for interface units and memory units, which is divided into memory and I/O address areas (Figure 4.5b). The advantage of this addressing technique lies in the fact that all instructions with memory access, as well as arithmetic, logic and compare instructions, can be used on interface registers. - In both cases the allocation of the address spaces is defined by memory maps in which contiguous memory areas are indicated by their beginning and end addresses, and interface units are indicated by their register addresses.

4.2.2 Card Selection and Component Selection

When a microprocessor system is designed, the necessary components have to be matched with addresses from the available address space. The number of necessary addresses can vary substantially. For instance, a 1K memory component uses 1024 addresses, whereas an interface component can manage with 2 to 16 addresses in all.

As long as single cards in a multiple-card system contain several addressable components, they require addresses for card and component selection. Thus, an address hierarchy is created, which includes card address, component address and register or memory address. The address ranges of these three levels are usually defined in powers of 2; i.e., the addressing of the single components can occur with a partition of the address. This division depends on the address decomposition

114

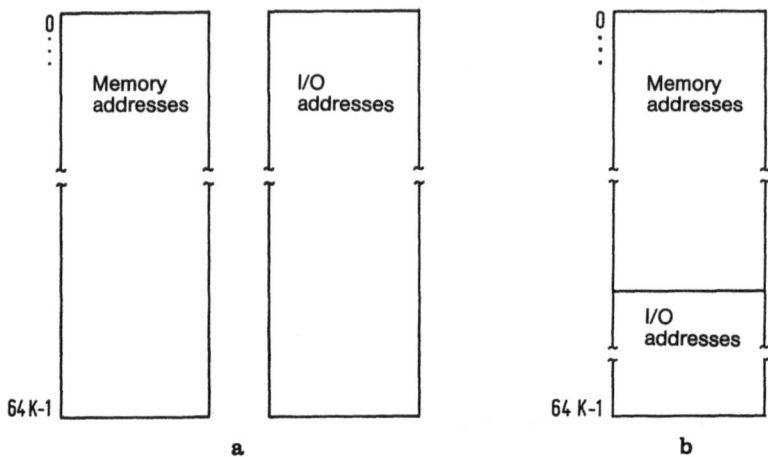

Fig. 4.5. Address space assignment for 16-bit addresses. a) isolated addressing, b) memory-mapped addressing

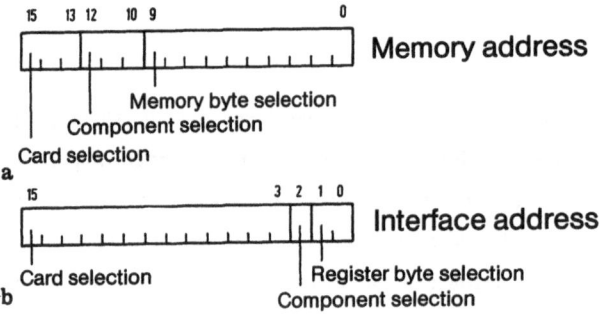

Fig. 4.6. Address partition for card and component selection

within the single cards and is thus managed by the addressing logic of each single card. Figure 4.6 shows two examples of a 16-bit address partition: a) an 8K byte memory card containing eight 1K byte memory chips, and b) an interface card containing two interface components with four 8-bit registers each.

The lowest level of address decoding is usually contained in the component itself, so that the lower address bits can be sent to the components directly. The addressing of the components on the card and the addressing of the card itself can occur either in coded form, by dividing the address in fields, or in uncoded form, by means of single bits. Coded addressing allows complete use of the address space, but it requires a decoder and comparison components to decode the address. It is preferably used with multiple-card systems with modular extensibility. Uncoded addressing, also called linear addressing, does not make full use of the address, but it does not need an address decoder logic. Thus, it is used with smaller limited systems, mostly single-card systems.

Figure 4.7 illustrates a complete address decoding circuit relative to the example of the address partition of an 8K byte memory card as in Figure 4.6a. The selection of cards takes place with a comparator which compares the three highest address bits A15 through A13 with a fixed 3-bit card address. If the two addresses correspond, the output signal $\overline{S}$ is set; it acts like a card selection signal and activates the Chip Enable input ($\overline{CE}$) of a 1-out-of-8 decoder. The 3-bit component address A12 through A10 is given to the decoder, and it activates exactly one of its eight outputs. This output signal works like a Chip Select signal ($\overline{CSi}$) for one of the eight memory components and, together with the $\overline{S}$ signal, it switches its data lines. The memory byte selection uses the 10 lower address bits A9 through A0, which are distributed to all eight memory components, but are only evaluated by the component that has been activated. According to the information in the 3-bit card address, the memory card can be used in one of the 8K byte areas of the address space, whose area limits are an integral multiple of 8K.

Figure 4.8 shows an example for incomplete address decoding. Two interface components with four registers each are selected with address bits A15 or A14 and one 1K byte memory component is selected with address bit A13 directly (uncoded selection). The decoding of address bits A1 and

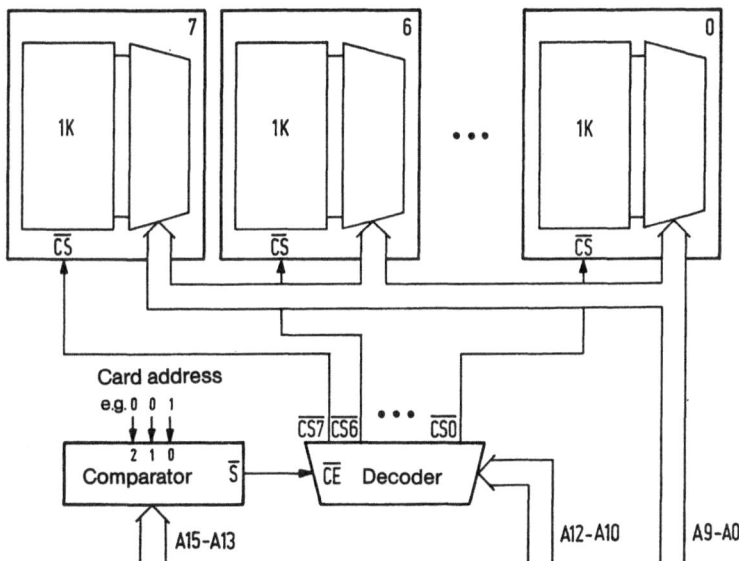

Fig. 4.7. Address decoding for an 8K-byte memory card (address area from 8K to 16K-1 indicated by card address 001)

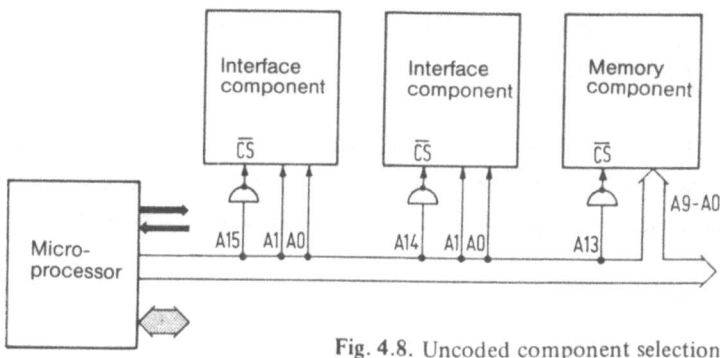

Fig. 4.8. Uncoded component selection

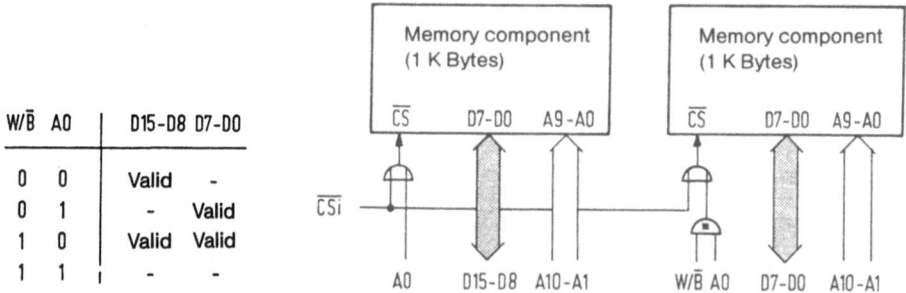

W/B̄	A0	D15-D8	D7-D0
0	0	Valid	-
0	1	-	Valid
1	0	Valid	Valid
1	1	-	-

Fig. 4.9. Memory word/byte selection

A0 of the interface components and the address bits A9 through A0 of the memory components occurs by means of the component-internal address decoder. In order to ensure an unequivocal component selection, only those addresses can be used in which only one of the address bits A15, A14 and A13 has value 1 (1-out-of-3 code). In this case, the address space of 64K addresses cannot be completely exploited.

4.2.3 Word/Byte Selection

Data transfer between the processor and the memory units connected with the system data bus takes place either in word or byte format. The distinction between the two formats is made with the processor's Word/Byte control signal (W/B̄). The higher or lower byte of a memory word is selected with address signal A0. Figure 4.9 presents an example of interconnection for processor-external word/byte selection on a memory card. 1K memory cells are illustrated, and higher and lower bytes are stored in different memory components. Both components are selected by signal C̄Si (see also Figure 4.7).

Depending on A0, byte transfers occur either on the higher (A0 = 0) or on the lower data bus half (A0 = 1). However, source or destination in the microprocessor are in the lower register half, as already mentioned in Subsection 2.1.2. The corresponding data path switching takes place in the microprocessor.

4.2.4 Memory Management

As shown in Subsection 2.1.3 with the example of 16-bit microprocessors Motorola MC68000, Zilog Z8000 and Intel 8086, the address word is not limited to 16 bits, but has up to 24 address bits depending on the processor. This allows direct addressing of up to 16 M bytes or 8 M words. The starting point for the following considerations will be a 24-bit address.

Extension of the Address Space. Programs and data are often kept in physically separated memory areas, programs are stored in ROMs for instance, and data are stored in RAMs. With such a division of the memory, the address space indicated by the 24-bit address can easily be doubled by using the processor status signal $P/\overline{D}$ (Program/Data fetch) as an additional address signal. In state 1 it indicates an instruction access; in state 0 it indicates an operand access of the microprocessor, and thus determines the choice between program and data memory. Both areas can use the whole address space of the 24-bit address.

Memory Protection for the System Area. In the case of microprocessor systems, which divide the available address space into a system area and a user area, the processor status signal $S/\overline{U}$ (System/User state) can be used to communicate access rights. In the example illustrated in Figure 4.10, the available address space is divided by the highest address bit A23 in a system area (A23 =

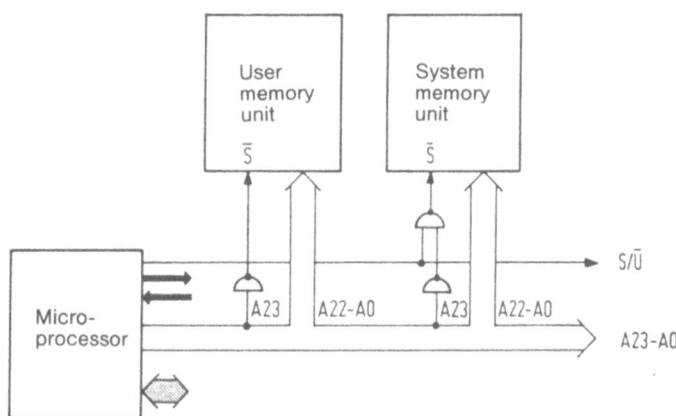

Fig. 4.10. Addressing of a user and of a system memory area with access protection for the system memory

0) and in a user area (A23 = 1) in a 1 : 1 ratio. (Other division ratios are possible through corresponding address decoding circuits.) By using the NAND gate, the system area is not accessible in user mode (S/$\overline{U}$ = 0), while both the system as well as the user areas are accessible in system mode (S/$\overline{U}$ = 1).

4.2.5 Memory Management Units

In larger microprocessor systems, the addressing of memory units is supported by Memory Managements Units (MMUs). These units allow the translation of machine addresses, as they are generated by the microprocessor (logic, virtual addresses), into memory addresses, as they are evaluated by the memory units (physical, real addresses). Thus, programs and data are not tied to the areas of the memory indicated by the programmer, but they can be shifted in the memory [3,20]. Address translation is used for areas of variable length called segments. Each segment can be assigned access rights, the observance of which is checked by the MMU at each memory access. Unauthorized accesses and accesses to logic segments, whose data are not in memory, lead to an interruption of the running program.

Address translation usually concerns the 16 higher bits of the 24-bit address bus; the eight lower bits bypass the MMU without being affected (Figure 4.11).

Address Translation through an Associative Memory. Figure 4.12 shows an MMU structure which could manage up to 32 program and data segments (see also Motorola MC68451 [21]). A segment includes between one and 64K blocks with 256 bytes each, i.e. up to 16 M bytes altogether. In each segment there are three 16-bit registers containing the higher bits of the logic segment base address, of the physical segment base address and one 16-bit mask. The mask registers are not explicitly drawn in the illustration, but their effect is indicated. They define an m-bit segment number in each base address entry. The remaining n bits (dotted areas) are not evaluated during address translation.

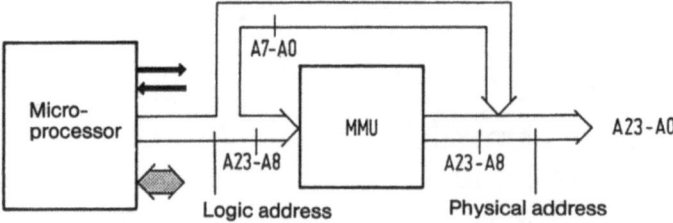

Fig. 4.11. Address translation with a memory management unit (MMU)

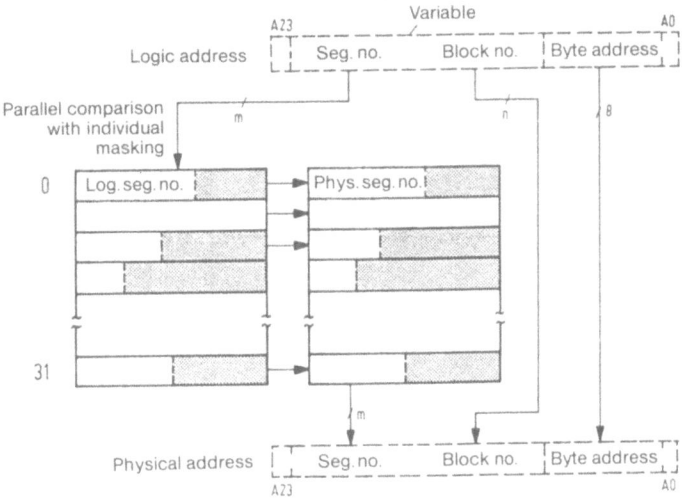

Fig. 4.12. Memory management unit with associative address translation

The 24-bit address (logic address) generated by the microprocessor defines the area of a 256-byte block in the logic space through the 16 higher address bits. These 16 address bits, including their individual mask, are compared with the 32 logic base addresses stored in the MMU, i.e. in the m significant bit positions that are specified through the segment specific mask (logic segment numbers, white areas in the left register block in Figure 4.12). The $n = 16\text{-}m$ non-significant mask bit positions indicate the maximum number of blocks in a segment and thus the maximum segment size. If the logic segment number sent by the processor corresponds to one of the 32 logic segment numbers stored into the associative memory, the addressed segment in the memory is indicated to be loaded and described by the MMU. The physical 24-bit address is obtained when the higher m bits of the logic address (logic segment number) are substituted by the corresponding m significant bits from the physical base address indication of the segment (physical segment number). - A status and control register, which is not included in Figure 4.12, is assigned to each segment e.g. to protect it from being written.

Figure 4.13 shows an excerpt of the logic address space with two segments divided into blocks on the left, and an excerpt of the physical address space with these segments' actual mapping in the memory on the right. Arrows indicate the mapping of the logic segment numbers to the physical segment numbers. Memory representation also illustrates the possible segment boundaries resulting from multiples of the segment lengths for each segment. In this situation, segments can also overlap.

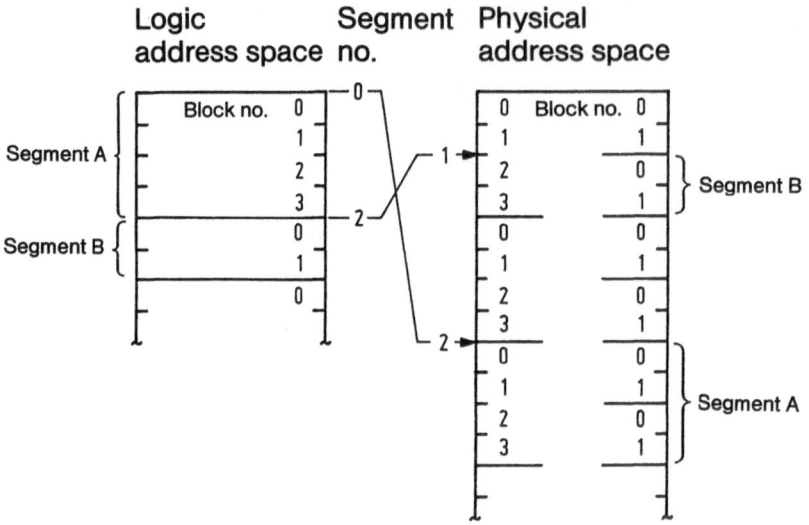

Fig. 4.13. Mapping of logic segments on the physical address space by means of an MMU according to Fig. 4.12

A test on the ownership of a segment by a user is not represented in Figure 4.12. To this purpose, each segment is given a user number. The actual user number results from a table stored in registers, which is chosen through the processor's status signals. A differentiation is made between system, user, program and data memory accesses. Thus, a segment access not only depends on the correspondence of the segments numbers, but also on the correspondence between the actual user number and the user number given to the segment. This comparison can also be performed associatively. Since individual masking is used here, the system software is also able to access user segments, whereas the opposite is impossible.

Address Translation through a Random Access Memory (RAM). Figure 4.14 shows another technique that can be used for address mapping with an MMU (see also Zilog Z8010 [3]). Up to 256 segments can be managed, and each segment can include up to 256 blocks with 256 bytes each, i.e. a maximum of 64K bytes. The eight highest bits in the logic address are used to select the segment (logic segment number). They address a RAM, which is used as a translation table, with 256 16-bit cells and select a physical 16-bit block number as the basis of the physical segment. This block number is added to the logic block number, and it results in the physical block number in the segment. The addressing within the block occurs through the eight lowest bits of the logic address (byte address). Once more, the resulting physical address consists of 24 bits, the physical block number and the byte address. - Two memory protection registers are associated with each segment and are evaluated when the segment is accessed.

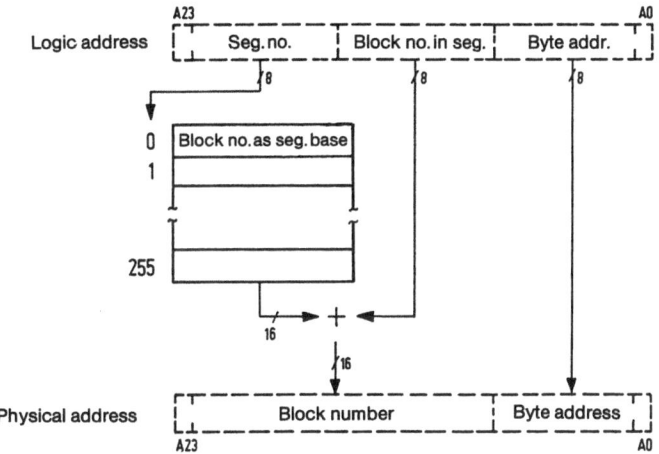

Fig. 4.14. Memory management unit with address mapping through a RAM

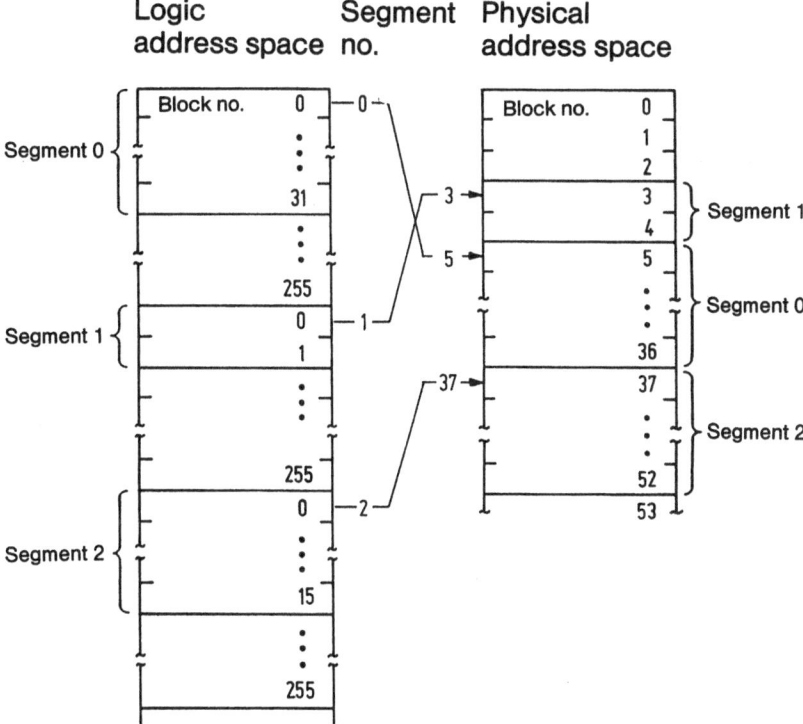

Fig. 4.15. Mapping of logic segments on the physical address space by means of an MMU according to Fig. 4.14

Figure 4.15 shows an example of address mapping between a logical address and a physical address space with the allocation of three segments. The mapping of the logic segment numbers to the physical block numbers stored in the MMU for the segment beginning is represented by arrows. The numbering of the blocks within the logic segments indicates the position of the blocks in the physical segments.

Memory Protection. As already mentioned, access rights to the segments are indicated by the contents of segment specific control registers. Some of the typical protection measures are:

- read only: only a read access is allowed;

- system only: access is only possible in system mode;

- instruction fetch only: only instruction fetching is permitted;

- not available: the segment is in memory, but access is not allowed;

- not resident: the segment is defined in the MMU, but is not in memory.

Access faults are indicated in the status register specific of that segment. Each access fault also causes the setting of an MMU trap signal, so that a program interruption is triggered in the processor. In the trap program, the access fault can be examined through the status information and the necessary steps can be taken. For instance, the access to a segment that is not loaded can cause the subsequent loading of the segment.

Both the loading of the MMU address and the control registers and the reading of the status registers is done in system mode. To this purpose, the MMU is equipped with a data bus port, an address input for register selection, a $\overline{CS}$ input for the selection of the unit and the necessary control signal connections for data transfer.

For an overview of memory management units see [22].

4.3 Data Transfer

In addition to functional unit addressing, the execution of data transfers includes a certain amount of control procedures, like the connection of the addressed unit to the system data bus, the direction selection during data transfer and the indication of the timing. To this purpose, the microprocessor has the following control signals: Address Strobe ($\overline{AS}$), Data Strobe ($\overline{DS}$) and Read/Write (R/$\overline{W}$). The addressed unit generates the Data Acknowledge signal ($\overline{DTACK}$).

4.3.1 Bus Coupling

As already mentioned, it is important to ensure that a functional unit works as the sender and an additional unit works as the receiver during data transfers. The data bus connections of the remaining units have to be disconnected from the system data bus. The logic required for this is often contained in the units themselves as data bus driver logic, which is controlled by $\overline{CS}$ (Chip Select) or $\overline{CE}$ (Chip Enable). With $\overline{CS} = 1$ or $\overline{CE} = 1$, the data bus connections are in high impedance state and are thus disconnected from the system data bus; with $\overline{CS} = 0$ or $\overline{CE} = 0$ they are switched on the system data bus. The data flow direction in the driver logic is determined by the Read/Write signal at the $R/\overline{W}$ input of the unit.

Oftentimes, bus coupling takes place through special driver units inserted between the functional unit and the data bus. Figure 4.16 shows such a bus driver, which is called bidirectional driver because the direction of its data flow can be switched. For each signal path Ai/Bi it has two amplifier sections (triangle symbol); either one is selected by the state of the $R/\overline{W}$ signal. The $\overline{CE}$ signal switches on the selected signal path or switches the amplifier outputs to high impedance state.

Apart from their three-state function, driver units also have the advantage of being able to drive a bigger bus load; i.e., the bus can be loaded with a higher number of units. This is why also address

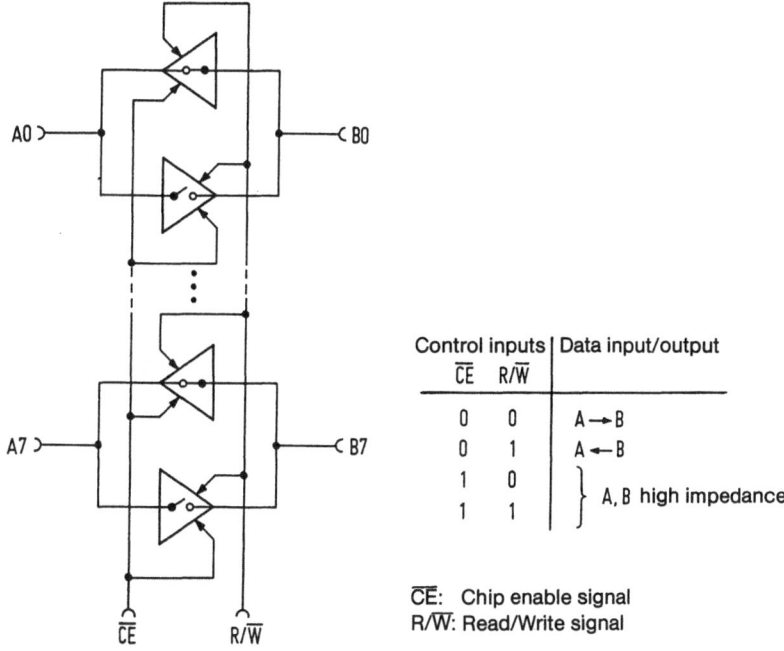

Control inputs		Data input/output
$\overline{CE}$	$R/\overline{W}$	
0	0	A → B
0	1	A ← B
1	0	} A, B high impedance
1	1	

$\overline{CE}$: Chip enable signal
$R/\overline{W}$: Read/Write signal

Fig. 4.16. Bidirectional bus driver with Three-State Logic

and control lines are often connected to the system bus with driver units, although in this case, the use of unidirectional drivers is sufficient. The microprocessor itself is also connected to the system with driver units due to the limited driving capabilities of its interconnections.

4.3.2 Data Transfer Control

Synchronous and Asynchronous Buses. Data transfer from the microprocessor to a functional unit attached to the system bus is either synchronous or asynchronous depending on the bus control. In both cases it is started by the microprocessor, which activates the functional unit with the control bus. In the case of a synchronous bus, the duration of the data transfer is determined by one or more bus clock frequency steps and is the same for all functional units. The microprocessor clock signal, or any other signal with lower frequency that is derived from it, is used as bus clock frequency. - On the other hand, in the case of an asynchronous bus, the duration of the data transfer depends on the data access time of the addressed functional unit. This unit reports the end of the access time with an acknowledge signal, and the processor finishes the transfer procedure (handshaking). Asynchronous buses require more control than synchronous buses, but they have the advantage of being able to connect functional units with very different data access times to the bus. - The whole procedure of either synchronous or asynchronous data transfer is also called bus cycle.

Figure 4.17 illustrates a possible interconnection for asynchronous data transfer of memory words with the processor signals described in Subsection 4.1.4. There is a memory card with card selection logic and a DELAY mechanism to produce the acknowledge signal $\overline{\text{DTACK}}$. The connection of the memory units to the data bus occurs through a bidirectional data bus driver which is selected with a Multiplexer (MUX) depending on the R/$\overline{\text{W}}$ signals.

Signal behavior for the read cycle and the write cycle during word transfers is represented in Figure 4.18. Signal transitions are caused by the positive and negative edges of the clock states Zi. Double lines for signals indicate the possibility of different signal levels in the case of several signal lines; signal lines in middle position represent the high impedance signal state of three-state signals.

Read Cycle. Starting from idle state Z0, the processor in state Z1 sends address signals A15 through A0 and control signals W/$\overline{\text{B}}$, S/$\overline{\text{U}}$ and P/$\overline{\text{D}}$ which are needed to address system bus units. In state Z2, it indicates the validity of these signals with the Address Strobe signal ($\overline{\text{AS}}$); the addressed functional unit creates the Select signal ($\overline{\text{S}}$) for card selection from these signals. Simultaneously with $\overline{\text{AS}}$, the processor sets the Data Strobe signal ($\overline{\text{DS}}$). This, together with $\overline{\text{S}}$, starts the delay device of the addressed unit.

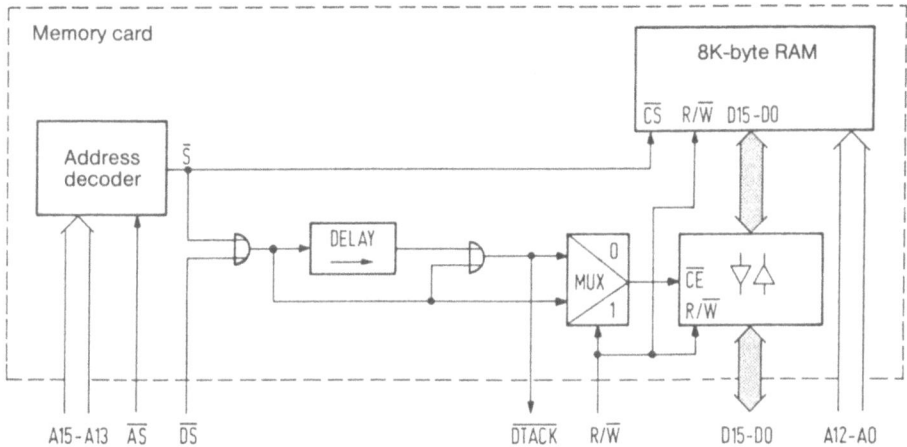

Fig. 4.17. Data transfer control for a memory unit

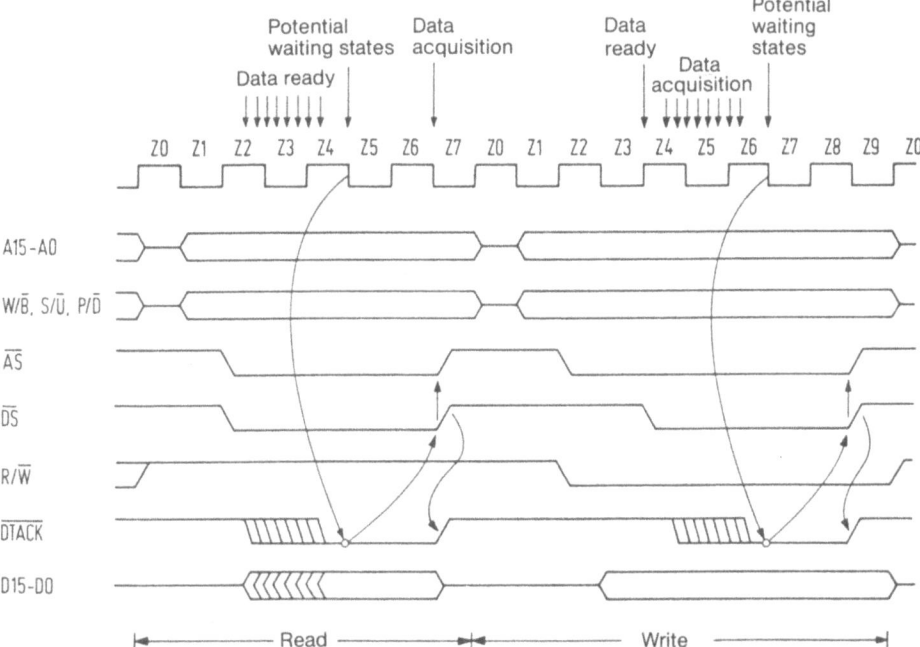

Fig. 4.18. Read cycle and write cycle

At the end of data access time, the delay device produces Data Acknowledge signal $\overline{\text{DTACK}}$. which switches the data bus driver to the system data bus and signals to the processor that the datum is ready. After two additional states, the processor tests the $\overline{\text{DTACK}}$ signal in state Z4 and introduces waiting conditions in the read cycle, if the signal is still not set. After arrival of $\overline{\text{DTACK}}$, the processor synchronizes in states Z5 and Z6 with the $\overline{\text{DTACK}}$ signal and reads the data signals D15 through D0 at the beginning of state Z7. In state Z7 it resets both strobe signals $\overline{\text{AS}}$ and $\overline{\text{DS}}$ and terminates the read cycle in state Z0. When $\overline{\text{DS}}$ is reset, also the $\overline{\text{DTACK}}$ signal is reset by the card control logic. The $\text{R/}\overline{\text{W}}$ signal has value one throughout the read cycle; it thus determines the data transfer direction for the reading from the addressed units and from the data bus driver.

Write Cycle. As was the case in the read cycle, the processor in state Z1 sends address signals from A15 through A0 as well as control signals $\text{W/}\overline{\text{B}}$, $\text{S/}\overline{\text{U}}$ and $\text{P/}\overline{\text{D}}$ to generate card selection signal $\overline{\text{S}}$. It indicates validity of the address in state Z2 by means of the $\overline{\text{AS}}$ signal; at the same time it sets the $\text{R/}\overline{\text{W}}$ signal to zero. In state Z3, the processor puts data on the data bus and indicates with the $\overline{\text{DS}}$ signal in state Z4 that the datum is asserted. The $\overline{\text{DS}}$ signal switches the data bus driver and starts, together with card selection signal $\overline{\text{S}}$, the delay device of the addressed unit.

At the end of the data acquisition time, the delay device sends acknowledge signal $\overline{\text{DTACK}}$. The processor checks this signal in state Z7 and, if it is still not set, inserts waiting states in the write cycle. After $\overline{\text{DTACK}}$, the processor synchronizes with the $\overline{\text{DTACK}}$ signal in states Z7 and Z8 and resets both strobe signals $\overline{\text{AS}}$ and $\overline{\text{DS}}$ in state Z9. One state later, it sets the $\text{R/}\overline{\text{W}}$ signal to 1 and ends the write cycle.

If the acknowledge signal $\overline{\text{DTACK}}$ is missing in a read or write cycle because of a hardware error, the microprocessor remains in waiting state. The system is not able to work, it is "hung". In order to avoid such a system breakdown, the hardware is equipped with a central watchdog timer. If $\overline{\text{DTACK}}$ is not available, this timer causes a program interruption after a fixed time, so that the processor can leave the waiting state and start with error handling.

4.4 Interrupt Systems

An interrupt is caused by the request signal of a functional unit to the microprocessor. In this situation, the processing of the running program is interrupted and an interrupt program, that is mapped to the interrupt source, is executed. Typical interrupt sources are for instance I/O devices, like keyboards and printers, and secondary memories, like floppy disk units, which send their requests to the processor by means of interface components. Also components near the processor, like watchdog timers and memory management units, or functional units far from the processor, e.g. units of an external industrial process, can behave as interrupt sources.

While interrupt handling was considered from the point of view of programming in Chapter 2, this section mainly deals with the realization of interrupt systems from the point of view of system structure. This includes assigning a priority to external interrupt requests and the signal exchange between interrupt source and microprocessor. Moreover, this Section will discuss special interrupts like system control signals $\overline{\text{BERR}}$ and $\overline{\text{RESET}}$ and the $\overline{\text{HALT}}$ signal.

4.4.1 Interrupt Priority and Interrupt Cycle

Priority Unit. In order to use the seven interrupt levels supplied by the microprocessor, the request signals of the interrupt sources have to be coded outside the processor through a priority encoder. Figure 4.19 shows the structure of such a component, which allows priority encoding of eight static interrupt signals.

The eight input signals $\overline{\text{INT0}}$ through $\overline{\text{INT7}}$ run through a priority logic, and each signal can be blocked by one bit of an 8-bit mask register (interrupt enable/disable). The priority logic maps $\overline{\text{INT0}}$ with the highest priority and $\overline{\text{INT7}}$ with the lowest priority. In the case of several simultaneous requests, it only lets that request through, which has the highest priority in the set of non-masked requests, and thus creates a 1-out-of-8 code. This code is translated by an encoder to a 3-bit interrupt code. Moreover, the output $\overline{\text{INT}}$ indicates whether a non-masked interrupt request is present or not. (The AND gate works like an OR gate because negated signals are used.) A non-masked request with lower priority arriving later is blocked as long as there is a non-masked request with higher priority. On the other hand, a non-masked request with higher priority immediately causes a change of interrupt code. In order to obtain an interrupt code 7 (no request), $\overline{\text{INT7}}$ has to be set to 0. (Figure 4.19 does not include the control and data connections necessary to load the mask register.)

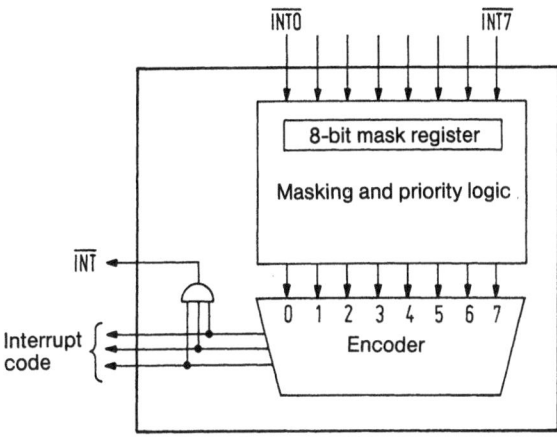

Fig. 4.19. Priority encoder

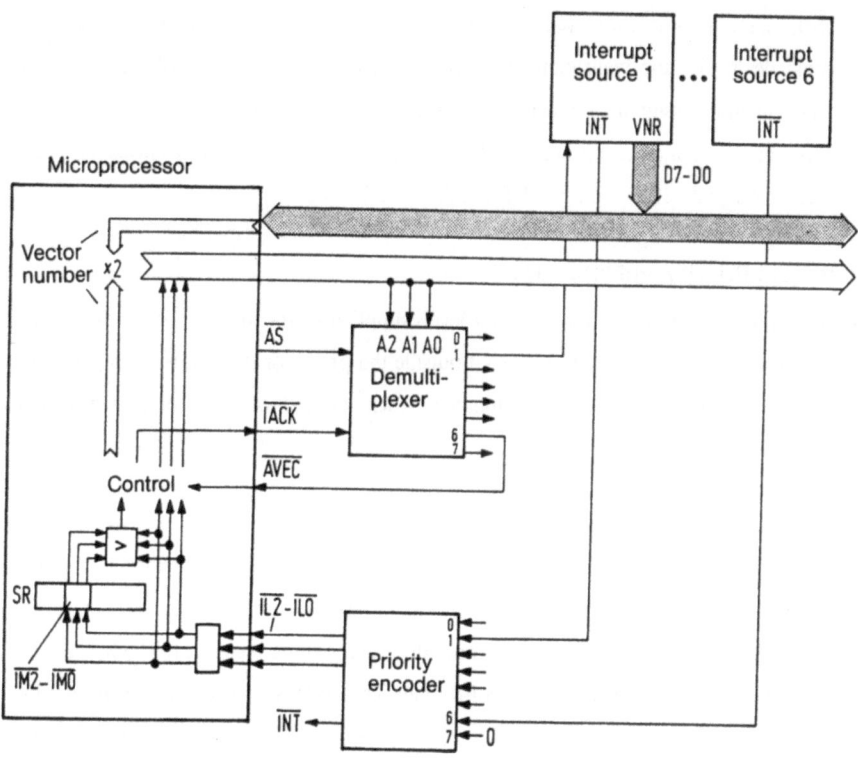

Fig. 4.20. System structure with coded interrupt requests

If a microprocessor system does not use more than one interrupt level, priority components do not have to be used. The interrupt line is directly connected with one of the interrupt inputs of the processor; the remaining two interrupt inputs are set to logic value 1 (no request).

Interrupt Cycle. Figure 4.20 shows the structure of a microprocessor system using a priority encoder. There are seven interrupt sources, two of them are illustrated: one with vector interrupt (source 1) and one with autovector interrupt (source 6). The value of input 7 of the priority encoder (lowest priority) is zero.

In connection with Figure 4.20, Figure 4.21 illustrates the signal exchange between interrupt source and microprocessor for vectorized interrupts. The interrupt source reports its interrupt request in form of a 3-bit interrupt code: At the end of the bus cycle, the processor in state 0 decides whether it will grant the request or not. To this purpose, it compares the interrupt code stored in a buffer register with the interrupt mask in the processor status register. If it grants the request, it first copies the content of its status register in an internal buffer register and then sets the mask equal to the accepted interrupt code. (Furthermore, it sets the system/user bit to system mode and resets the trace bit.) It notifies the interrupt source in state Z1 by setting the acknowledge signal $\overline{\text{IACK}}$. At the same time, it asserts the accepted interrupt code on address lines A2 through A0 and indicates this with the $\overline{AS}$ signal. Address lines A15 through A3 are set to 1. The interrupt code is used to direct the $\overline{IACK}$ signal to the accepted interrupt source with an external demultiplexer.

In the case of a vector interrupt ($\overline{AVEC} = 1$), the processor in state Z2 starts the acquisition of the vector number by setting Data Strobe signal $\overline{DS}$. Then the interrupt source prepares its Vector Number (VN) on the lower data bus half and signals this to the processor by setting the $\overline{DTACK}$ signal. The processor takes the vector number at the beginning of state Z7, then it resets its two strobe signals and ends the acquisition in the next state. (The acquisition of the vector number corresponds to the read cycle described in Subsection 4.3.2, although the interrupt source is not addressed with address signals A15 through A0, but with the $\overline{IACK}$ signal conveyed by the demultiplexer.) The processor first saves its status (PC, copy of SR) on the system stack. Then, by using the vector number, it addresses the associated interrupt vector in the vector table, loads it as the start address of the interrupt program in the program counter and begins the execution of this program.

In the case of an autovector interrupt ($\overline{AVEC} = 0$), the vector number is not read, and after saving the status the processor loads the autovector from the vector table indexed by the interrupt level

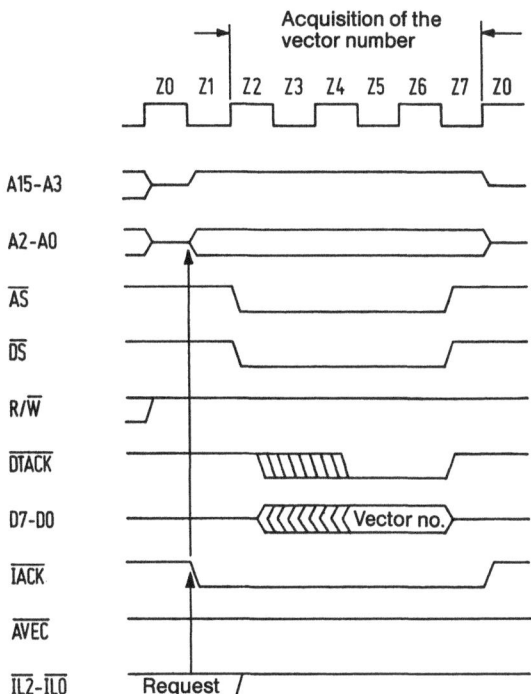

Fig. 4.21. Interrupt acknowledge
cycle for vectorized interrupts

immediately into the program counter. As shown in Figure 4.20, the $\overline{AVEC}$ signal is created with the $\overline{IACK}$ signal relative to the interrupt source. If there are several sources with autovector interrupts, the $\overline{AVEC}$ signal can be created for instance with an OR connection of the single $\overline{IACK}$ signals. - The whole procedure between the acceptance of an interrupt request by the processor and the beginning of the corresponding interrupt program is called interrupt cycle, whereas the included signal exchange for the acquisition of the vector number is called interrupt acknowledge cycle.

4.4.2 Allocation of Interrupt Levels

If the seven interrupt levels provided by the processor are not sufficient for priority allocation, these levels can be further subdivided according to priority with external circuitry. This can either be a centralized procedure through a priority encoder or a decentralized procedure, e.g. chaining interrupt sources within one interrupt level.

Centralized Allocation. As an addition to Figure 4.20, Figure 4.22 shows the allocation of one of the seven interrupt levels into eight priorities. To this purpose, a second priority encoder is used, whose $\overline{INT}$ output is tied to the corresponding input of the first priority encoder. The 3-bit code of the priority encoder is used to convey this level's $\overline{IACK}$ signal to the requesting interrupt source with an additional demultiplexer. In order to hold the code signals, they are stored in a buffer register at the beginning of the interrupt acknowledge cycle. The identification of an interrupt source is done by the vector number it delivered. If the processor accepts an interrupt request, it blocks each additional request on this level by setting the interrupt mask in the status register (exception: level 0).

Figure 4.23 shows a variant of the circuit represented in Figure 4.22, it is designed for interrupt sources that are not able to deliver vector numbers themselves. In this case, the vector numbers are created from the 3-bit code of the priority encoder. This is carried out by means of a three-state driver unit, which sends the 3-bit code, during the vector number read cycle, together with five previously determined bits as 8-bit vector number on the data bus. The connection of the driver component to the data bus occurs with additional logic selected by the $\overline{IACK}$ signal level.

Decentralized Allocation. Another possibility to subdivide the available interrupt levels according to their priorities is the connection of interrupt sources in what is called daisy-chain. The source, that is closest to the processor card in the rack, has the highest priority in the chain. The priorities of the following interrupt sources decrease with the increasing distance from the processor card.

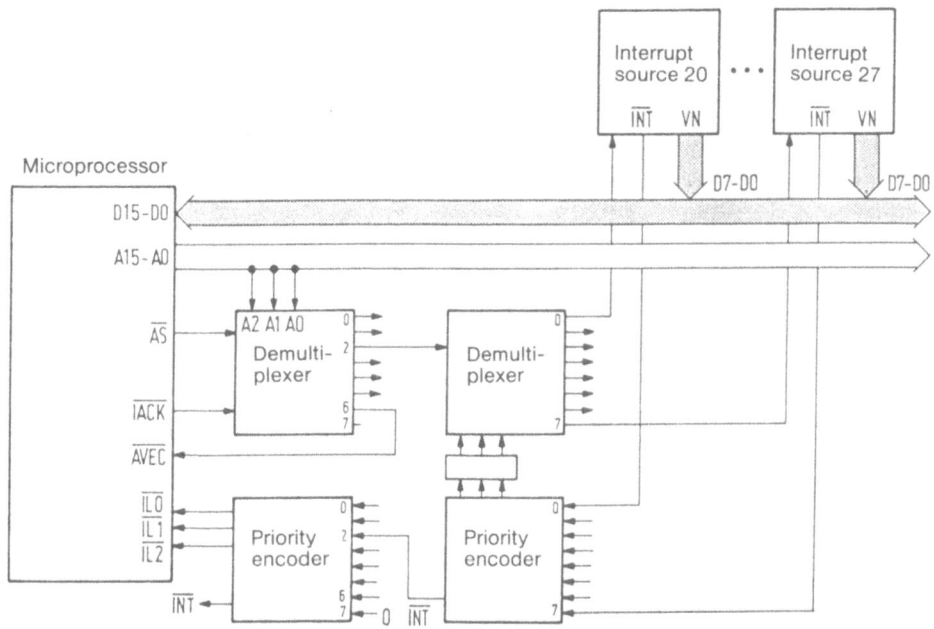

Fig. 4.22. Partition of an interrupt level by means of a priority unit; identification of the interrupt sources through their vector numbers

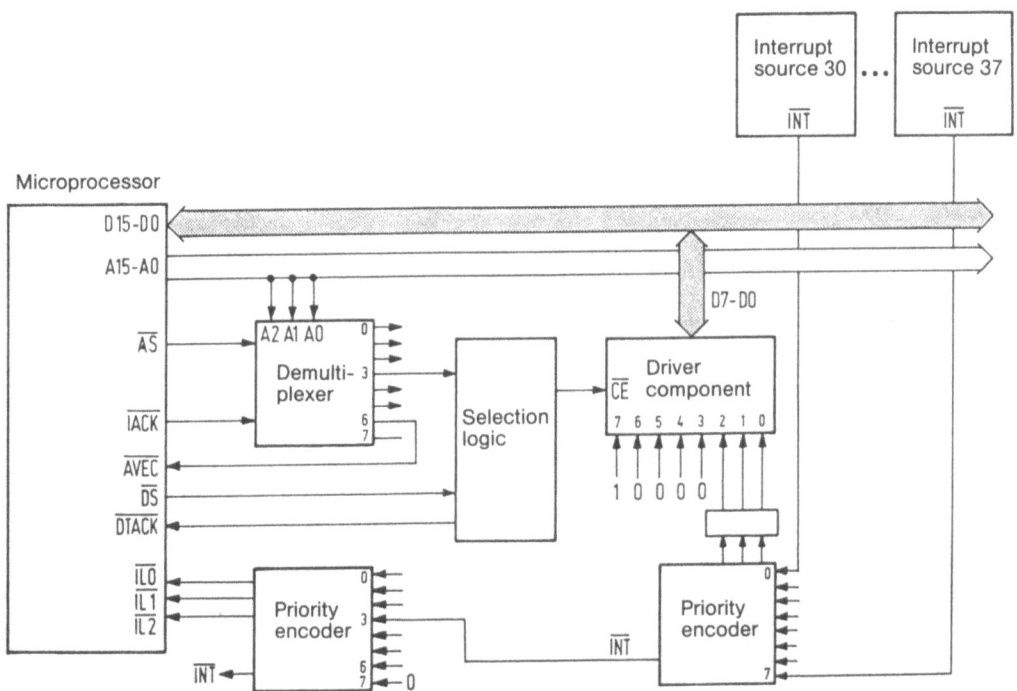

Fig. 4.23. Partition of an interrupt level by means of a priority unit; identification of the interrupt sources through the 3-bit code of the component

Figure 4.24 shows the basic structure of a daisy-chain. The request lines $\overline{INT}$ of the single interrupt sources of an interrupt level are connected through wired-or (circle) and are sent directly to the priority encoder. The acknowledge signal level $\overline{IACK}$ has two functions. On one hand it is directly sent to the interrupt sources to block the requests that were made during the interrupt acknowledge cycle and thus exclude them from the priority procedure in progress. On the other hand, it is sent to the chain input $\overline{IACKIN}$ of the first source in the daisy-chain in order to start the priority procedure for the existing requests. If one of the sources made a request, its chain logic blocks the transmission of the $\overline{IACK}$ signal to the following chain members. If there are several simultaneous requests, this allows only the interrupt source that is closer to the processor in the chain and thus has the highest priority of all requests, to receive the acknowledge signal. Here, the term "simultaneous" refers to the time between the arrival of a request and the activation of the $\overline{IACK}$ signal. When the $\overline{IACK}$ signal is received, the interrupt source sends its vector number on the data bus; if the $\overline{IACK}$ signal is reset by the processor, the block of the priority logic is removed.

If the microprocessor accepts an interrupt request from the daisy-chain, it blocks any additional request in this interrupt level by setting the interrupt mask in the status register (exception: level 0). However, the interrupts contiguous to the daisy-chain are maintained by the interrupt sources, so that they are not lost. When the level is released, it is the turn of the highest priority request.

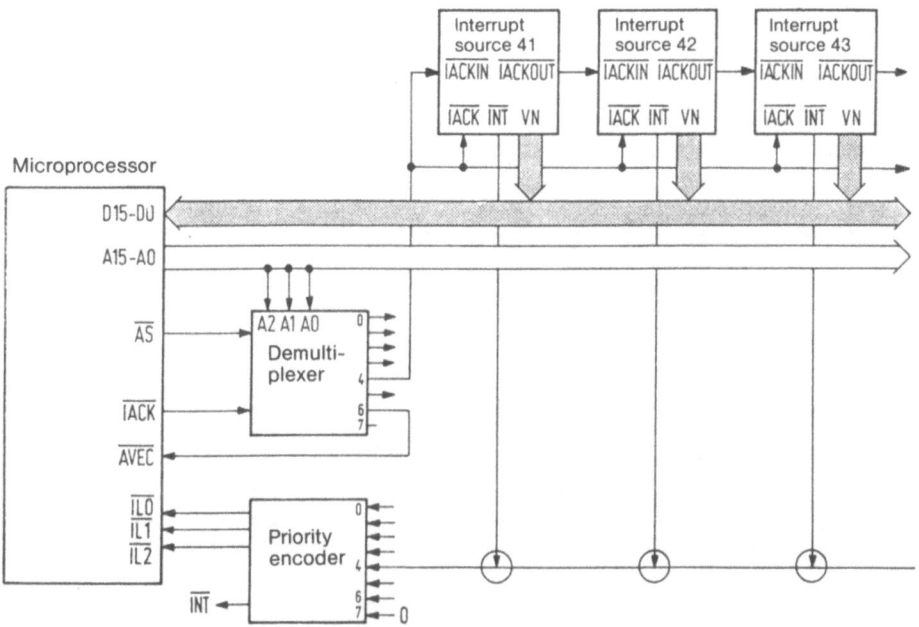

Fig. 4.24. Combination of several interrupt sources by connections in a daisy chain; identification of the interrupt sources through their vector numbers

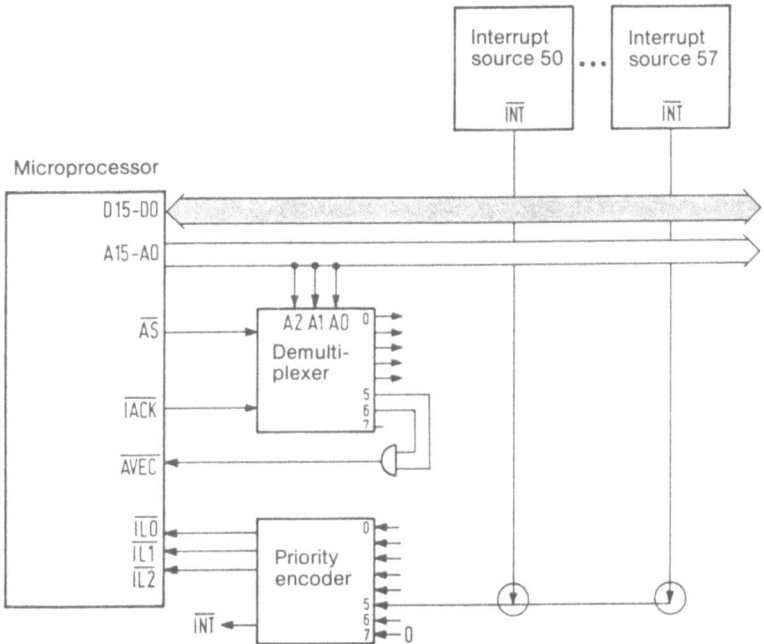

Fig. 4.25. Combination of several interrupt sources through wired-or; priorization and identification of the interrupt sources through the interrupt program

Figure 4.25 shows another possibility of decentralized allocation of an interrupt level for autovector interrupts. The request lines of the single interrupt sources are connected by wired-or, as in a daisy-chain, and are thus sent to the priority encoder. The $\overline{\text{IACK}}$ signal of the level is used to set the $\overline{\text{AVEC}}$ signal for autovector interrupt handling. Through the autovector of its level, an interruption leads to an interrupt program that all interrupt sources of this level will have in common. A polling routine in which the interrupt program evaluates the status information of the single interrupt sources determines the requesting source. The priorities of the single interrupt sources are defined by the sequence of accesses.

When compared to the centralized allocation of interrupt levels, decentralized allocation has the advantage of being able to utilize less signal lines on the system bus. This is particularly important when the system bus lines are not sufficient for centralized allocation due to the limited connector pins of the cards. As another application, decentralized allocation is mainly used in simple microprocessor systems with only one interrupt level, where the request line, which is shared by all interrupt sources, is directly connected with one of the interrupt inputs of the processor.

4.4.3 System Control Signals

Apart from interrupt inputs $\overline{IL2}$ and $\overline{IL0}$, the microprocessor has two additional inputs for special interrupts, Bus Error input $\overline{BERR}$ and $\overline{RESET}$ pin. Both signals are used to control the system together with an additional signal pin $\overline{HALT}$. Signals $\overline{BERR}$ and $\overline{RESET}$ work as trap signals. They trigger a program interruption and activate an interrupt program; however, no signal exchange takes place for processor-external interrupt handling (compare Subsection 2.3.1).

Bus Error Signal. The signal $\overline{BERR}$ is used to indicate to the processor mistakes that are recognized by the hardware in the processor environment. Frequently, this signal is used to connect a watchdog timer. If a $\overline{DTACK}$ signal is missing, it makes it possible to terminate the waiting state and to continue execution in an error handling program. An interrupt request, caused by a watchdog timer through a $\overline{BERR}$ input, has second highest priority in the whole trap and interrupt system due to its importance for system safety.

Reset Signal. The $\overline{RESET}$ signal is used to initialize the whole microprocessor system and therefore has highest priority of all interrupt signals. It starts the initialization of the processor hardware, where the system stack pointer register is loaded from the vector table and the other registers are loaded with zero. Then it leads to an initialization program, whose start address is also in the vector table. This program itself initializes all function units that depend on the system software and then returns the program control to the user. The $\overline{RESET}$ signal is usually activated by hand with a reset switch. Moreover, it can be connected to the power supply circuitry (reset logic), so that the initialization occurs automatically when the power supply is switched on (power-on reset).

The $\overline{RESET}$ pin of the microprocessor is bidirectional, so that the processor can send a $\overline{RESET}$ signal by means of a RESET instruction. Thus, the programmer has the possibility to initialize the system components that are attached to the external reset line with their $\overline{RESET}$ inputs.

Halt Signal. The $\overline{HALT}$ signal puts the microprocessor in a waiting state when the present bus cycle is terminated. In this case, all three state outputs of the processor are high impedance, so that the system bus is available for other system components with processor capabilities.

The $\overline{HALT}$ signal allows the realization of the operations *halt, run* and *single-step* by means of additional logic. There is no processing in halt mode, the program is executed in run mode. In single-step mode, the processor is first brought into run mode until it starts a bus cycle. This is indicated by $\overline{AS} = 0$. When at $\overline{AS} = 0$, it is switched to halt mode, so that it can only execute one bus cycle. This enables the user to execute processor operations stepwise and thus to test the system.

4.5 Bus Allocation

The basis for the allocation of a shared system bus to the different components of a microprocessor system is the master/slave principle. The microprocessor or a DMA controller takes over the bus control, it becomes an active component and is thus the master. Memory and interface components are passive functional units and are thus considered slaves. During data transfer, only one master and one slave can be switched on to the bus. In simple systems with one master only, the master is permanently assigned to the system bus and it chooses a slave through the address bus. In more complex systems with several masters, it is important that always only one master be assigned to the bus. The control of bus allocation is called bus arbitration.

In multiple-master systems, we distinguish between two kinds of bus allocation, local and global, depending on the complexity of the system structures.

4.5.1 Local Bus Allocation

Systems with local bus allocation have a system bus which is assigned to the microprocessor as a local bus. Depending on the need, additional masters in the system request the bus from it. Generally, these masters are controller components with very limited processing functions, like a DMA controller for instance. The bus allocation occurs through the processor with bus arbitration signals $\overline{\text{BREQ}}$, $\overline{\text{BGT}}$ and $\overline{\text{BGACK}}$ (see Figure 4.26) and is supported by a processor-external priority logic.

A DMA controller for example, which would like to execute a data transfer, requests the microprocessor system bus by setting the Bus Request signal ($\overline{\text{BREQ}}$). The microprocessor, which always has the lowest priority, first terminates its bus cycle, then it releases the bus. It also switches its address and data pins and the three-state control pins to high impedance state. At the same time, it reports the bus release by setting the Bus Grant signal ($\overline{\text{BGT}}$). This signal is sent to the DMA controller that requested the bus. The DMA controller takes control of the bus and indicates this by setting its Bus Grant Acknowledge signal ($\overline{\text{BGACK}}$); it also negates its $\overline{\text{BREQ}}$ signal. Then the processor resets its $\overline{\text{BGT}}$ signal. The DMA controller executes the data transfer, which can include one or more bus cycles. Then it releases the bus and indicates this by resetting the $\overline{\text{BGACK}}$ signal. The microprocessor is again connected to the bus.

In the simplest case, there is only one additional master beside the microprocessor. If there are several masters in the system, their bus requests have to be managed by a processor-external priority logic. Figure 4.27 shows the example of two DMA controllers in a daisy-chain, whose Bus Requests $\overline{\text{BREQi}}$ are combined on a shared $\overline{\text{BREQ}}$ line through wired-or. The daisy-chain is driven by the processor's grant signal $\overline{\text{BGT}}$ (see also interrupt daisy-chain in Subsection 4.4.2). Bus

136

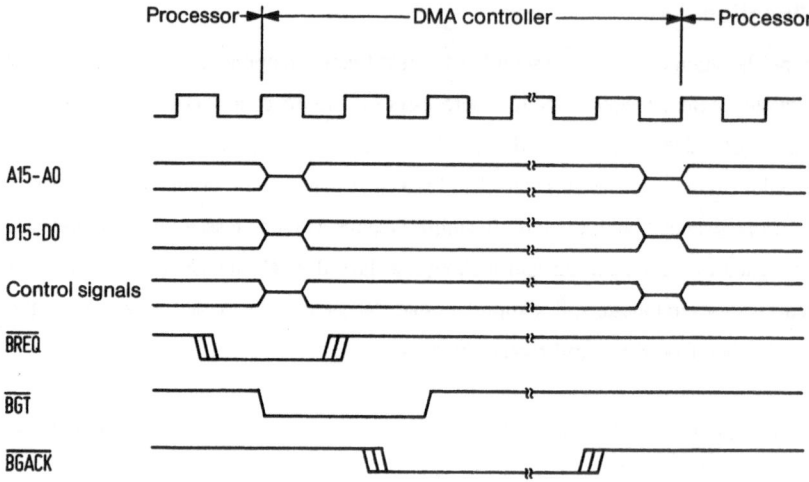

Fig. 4.26. Bus allocation cycle

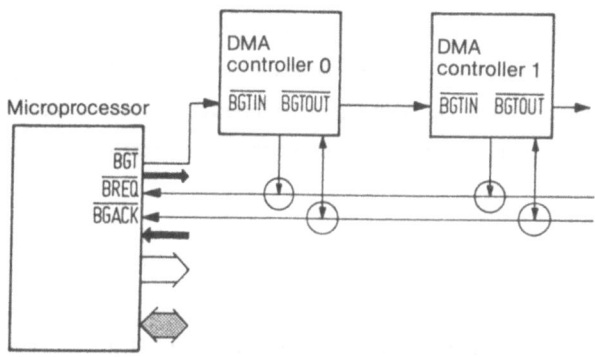

Fig. 4.27. Bus allocation of a local bus with priorization in a daisy chain

allocation or release through a DMA controller is indicated by the Bidirectional Acknowledge signal ($\overline{\text{BGACK}}$). - During a bus allocation cycle, the first element making a request in the chain receives the active level of $\overline{\text{BGT}}$ and sends a passive $\overline{\text{BGT}}$ signal to the next element in the chain. It only takes control of the bus when its availability is indicated through the $\overline{\text{BGACK}}$ line; i.e., a new requester, which finds the $\overline{\text{BGT}}$ active level at its chain input, does not interject with the current bus cycle as long as $\overline{\text{BGACK}}$ is held active. (The connection of DMA controllers is described in detail in Subsection 6.1.1.)

4.5.2 Global Bus Allocation

A system with global bus allocation consists of several processors (central processing units, I/O processors) or microcomputers (autonomous microprocessor systems with a local bus), all of which have access to a common global bus. Differently from local bus allocation, the shared bus is not assigned to one master, but is only available on request according to priority. The control needed for this procedure is provided by special control components (bus arbiters, priority components).

Figure 4.28 shows the example of part of a system with several local microprocessor systems (multiprocessor system) all of which have access to a shared memory by means of a global bus. One of the local systems is represented in detail with its bus arbiter; moreover, the priority logic with central priority allocation and the global bus with the shared memory are illustrated (see also [23,24,40]).

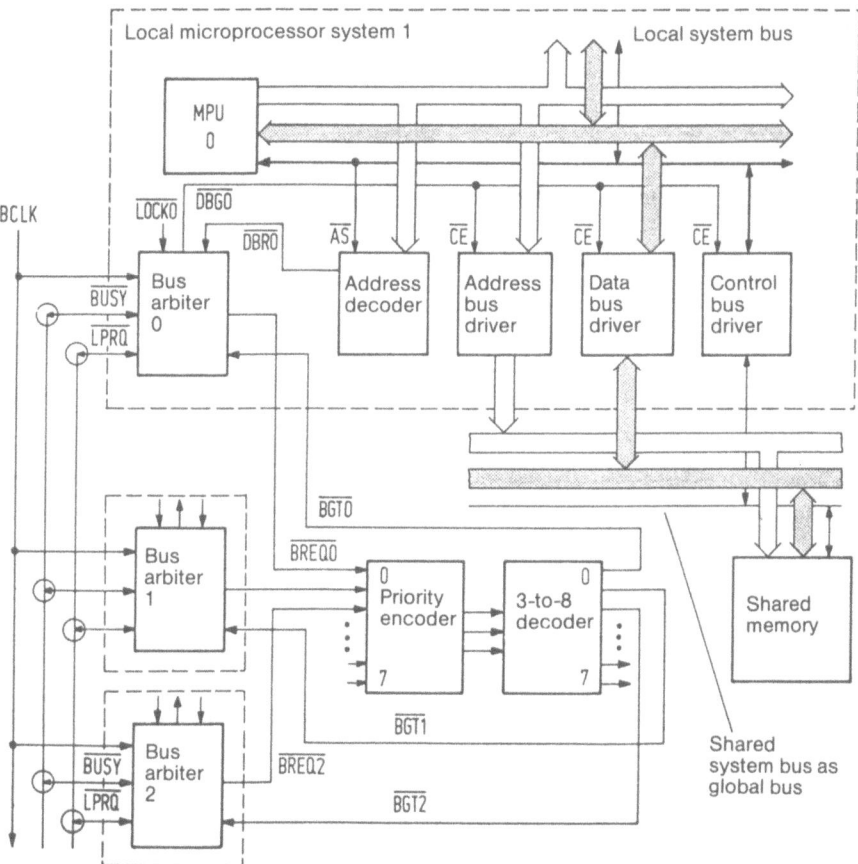

Fig. 4.28. Section of a multiprocessor system; bus allocation by bus arbiters in connection with a central priority control

The access to the shared memory is started by the microprocessor like a local memory access by sending the memory address and the $\overline{\text{AS}}$ signal. A decoder, which recognizes the address to be a shared memory address, generates a Device Bus Request signal ($\overline{\text{DBR}}$) for the local bus arbiter. The arbiter transmits the request as a $\overline{\text{BREQ}}$ signal to the priority encoder with a 3-to-8 decoder. If no higher priority request is present, the encoder confirms the granting of the request to the bus arbiter by means of the $\overline{\text{BGT}}$ signal. At the same time, the priority encoder removes the $\overline{\text{BGT}}$ signal from a lower priority bus arbiter if it is using the bus at that time. This bus arbiter will release the bus at the end of its present bus cycle ($\overline{\text{AS}} = 1$). It indicates the bus release by resetting its $\overline{\text{BUSY}}$ signal. Then, the higher priority bus arbiter, which is reading the $\overline{\text{BUSY}}$ line, takes over the shared bus. To this purpose, it connects the bus drivers of the local system to the shared bus by means of its Device Bus Grant output ($\overline{\text{DBG}}$). Simultaneously, it indicates the use of the bus to the other bus arbiters by setting its $\overline{\text{BUSY}}$ output. The requesting processor is in waiting state until the bus is allocated.

In order to avoid requesting the shared bus for each data transfer, which would be very time-consuming, the bus arbiter keeps the bus as long as it is not substituted by a higher priority request on the bus. In any case, the bus master is also removed from the bus during a lower priority request if it is not executing a bus cycle on the shared bus. To this purpose, the requesting bus arbiter sets its wired-or output $\overline{\text{LPRQ}}$ (Lower Priority Request) beside the $\overline{\text{BREQ}}$ signal. The bus arbiter, that is using the bus and that recognizes this request through its bidirectional $\overline{\text{LPRQ}}$ pin, resets its $\overline{\text{BREQ}}$ signal, which causes the priority logic to reset the corresponding $\overline{\text{BGT}}$ signal and to set the $\overline{\text{BGT}}$ signal of the requesting bus arbiter. - All request and grant signals are synchronized by their own Bus Clock (BCLK) in the bus arbiters. Thus, local microprocessor systems are independent as far as their clock frequencies are concerned.

In the procedure described above, bus allocation is controlled by the hardware (bus arbiters). On the contrary, microprocessors with so-called multimicro signals can exercise a form of control that is basically managed by the software (see Zilog Z8000 [3]). In this case, a multimicro signal output is used to send a request or to indicate the state of an operational device. The state of an operational device can be tested with a multimicro signal input. Since the instructions needed for this procedure are privileged, they can only be executed in system mode.

5 Input/Output Organization

The main activity when performing input/output is the transfer of a single datum between the microprocessor or the main memory, on one side, and a peripheral on the other. Data transfer, described in Section 4.3, between the microprocessor and a memory cell of the main memory is the basis for this transmission; however, data transfer with peripherals generally requires more control. The reasons are that peripherals have to be started and stopped, that synchronization and control signals for data transfer are required, and that data is not always received and sent by the peripheral in a bit-parallel way, as on the system bus, but it is often received and sent bit-serially. For this reason, other transfer paths are necessary which are partly very different from the system bus and therefore require their own control mechanisms. The interconnection of the system bus with the transfer paths occurs through interface adapters that are called interfaces or I/O controllers (Figure 5.1).

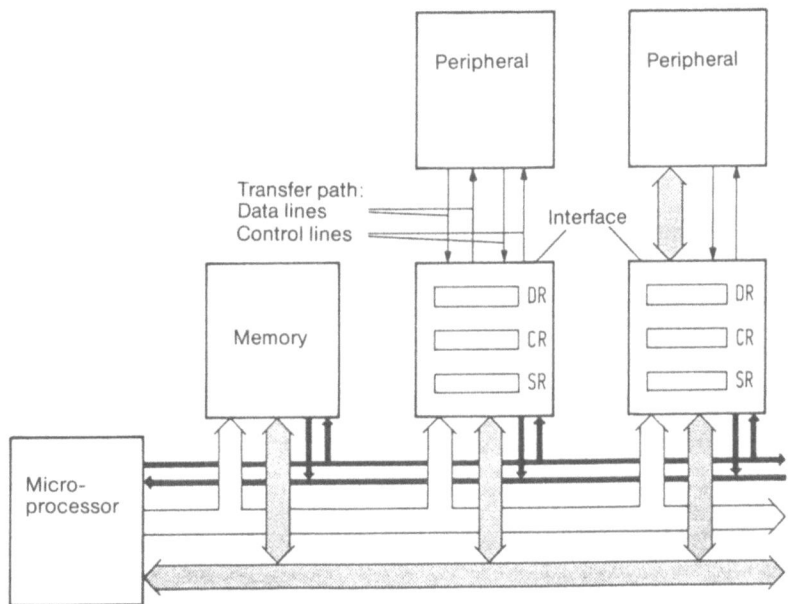

Fig. 5.1. System structure with interface modules for data input and data output

An interface has at least one Data Register (DR) to buffer data between the system bus and the peripheral transfer path. The interface interconnection with the system bus is designed so that the data register can be read and written like a memory cell; i.e., a single data transfer with the peripheral, apart from the synchronization, is like a memory access as far as the microprocessor is concerned. The differences between interfaces are in the interface interconnections with the peripheral (e.g. parallel or serial data transfer, type and number of control lines) and in the control mechanism necessary for data transmission between interface and peripheral.

By loading some control information into one or more Control Registers (CR), several operations of an interface can be controlled by the program, i.e. can be programmed. The current state of the interface is indicated in one or more Status Registers (SR). The control and status registers are also writeable or readable like memory cells. Often, control information and status are also combined in a single register.

Section 5.1 describes some possible I/O organizations in which the microprocessor takes over the control of the data transfer (microprocessor controlled I/O). In this case, the emphasis is on the synchronization of single-data transfers and on programming techniques. Section 5.2 deals with some physical and functional characteristics of transfer paths between interface and peripheral, as well as with aspects of remote data transmission. This section is the basis for the description of the three most important interfacing techniques and their corresponding interface modules: the parallel, the asynchronous serial and the synchronous serial data transfer. They are described in detail in Sections 5.3, 5.4 and 5.5. The descriptions of the components concentrate on the most important functions of the commercially available interfaces.

5.1 Input/Output Control with the Microprocessor

As already mentioned, the transmission of data between microprocessor and peripheral requires the synchronization of the two transfer partners. The reason for this lies in the different transmission speeds. The synchronization occurs with an exchange of control information between microprocessor and interface on one side, and interface and peripheral on the other side. There are several possibilities to communicate control information, which can also be combined on the two transmission connections:

1. the control information is transmitted with its own control lines,

2. the control information is contained in the data information (in the data frame), and

3. the control information is transmitted as data (control character).

As far as the synchronization itself, there are several possibilities that differ in the processing by the processor, in the programming techniques and in the reliability of the data transmission. In the following, we will consider the most important synchronization alternatives in microprocessor controlled I/O. In this case, the processor manages the control of each data transfer with the interface and exchanges control information with it.

5.1.1 Synchronization with Busy Waiting

During the synchronization with busy waiting, the microprocessor waits for the interface to be ready before it outputs or inputs data; the readiness of the interface is indicated by a status bit (ready bit) in its status register (Figure 5.2). This bit is set by a control signal (READY) of the peripheral after reading the content of the interface data register (output) or loading the data register (input). The microprocessor is either in a waiting loop, in which it continuously checks the ready bit of the status register, or it executes the read operation at fixed intervals while continuing to process in the meantime. If the ready bit is set, it branches into the I/O instruction sequence (see also Subsection 5.1.3, Example 5.1). There, the datum is written or read and the ready bit is reset, so that the next transfer request can be performed by the interface. Depending on the component, the reset of the ready bit is performed for example with a read access to the interface data register.

The drawback of busy waiting lies in the fact that the microprocessor needs some of its processing time to read the ready bit during an I/O procedure, whether or not a transfer request was made. If the microprocessor is in a waiting loop, it is only waiting and is thus badly utilized. Moreover, a prerequisite for busy waiting is that the microprocessor's processing speed be higher than the speed of the peripheral. Time can become a problem when, for instance, the microprocessor has to process several I/O operations at the same time.

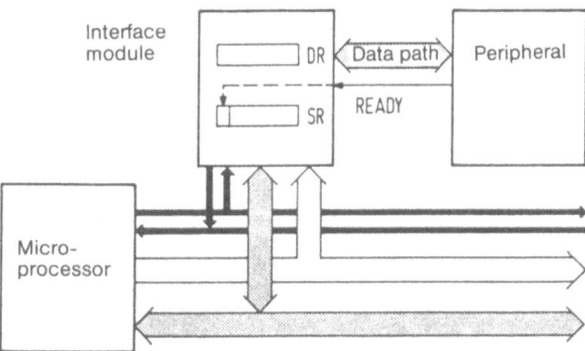

Fig. 5.2. Synchronization through busy waiting

142

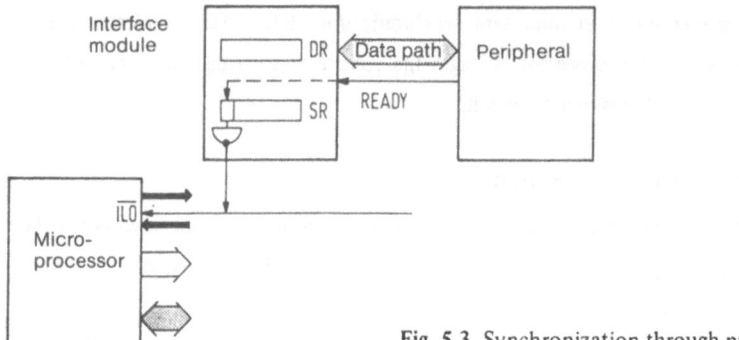

Fig. 5.3. Synchronization through program interruption

5.1.2 Synchronization with Program Interruption

If synchronization is carried out with a program interruption, the state of the interface status bit, set by the ready signal of the peripheral, is passed on to the microprocessor as an interrupt request, i.e. the ready bit has the effect of an interrupt signal (Figure 5.3). Thus, the program does not constantly read the state of the status bit, like in busy waiting, but receives it directly as interrupt signal. If the microprocessor accepts the interrupt request, it reacts with a program interruption and it branches to an interrupt program, which executes the I/O (see also Subsection 5.1.3, example 5.2).

Compared to the synchronization with busy waiting, here the processor achieves a certain independence from the I/O activities of the peripheral, and it can use the time between program interruptions for other tasks. Again, the prerequisite for a faultless transfer is that the processing speed of the microprocessor be higher than that of the peripheral.

5.1.3 Synchronization with Handshaking

In order to have a safe data transmission even in cases where the peripheral has to wait for the microprocessor, the transfer control is expanded so that the microprocessor - or the interface in its place - reports its readiness by setting an acknowledge signal. For example during data input, the microprocessor takes one datum from the interface data register only when the transfer of data is confirmed as usual by the peripheral. The peripheral itself only transfers data when the microprocessor has acknowledged the acceptance of the last datum. This procedure, in which both transfer partners perform a sort of shake hands, is called handshaking (acknowledge mechanism).

Figure 5.4 is an expansion of Figure 5.2 and 5.3, and it shows the block diagram of handshaking at the control signal level. When the interface data register is either read (input) or written (output) by the microprocessor, the peripheral receives the Acknowledge signal $\overline{\text{(ACKN)}}$ from the interface.

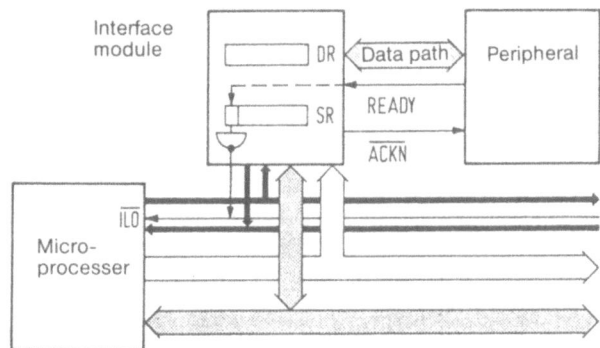

Fig. 5.4. Synchronization through handshaking

On its part, the peripheral reports the data transfer or the data acquisition from the data register with the READY signal, like it did before. The processor either evaluates this signal as status information (handshaking with busy waiting) or as an interrupt signal (handshaking with program interruption). An interrupt enable bit in the control register of the interface allows the differentiation between the two operations.

Example 5.1. Synchronization of a data input through handshaking with busy waiting. 128 data bytes have to be read into a memory area at the address BUFFER by means of an 8-bit interface Data Register (DR). In order to synchronize the transmission, the peripheral sends a READY signal every time one datum is transferred to DR; this is indicated by a one in the bit position 7 (ready bit SR7) of the 8-bit interface Status Register (SR). This bit's state has to be evaluated with busy waiting. To this purpose, the interrupt enable bit in the control register of the interface is reset during the initialization, so that the interrupt signal connected to the ready bit is inhibited.

At the beginning of the input program, registers R5 and R6 are initialized as buffer pointers with the buffer starting address BUFFER and with the buffer end address BUFFER + 128 for the determination of the loop's end. The ready bit is read in a waiting loop by means of the Bit Test instruction (BTSTB) with mask $80. If the ready bit is set, the DR content is read into the buffer area addressed with the autoincrement of R5. This read procedure causes the status bit to be reset by the interface and the Acknowledge signal ($\overline{\text{ACKN}}$) to be sent to the peripheral. The $\overline{\text{ACKN}}$ signal indicates to the peripheral that the datum is acquired by the processor. The procedure is repeated until the buffer pointer in R5 coincides with the buffer end address in

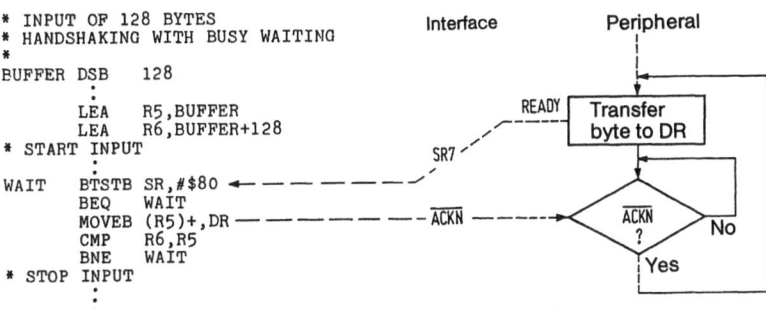

R6 incremented by one and therefore indicates that the buffer is full. - The input operation was programmed without the initialization of the interface or its starting and stopping (see Section 5.3, Example 5.3). ■

Example 5.2. Synchronization of a data input through handshaking with program interruption. The input of 128 bytes described in Example 5.1 has to be modified so that the transfer of a datum to the Data Register (DR) of the interface causes a program interruption and the data acquisition occurs through an interrupt program in the processor. To this purpose, the interrupt enable bit was set in the control register of the interface during its initialization, so that the interrupt signal, connected to the ready bit, is enabled.

```
* INPUT OF 128 BYTES
* HANDSHAKING WITH PROGRAM INTERRUPTION
* MAIN PROGRAM
*
         REF    BPTR,BEND
BUFFER DSB    128
         :
         LEA    BPTR,BUFFER
         LEA    BEND,BUFFER+128
* START INPUT
         :
```

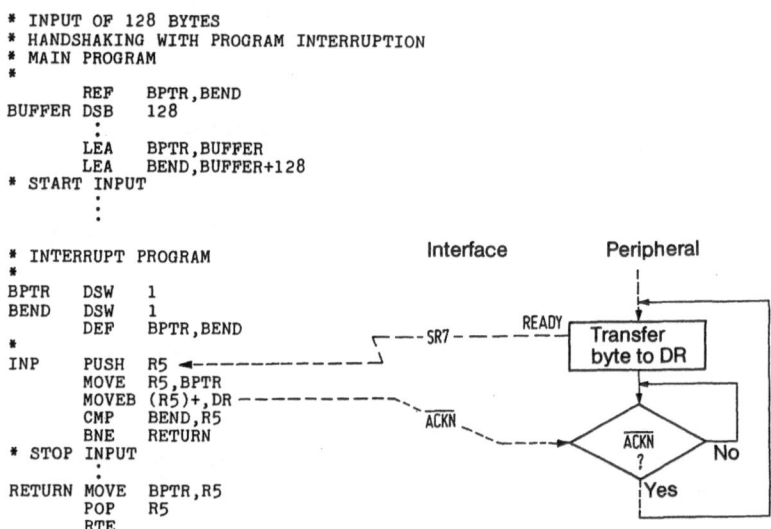

```
* INTERRUPT PROGRAM
*
BPTR    DSW    1
BEND    DSW    1
        DEF    BPTR,BEND
*
INP     PUSH   R5
        MOVE   R5,BPTR
        MOVEB  (R5)+,DR
        CMP    BEND,R5
        BNE    RETURN
* STOP INPUT
         :
RETURN  MOVE   BPTR,R5
        POP    R5
        RTE
```

A program interruption, triggered by the ready signal, leads to the Interrupt Program (INP), which transfers one data byte from the Data Register (DR) to the buffer for each call. In order to be able to address the buffer and to count the bytes, the main program initializes the global variables BPTR and BEND with the buffer start address BUFFER and the buffer end address incremented by one BUFFER + 128. The interrupt program loads the Buffer Pointer (BPTR) to R5 and reads the DR content into the buffer area which is addressed with the autoincrement of R5. Finally, it assigns the buffer pointer incremented by one again to the variable BPTR. In order to avoid writing over its original content, R5 is first saved on the system stack. When reading DR, the ready bit in the status register is reset by the interface, thus the interrupt request is negated. At the same time, the interface sends the Acknowledge signal ($\overline{ACKN}$) to the peripheral and thus reports the data acquisition. ■

5.1.4 Simultaneous Handling of Several Input/Output Activities

I/O processing is not limited to single I/O activities, but it often requires simultaneous handling of several similar procedures by the microprocessor. A simple example is represented by a system in which several terminals can make simultaneous transfer requests to the microprocessor (e.g. a time sharing system). Depending on whether the single transfer requests will be handled with busy waiting or with a program interruption, their handling requires different programming techniques.

Polling. In the case of peripheral units, whose transfer requests are processed by means of busy waiting, the test of each ready status bit is performed consecutively in a testing sequence (polling

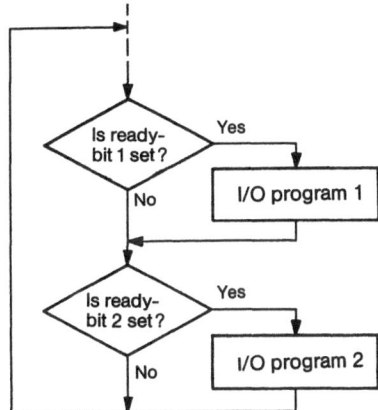

Fig. 5.5. Testing of transfer requests through polling

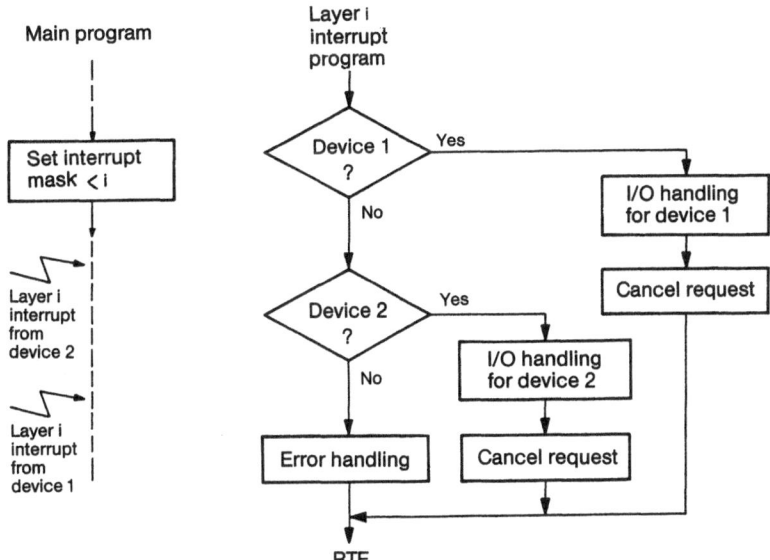

Fig. 5.6. Identification of interrupt requests through polling

routine). The testing sequence will run repeatedly until one of the interfaces has a transfer request; at this point, there will be a branching to the corresponding I/O program (Figure 5.5). This program is also called polling program.

In the case of peripheral units, whose transfer requests are processed by means of program interruption and in which the requests as autovector interrupts of the same level share an interrupt program, the identification of the single requests is carried out by polling (see also Subsection 4.4.2). To this purpose, the single ready status bits are tested in the interrupt program. When the ready bit that is causing the program interruption is found, there is a branching to the corresponding I/O program (Figure 5.6) that negates request by resetting the ready bit.

Interruptibility of Input/Output Programs. In polling, the priority assignment to the transfer requests is determined by the sequence of tests, i.e. a running I/O program cannot be interrupted. In the case of interrupt requests, that identify themselves by means of an external vector number or an internal autovector, polling is not necessary, and the priority distribution is managed by the hardware (see Section 4.4). Here, a running I/O program (interrupt program) can be interrupted by a request at a higher priority interrupt level. This leads to the nesting of interrupt program executions, where the same requirements as with reentrant subprograms are to be observed for saving and loading the status (see Subsection 3.3.4). Since the call point is unknown, the status has to be saved immediately after input in the interrupt program, and it has to be reloaded when the program is exited. By using the system stack, the processor can do this for the contents of registers PC and SR. The MOVEM instruction can be used for the contents of the general purpose registers. The system stack is also used, since the interrupt structure is identical to the structure of subprogram nesting and thus follows the LIFO principle.

An interrupt program of level i ($1 \leq i \leq 6$) cannot usually be interrupted by interrupts of similar or lower priority, because the processor sets the interrupt mask in the processor status register on value i before calling the interrupt program. The old processor status - containing PC and SR - and thus the original interrupt mask are reloaded only when the interrupt program is exited by means of the RTE instruction, so that a new program interruption at level i is possible. If, exceptionally, similar or lower priority interruptions were to be granted anyway, the interrupt mask can be set to a value > i by the running program. This can only be obtained by the privileged instruction MOVSR which can alter the processor status. The priorities determined by the interrupt levels of the processor can be subverted by these procedures.

5.2 Data Transmission Systems and Remote Data Transmission

Data transmission systems basically consist of a data transfer path and of Data Terminal Equipment (DTE). Data terminal equipment includes for instance the microprocessor system with its interface on one end and a peripheral with its control logic at the other end of the transfer path. Data terminal equipment can also include two or more microprocessor systems. If the distance is limited, data transfer paths consist of one or more signal lines and one common return line. For bigger distances, lines and communication devices from the national remote telecommunication equipment are used. These transfer paths (communications channels) for Remote Data Transmission (RDT), like voice telephone lines for instance, require additional Data Communications Equipment (DCE) at their ends, e.g. modems, for signal adaptation between data

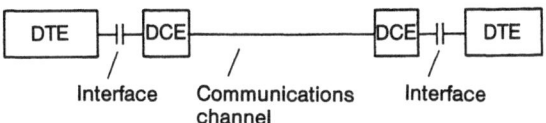

Fig. 5.7. Components of a data transmission system

terminal equipment and data transfer path (Figure 5.7). This way, computer systems that are very distant from each other can be connected by means of dial-up lines, by specialized data nets for digital data transmission, or by radio communication. Such a connecting system, called computer net, includes the computers of the participants (host computers) as well as computers that are only used to transfer data through the net paths (communications computer).

The techniques of data transfer over a public telephone net and over public data nets are regulated by national and international standards and are documented for example in the so-called V.- and X.-Recommendations of the CCITT (Comite Consultatif International Telegraphique et Telephonique). These recommendations also include electrical, physical and functional characteristics of the interfaces between data terminal equipment and data communications equipment. Some of these characteristics are discussed in this section as an introduction to the following sections. Furthermore, we will deal with data checking during data transfer. For a more detailed presentation see for instance [25-27].

5.2.1 Data Transfer Techniques

Operations. There are three kinds of modes, used for signal transmission, that differ in their use of signal lines: the simplex mode, the half-duplex mode and the full-duplex mode. In simplex mode, the transmission is possible only in one direction. On the one end of the transfer path there is a sender and at the other end there is a receiver. Such a connection is also called unidirectional. In half-duplex operation, the signal transfer is possible in both directions but not at the same time. Both ends each have one sender and one receiver that are connected to the signal lines depending on the direction of the transfer. Such a connection is also called bidirectional. In full-duplex operation (for short, duplex operation), signal transfer is possible in both directions at the same time. To this purpose, each direction is equipped with its own transfer lines. If compared to the half-duplex operation, the performance is doubled; the command for sender/receiver switching at the terminal ends is not necessary.

Serial and Parallel Data Transmission. In serial data transmission, the single bits of a character are transferred one after the other at a fixed transmission frequency on one single data signal line; this is also called bit-serial data transfer. In parallel data transmission, each character bit can have its own signal line; bit transmission occurs simultaneously. This is also called bit-parallel character-serial data transfer. An exception is represented by the encoding of several bits within a frequency carrier, which is achievable by means of modulation techniques. In this case, several bits are transferred simultaneously over one signal line.

Synchronous and Asynchronous Data Transmission. Synchronous data transmission occurs in a fixed time frame that is maintained for the duration of the transfer. The time frame is either determined by a frequency generator shared by the sender and the receiver, or sender and receiver have two frequency generators with the same frequency that are synchronized through the transferred data signal.

Time intervals between the single data transfers are variable in case of asynchronous data transfer. Sender and receiver have two frequency generators with the same frequency that are synchronized every time there is a data transfer, i.e. a character transfer. The information needed for the synchronization is transmitted with the characters.

Bit Rate, Transmission Rate and Transfer Rate. Bit rate is indicated by the number of the transmitted bits per second in the unit of measurement bit/s. Transmission rate is defined by the transmission frequency per second and is measured in baud. Usually, these two speed specifications are the same for serial data transmissions. If the bits are transmitted in parallel, the number of bits per second is bigger than the baud rate by the factor of parallelism. This is also true for the exception described above, where the transmission is executed on a single signal line.

If part of the transmitted bits is used for error detection, the actual bit rate of the real data bits is reduced. This speed is called transfer rate.

5.2.2 Remote Data Transmission

Data Transmission Services. Data transmission within a building is usually under the responsibility of private institutions. If this limited range is trespassed, data transmission is under the authority of public institutions or telephone companies and it has to comply with certain conditions. In Germany for example, the Post Office offers several services (Dateldienste) [28,29] for data transmission with different transmission techniques, bit rates and user costs. These are:

- the public telex net: 50 bit/s (low speed),

- the public voice telephone net: from 300 to 4800 bit/s (medium speed),

- the public datex net with switched lines for digital data transmission (DATEX-L): from 50 to 9600 bit/s (high speed),

- the public datex net for packet switching (DATEX-P): 2400 to 48000 bit/s (high speed), and

• the public direct call net with leased lines for the transmission of digital information: from 2400 to 48000 bit/s (high speed).

The lines used in these nets are telegraph lines, voice telephone lines and so-called broad band lines. In addition, if the data are not transmitted over long distances, d-c coupled lines are used.

Connections. Data transmission paths can be implemented with switched or leased lines. In the case of leased lines, the transmission path is assigned to the two transmission partners and is thus always available. Due to the high renting expenses, this solution is only advantageous if it is used frequently. Apart from its availability, its advantage also lies in its low error rate, because there are no moving contacts on the transmission path and the data transmission equipment is adjusted to the transmission path. In the case of switched lines, the connection is established when needed, as it is in telephone traffic. It is cost effective if the transmission path is only used from time to time. Its availability is lower than what offered by the direct lines, since the transmission path can be in use when a transfer is requested; moreover, connection generation requires some time.

Within the limits of a building, fixed connections are used because, unlike public nets, they do not need to be rented. Furthermore, the distances between different data terminal equipment units are usually small, e.g. for the direct connection of a terminal to a microprocessor system. Data communications equipment is not needed in this case.

Interface Standard. The most popular interface is defined as a bit-serial interface for transmitting digital characters over the telephone net in CCITT Recommendation V.24 (based on EIA RS-232C - Electronic Industries Association, comparable to DIN 66020 - Deutsche Industrie Norm [30]). The Recommendation contains the functional characteristics of the interface lines between data terminal equipment and data communications equipment for data, clock frequency, selection, status and control signals as well as for analog signals. Figure 5.8 shows the most important of the 25 interface lines.

The protective ground is used for personal safety against electric shock; the signal ground represents the common return conductor for all interface lines except protective ground. Figure 5.8 shows the following signal lines: one data line (TD,RD) for each transmission direction, two control lines to switch single functions of the data communications equipment (DTR, RTS), three status lines for reading the operational status of the data communications equipment (DSR, CTS, DCD), and four clock frequency lines for the mutual supply of clock frequency whose use depends on the unit in which the clock frequency is produced.

The typical electrical characteristics of the interface V.24 are described in the V.28 CCITT Recommendation. This Recommendation also defines the thresholds for the logical values 1 and 0

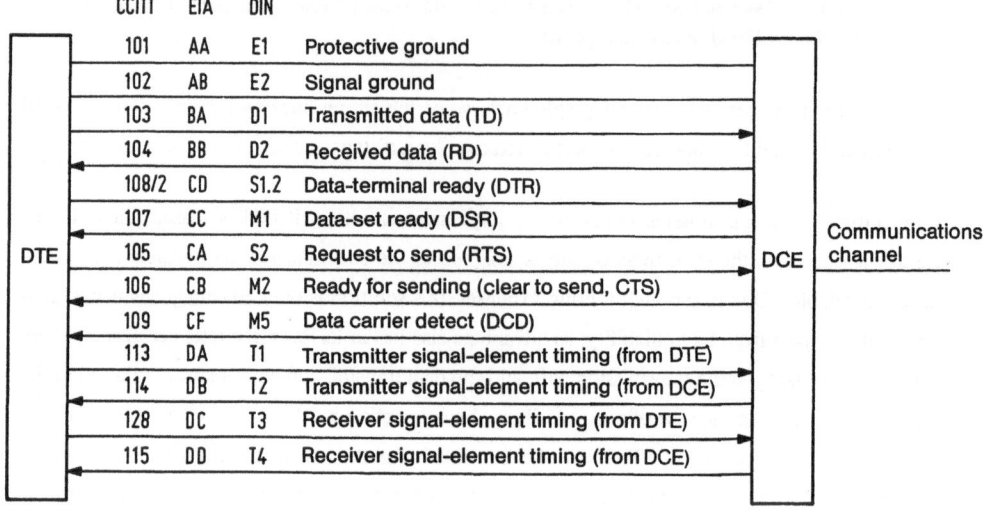

CCITT	EIA	DIN	
101	AA	E1	Protective ground
102	AB	E2	Signal ground
103	BA	D1	Transmitted data (TD)
104	BB	D2	Received data (RD)
108/2	CD	S1.2	Data-terminal ready (DTR)
107	CC	M1	Data-set ready (DSR)
105	CA	S2	Request to send (RTS)
106	CB	M2	Ready for sending (clear to send, CTS)
109	CF	M5	Data carrier detect (DCD)
113	DA	T1	Transmitter signal-element timing (from DTE)
114	DB	T2	Transmitter signal-element timing (from DCE)
128	DC	T3	Receiver signal-element timing (from DTE)
115	DD	T4	Receiver signal-element timing (from DCE)

Fig. 5.8. The most important V.24 interface lines

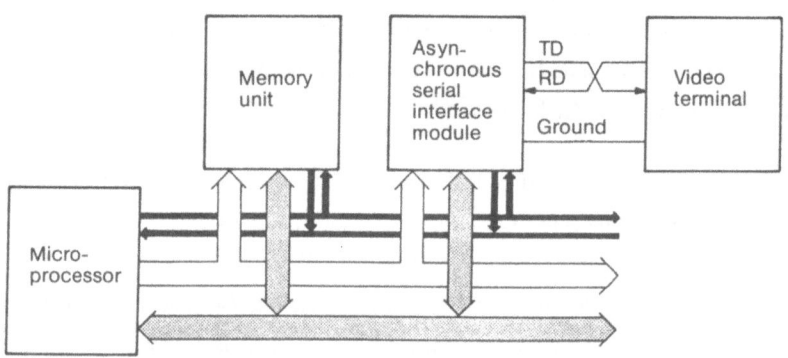

Fig. 5.9. Terminal attachment with V.24 interface

by means of voltages between +3 V and +15 V or -3 V to -15 V; commonly, these values are +12 V and -12 V. The bit rate is limited to 19200 bit/s; standard values are 50, 75, 110, 150, 300, 600, 1200, 2400, 4800, 9600 and 19200 bit/s. (The same is true for RS-232C.)

The V.24 interface is not only used for the interconnection of data transmission devices in remote data transmission, but also for the direct connection of peripheral devices like terminals and printers. Often only the two data signal lines TD and RD and the signal ground are used as connection lines.

Figure 5.9 shows the example of the connection of a video terminal to a microprocessor through an asynchronous serial interface. The synchronization information is contained in the data signals of TD and RD (see also Subsection 5.4.3). The crossed data lines correspond to the connector defined in the V.24 Recommendation: the sender connection on one side has to be connected with the receiver connection on the other side.

The interface for bit-parallel remote data transmission is defined in CCITT Recommendations V.30 and V.31 that will not be discussed here because of their secondary role in microprocessor technology. In microprocessor technology, the main application of bit-parallel data transmission is not in remote data processing and in the connection of I/O devices with V.30 interfaces, but in the transmission of data, control and status information for special applications (for instance: a process control peripheral). Thus, the transmission path is tailored to the application (see also Section 5.3). - An overview of CCITT Recommendations can be found in [31].

Data Communications Equipment (DCE). Lines, that are designed like voice telephone lines for the transmission of alternate current signals, need a data transmission device at each end of the transmission path in form of a modem (modulator/demodulator). The modem on the side of the sender transforms the direct current signals corresponding to the logical quantities 0 and 1 into alternate current signals, for instance with two different frequencies (modulation); the modem on the receiver's side reverses this transformation (demodulation). In the case of telephone lines, both frequencies are chosen in the range from 300 Hz to 3400 Hz (US: 3000 Hz), the frequencies needed for the transmission of voice. This modulation technique is called Frequency-Shift Keying (FSK) modulation. Depending on the kind of line and on the bit rate, other modulations are used beside the frequency modulation, for example Amplitude Modulation (AM) and Phase Modulation (PM) [32,33]. - Modems are also used for data transmission on current switched lines, for signal conditioning and signal correction.

5.2.3 Data Checking

Data are checked during remote data transmission, because of noise on the transmission paths, but also during data transmission over short distances. To this purpose, data are augmented with additional information by the sender; this helps detect transmission errors at the receiver's side. If an error is found, the transmission procedure can be either repeated or interrupted by issuing an error message.

Characterwise Checking. With characterwise checking, each character is completed by a so-called parity bit (vertical parity). Depending on what agreed upon, the value of this bit is created so that the sum of all bits of the augmented characters is either even (even parity) or odd (odd parity). Thus, all transmission errors with an odd amount of single bit errors can be detected, since non-

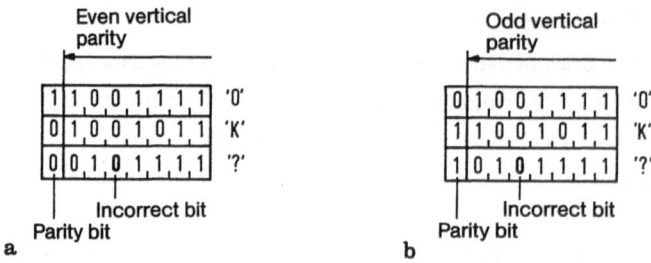

Fig. 5.10. Data checking through parity bit. a) even parity, b) odd parity

valid code words are created in these circumstances. According to [27], the safety factor is about 100 compared to the unchecked data transmission. In Figure 5.10 there are two examples that each include three 7-bit ASCII characters, where the last character has been transferred with an error in bit position 4.

Blockwise Checking. With blockwise data checking, a data block is completed with a Block Check Character (BCC) at the end of the block (longitudinal parity). Depending on the agreement, the values of the check bit are created so that the longitudinal sum, i.e. the sum of all bits in the same bit position, is either even or odd. This kind of checking is particularly advantageous when there is no space for an additional vertical parity bit in the data format and when there is also no additional signal line for the parity bit during parallel data transmission. As for characterwise checking, the safety factor is about 100 [27].

As an example of block checking, Figure 5.11a shows a data block with three 7-bit ASCII text characters that are expanded to 8-bit characters by an additional zero bit in the highest bit position. The beginning and end of the block are defined by the ASCII control characters STX (Start of Text) and ETX (End of Text). Block checking includes the characters STX and ETX.

Cross Checking. Cross checking is a combination of character and block checking. Its application brings the safety factor up to 1000 [27], which represents a substantial increase in safety compared to the two procedures described above. Figure 5.11b shows the ASCII character sequence introduced in Figure 5.11a with cross checking. Here, the eighth character bit was used to create the vertical parity.

Cyclic Block Checking. With cyclic block checking, the data block is terminated by one or two 8-bit CRC characters, the so-called Cyclic Redundancy Check code. For the creation of CRC characters, the sender considers the bit sequence of the character string as the coefficient of a polynomial and divides this polynomial by a fixed so-called generator polynomial. The binary coefficients of the resulting rest polynomial make up the CRC information. On the side of the receiver, the bit

153

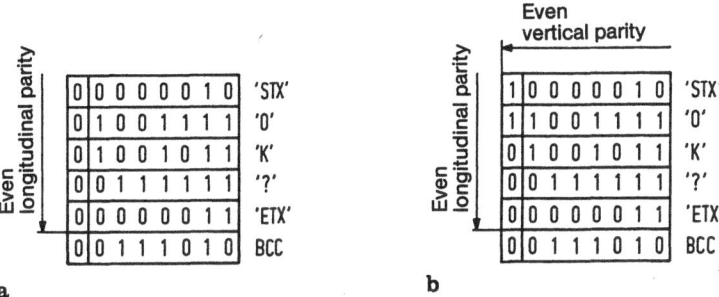

Fig. 5.11. Data checking with even parity. a) block checking, b) cross checking

sequence of the data block including the CRC character has to be divisible by the generator polynomial without rest. By choosing the appropriate generator polynomial, the check procedure can be tailored to specific errors. Safety factor in this procedure is about 100000 [27]. - See also [5] on data checking.

5.3 Parallel Data Transmission

As already mentioned, several bits are transferred simultaneously during parallel data transmission. For this reason, either each bit has its own signal line or the bits are coded with modulation techniques and transferred over one single signal line. This is called bit-parallel transmission, or character-serial transmission, if it occurs bytewise. Parallel data transmission allows the exchange of data, control and status information with different data formats. Thus, it offers a wide range of applications especially in automatic control techniques.

5.3.1 Data Formats

Within a microprocessor system, the data transfer takes place on the system data bus in parallel with 8-bit or 16-bit words. Parallel interface modules are used for the connection of peripheral units with parallel transmission. They are equipped with a system bus interface with the data, address and control lines necessary for reading and writing the interface register, and with a peripheral interface made of one or more I/O ports. Each one of these I/O ports includes up to 8 or 16 data lines and several control lines. The use of the data lines depends on the data formats to be transferred.

ASCII characters are transmitted as 8-bit characters, the highest bit is either set to zero or is used as parity bit. Peripherals, which work exclusively with decimal digits, transfer them in packed representation as 4-bit BCD characters. Four data lines are sufficient for this data format (half byte). Analog measurement values and adjust variables that are input through an analog-to-digital converter or are output through a digital-to-analog converter can include up to 16 bits, depending on the precision of such data. Finally, binary information that is used to control (control signals) or sense (sense signals) specific conditions of the peripheral can be transmitted. In this case, data formats include between one bit and the maximum number of bits allowed by the I/O ports.

5.3.2 Parallel Interface Module

In the following, we will discuss the basic structure and functionality of a parallel interface module. Due to the predominantly byte-oriented information structure of the peripheral, this module is connected to the system bus side with 8 data signals, i.e. it uses one half of the 16-bit system data bus for data transmission. On the side of the peripheral it has two independent I/O ports with one 8-bit data bus each. The module manages data buffering and synchronization of the data transfer. - The basic difference between commercially available parallel interface components lies in their number of I/O ports and in the degree of support for the synchronization with the peripheral. A market survey on parallel interface components is reported in [22].

Block Structure. Figure 5.12 shows the structure of a parallel interface module with its two I/O ports A and B; the representation of port A is more detailed because it includes the data flow. Beside the two central data registers DRA and DRB for data storage, the module also includes a control unit with three registers CR, DDR and IMR for the control of the two I/O ports. Each one of these ports has a control logic for the synchronization with the peripheral and for the generation

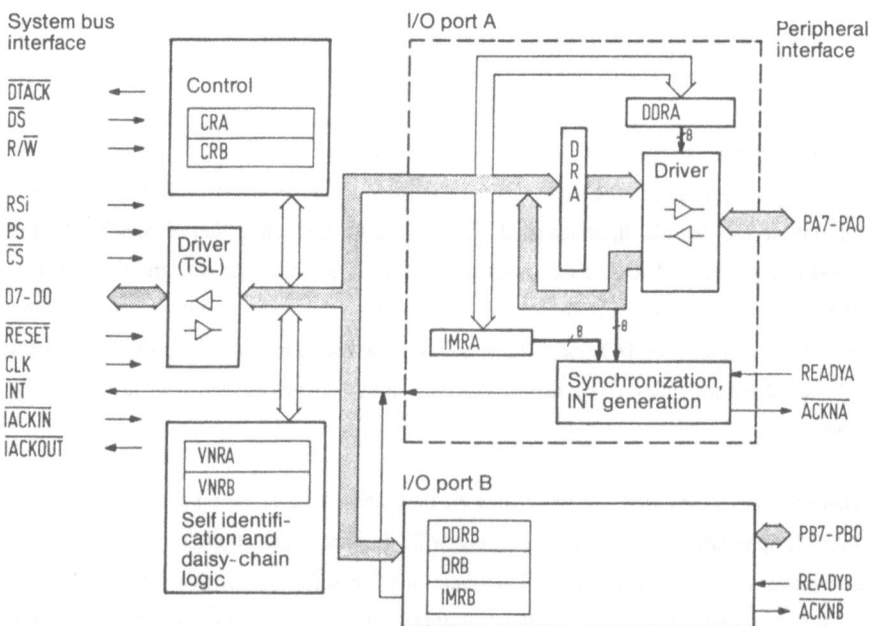

Fig. 5.12. Structure of a parallel interface module

of the Interrupt signal ($\overline{\text{INT}}$). Moreover, there is a device for self-identification of the two ports as interrupt sources and for the use of the $\overline{\text{IACK}}$ signal in a daisy-chain. It is internally predetermined that port A has priority over port B. (Self-identification and chain logic are missing in simpler modules.)

The following signals are necessary for interfacing with the system bus: eight bidirectional data lines from D7 to D0 with Three-State Logic for writing or reading the module registers, one Chip Select input ($\overline{\text{CS}}$) to select the module, one Port Select input (PS) to differentiate between ports during the selection of registers, several Register Select inputs (RSi) to select a register within one port, and the signals R/$\overline{\text{W}}$, $\overline{\text{DS}}$ and $\overline{\text{DTACK}}$ that have to be added for data transmission. Furthermore, there is the open collector output $\overline{\text{INT}}$ shared by both ports as interrupt line and the signals $\overline{\text{IACKIN}}$ and $\overline{\text{IACKOUT}}$ for chaining in a daisy-chain. The module is put in initial state by the $\overline{\text{RESET}}$ input; the CLK input supplies the clock frequency, e.g. the system clock frequency.

The interface with the peripheral requires both ports to be equipped with eight bidirectional data lines P7 through P0 as well as two control lines READY and $\overline{\text{ACKN}}$ that are used to synchronize data transmission.

Behavior. The operation of the interface components is indicated in one 8-bit Control Register (CR) for each port that is loaded with a control byte. Figure 5.13 shows the effect of the single control bits. Bit CR1 allows a differentiation between two types of operation, data mode and control mode, that are specified by the bits CR4 through CR7 or CR2 through CR3. Bit CR7 is an exception, because it is not a control bit but a status bit. The addition of this bit in the control register makes the separate creation of a status register unnecessary. (CR7 corresponds to the ready bit described in Subsection 5.1.1.)

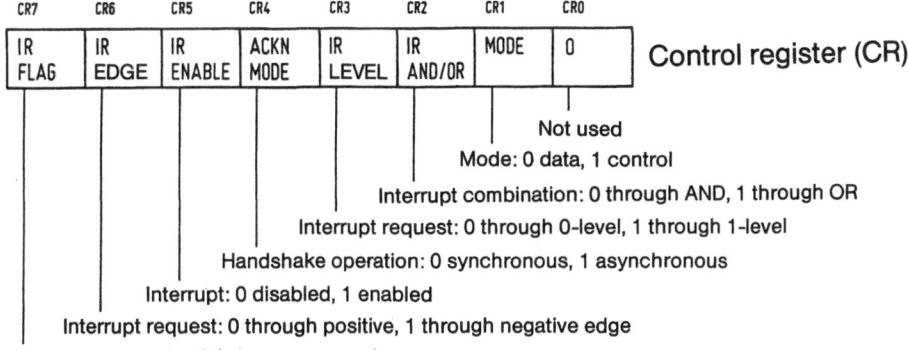

Fig. 5.13. Control register of the parallel interface module

Data Mode. The exchange of data between microprocessor and peripheral occurs in data mode. The direction of the transmission of data signals of the peripheral interface can be programmed individually through the corresponding bits of an 8-bit Data Direction Register (DDR): the data signal i is switched to output with DDRi = 0 and to input with 1. Thus, single data lines can be identified as outputs, e.g. for control signals, and others as inputs, e.g. for status signals. During the output, the microprocessor writes a data byte in the 8-bit Data Register (DR); the bits that are set to output are written to the peripheral data bus. During data input, the microprocessor reads a data byte directly from the peripheral data bus which is addressed with the address of the data register. All data signals of the data lines programmed as inputs have to be stable until the processor has completed the data acquisition.

The synchronization of the data transmission of an I/O port occurs over the two control lines READY and $\overline{ACKN}$. A ready signal arriving on the READY line, represented by a transition of the signal, is stored in bit position 7 in the control register as status bit IR-FLAG (interrupt bit, ready bit). The state of the IR-FLAG bit can be either read by the processor by reading the register content (READY has the effect of a sense signal), or it can be passed on to the processor as interrupt request through the $\overline{INT}$ line (READY operates like the interrupt signal). The control register bit IR-ENABLE decides about the transmission of the interrupt signal. An additional control register bit determines whether the IR-FLAG bit is set by a positive or by a negative edge on the READY line. Since the IR-FLAG bit is a status bit, it is not changed when the control register is loaded (read only bit); instead, it is reset when the data register is read. - The I/O port that caused the program interruption identifies itself in the interrupt handling procedure. The daisy-chain control causes the port to send its interrupt vector number, stored in an 8-bit Vector Number Register (VNR), to the system data bus.

The $\overline{ACKN}$ signal informs the peripheral of the end of the output or input of a data byte by the microprocessor. It is used with the READY signal for the handshake synchronization. The criterion for setting the $\overline{ACKN}$ signal is different for the two ports. In port A it is done when the loading of the data register is completed (output), in port B it is done when the reading of the data register is terminated (input). Thus, port A is mainly designed for output and port B for input. However, if port A is used for data input, a data write instruction, whose data will not be considered (dummy write), has to be added after the data read instruction in order to activate the $\overline{ACKN}$ signal. The same is true for port B; an additional read instruction (dummy read) is required during output.

The negation of the $\overline{ACKN}$ signal is the same for both ports. It is carried out in two ways, that are indicated in the control register of each port by the ACKN MODE bit. In asynchronous mode, it occurs after the arrival of a READY signal, i.e. it depends on the state of the peripheral. In

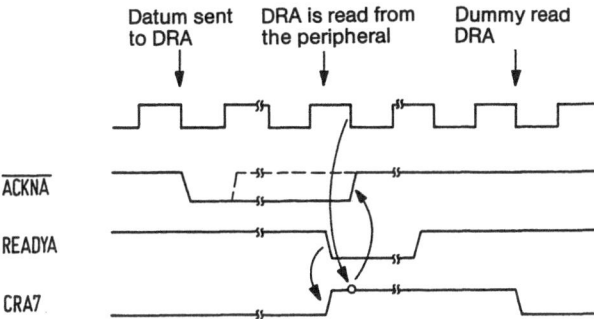

Fig. 5.14. Handshake synchronization during data output from port A

synchronous mode, it occurs by itself after a clock cycle, i.e. one single pulse is sent on the $\overline{\text{ACKN}}$ line. Therefore, this operation is also called pulse strobe mode.

Figure 5.14 shows the signal diagram of the handshake synchronization for the output of one datum through port A in asynchronous mode (CRA4 = 1, $\overline{\text{ACKNA}}$ signal as a continuous line) and in synchronous mode (CRA4 = 0, $\overline{\text{ACKNA}}$ signal as a dotted line). The signal READYA of the peripheral sets the ready bit CRA7 with its negative edge (CRA6=1); CRA7 is reset by a dummy read operation.

Control Mode. In control mode, the data lines programmed for output work like in data mode. They are mainly employed to transmit binary control signals (control lines). On the other hand, data lines that are programmed for input have the function of interrupt lines. Unlike the READY signal, interrupt signals are represented by a signal level. The signal level, either 0 or 1, is generally controlled by the register bit IR-LEVEL for all data lines that are programmed as interrupt lines. Moreover, each interrupt line can be individually masked by the bits of an 8-bit Interrupt Mask Register (IMR): with IMRi = 0, the interrupt line i is inhibited; with IMRi = 1, it is enabled. Furthermore, the control register indicates with the IR AND/OR bit, whether the transmission of the interrupt request to the microprocessor occurs through an AND or an OR function of all non-masked interrupt lines. The identification of an I/O port as interrupt source takes place through the corresponding vector number register like in data mode. The processor can determine on which line the interrupt occurred by reading the data lines that are programmed as interrupt lines. The control line READY and $\overline{\text{ACKN}}$ do not have any effect in control mode.

Figure 5.15 shows the example of an application of the control mode. In an industrial process, the pressure of a furnace has to be kept within a certain pressure range by means of a heating element and an excess pressure valve. Two alarm signals indicate when the pressure range has been exceeded; an additional alarm signal indicates that the fixed limit temperature has been exceeded.

158

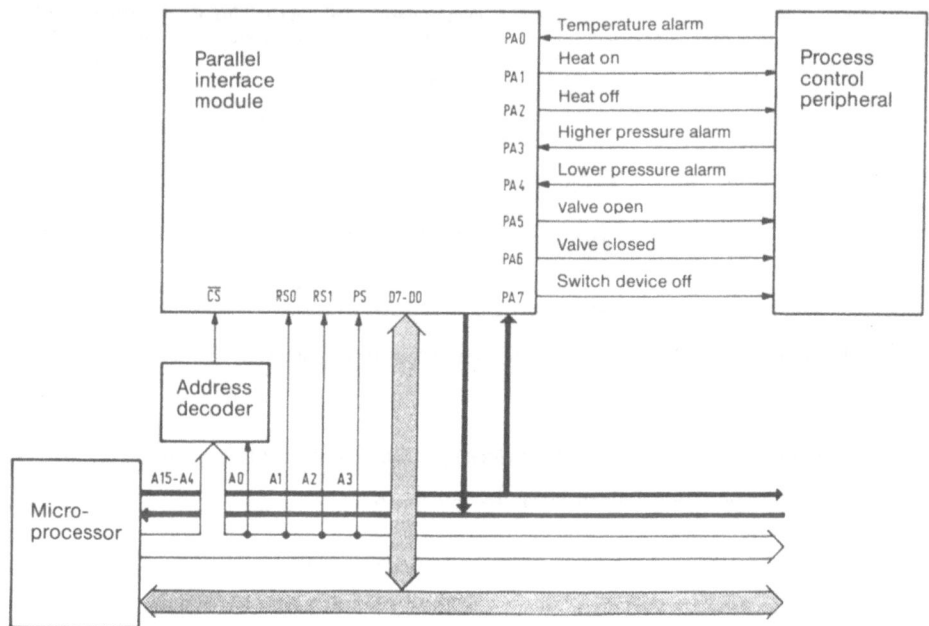

Fig. 5.15. Process control with a parallel interface mocule operating in control mode

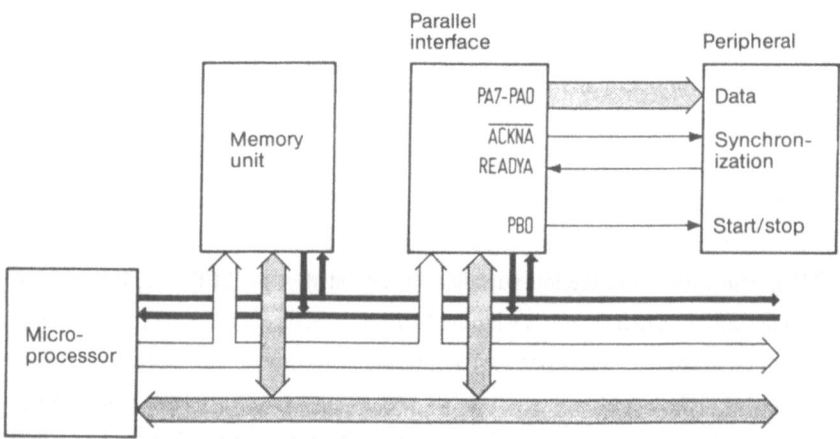

Fig. 5.16. Connection of a peripheral to a parallel interface module

The alarm signals are sent on the data inputs PA0, PA3 and PA4 as interrupts, the control signals are put on the data outputs PA1, PA2, PA5, PA6 and PA7 of the I/O port A. The assignment of inputs and outputs is controlled by the Data Direction Register (DDRA).

Example 5.3. Data output through a parallel interface component. Similarly to what described in Example 5.1 (Subsection 5.1.3), 128 data bytes have to be sent to a peripheral through the parallel interface component described above (Figure 5.16). Data transmission has to be 8-bit parallel and has to occur over the I/O port A through handshaking with busy waiting (asynchronous mode, negative edge as READYA signal). The peripheral has to be started by asserting a one on the data line PB0 (port B), and it has to be stopped with PB0 = 0 at the end of the transmission.

In order to initialize the interface, the Data Direction Registers of both ports DDRA and DDRB are first loaded with the control byte $00 which switches all signals to output, even those which are not used. Then, both control registers CRA and CRB are initialized with the control bytes $50 and $00, which define the data mode for both ports and set the synchronization modes specified in the example. CR5 = 0 inhibits the interrupts in both ports.

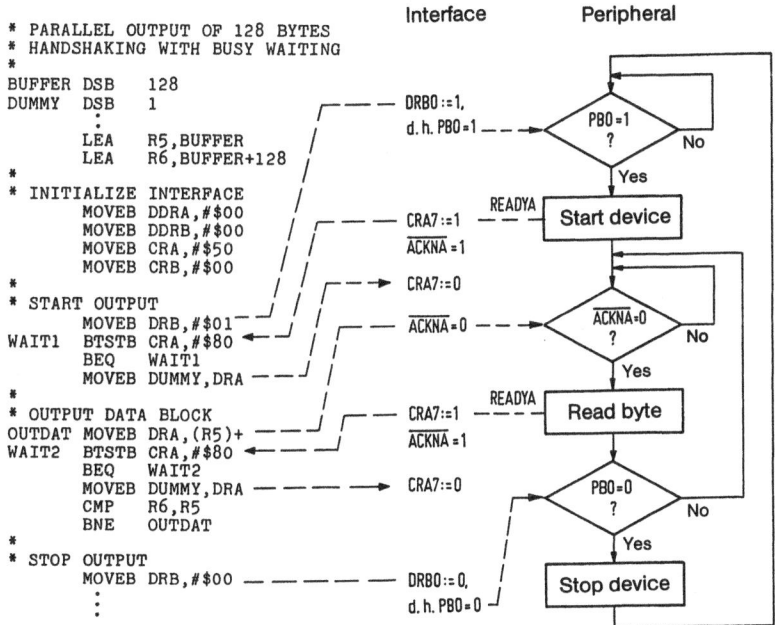

```
* PARALLEL OUTPUT OF 128 BYTES
* HANDSHAKING WITH BUSY WAITING
*
BUFFER DSB    128
DUMMY  DSB    1
         .
         .
       LEA    R5,BUFFER
       LEA    R6,BUFFER+128
*
* INITIALIZE INTERFACE
       MOVEB  DDRA,#$00
       MOVEB  DDRB,#$00
       MOVEB  CRA,#$50
       MOVEB  CRB,#$00
*
* START OUTPUT
       MOVEB  DRB,#$01
WAIT1  BTSTB  CRA,#$80
       BEQ    WAIT1
       MOVEB  DUMMY,DRA
*
* OUTPUT DATA BLOCK
OUTDAT MOVEB  DRA,(R5)+
WAIT2  BTSTB  CRA,#$80
       BEQ    WAIT2
       MOVEB  DUMMY,DRA
       CMP    R6,R5
       BNE    OUTDAT
*
* STOP OUTPUT
       MOVEB  DRB,#$00
         :
         .
```

The peripheral is started by sending $01 to the Data Register DRB; PB0 is set to one. The device announces its availability through the READYA signal and sets the ready bit CRA7 in port A on one. The program waits for this bit to be set in a waiting loop WAIT1 (busy waiting) and then resets it through a dummy read operation with the Data Register DRA so that it can begin with the data transmission. When a data byte is transmitted to the DRA, the interface sends its ACKNA signal. Then the peripheral reads the datum and acknowledges the acquisition by setting the READYA signal, so that the ready bit CRA7 is set and the ACKNA signal is reset. The program waits for the READYA signal in a waiting loop WAIT2 (busy waiting), resets CRA7 and sends the next data byte. When the transmission of the last data byte is completed, the peripheral is stopped by sending a zero on the PB0 data line. ■

5.4 Asynchronous Serial Data Transmission

During serial data transmission, the bits of a character are transferred consecutively on the same data line. They are sent at a fixed frequency to which the receiver has to conform in order to be able to acquire data. In the case of asynchronous serial data transmission, the time intervals between the single characters can vary. Therefore, the receiver has to synchronize itself to the clock frequency of the sender for the transmission of each single character.

The asynchronous serial data transmission, whose transmission speed is at most 19,200 bit/s, is mainly used to interface peripherals that cannot send or receive continuous characters, e.g. in the case of slow printers or of character output by video terminals equipped with an input keyboard. Another microprocessor system can also be a transmission partner. The devices are either connected to the microprocessor system over the telephone or over fixed connections. The advantage of this transmission technique lies in the comparatively low complexity of the sender and receiver equipment.

5.4.1 Communications Protocol

Contrary to parallel data transmission, in which the synchronization of the data transmission usually occurs through specially designed control lines, control information has to be transmitted on the data line in the case of serial transmission. In order to allow a distinction between control and data information and to guarantee an unambiguous transmission, conventions have been collected in so-called communications protocols. Included in these rules are for instance agreements on the bit rate, the synchronization mechanism, the data format (character code) and the kind of data checking. Moreover, the protocol determines the transmission of related transmission blocks and defines the flow control in terms of a transmission procedure. The flow control describes the information exchange between transmitter and receiver to start, execute and terminate the data transmission. This includes for example counting the transmitted block, indicating wrongly transmitted blocks, correcting the errors by repeating the block transmission, and so on. - An example of flow control for synchronous serial data transmission is described in Subsection 5.5.2.

5.4.2 Data Formats

Figure 5.17 shows the basic representation of a character as a timing diagram of the signal level on the transmission line. The value 0 of a bit is represented by the space line (e.g. 0 V) and the value 1 by the mark line (e.g. +5 V). In the case of a transmission over a V.24/V.28 or an RS-232C interface, the level has to be adjusted to -12 V and +12 V for example.

Depending on the convention, a character includes 5 , 6, 7 or 8 data bits and starts with the lowest bit D0. It is alternatively completed by a Parity bit (P) for even or odd parity (vertical parity). Both the character and the parity bit are enclosed by a start bit (space) and, depending on the convention, one, one and a half or two stop bits (marks). This frame indicates the beginning and the end of the

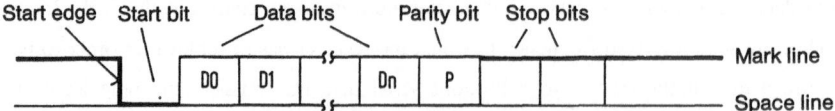

Fig. 5.17. Character representation in asynchronous serial data transmission

character transmission to the receiver. Thus, this transmission procedure is also called start/stop mechanism. Due to different possible standardizations, there are several data formats with a different number of bits. The transmitter sends a constant 1 level as idle signal between two character transmissions.

5.4.3 Bit and Character Synchronization

In order to be able to receive the individual bits, the receiver generates a pulse, whose frequency is equal to the sender frequency; this frequency is derived from the 16 or 64 times higher frequency of the receiver pulse generator through frequency division. The synchronization of the receiver pulse with the sender pulse occurs at the beginning of a character transmission with the falling edge of the start bit. Through frequency division, the receiver pulse is delayed by half the frequency period in relation to the start bit edge, so that the data acquisition edges of the receiver pulse are in the middle of the transmission steps. The signal levels of the single data bits sampled at these points are stored consecutively in a shift register, where the character will be picked up in the receiver data register.

Thus, the start bit determines the beginning of a character (character synchronization) and indicates the point of reference for the bit acquisition (bit synchronization). Since the start bit level should be asserted after the duration of a half bit, the receiver can determine if the received edge belongs to a start bit or if it was only the edge of a short faulty pulse within the transmission pause. Furthermore, it checks whether the transmission of the character was completed successfully by checking the stop bit or stop bits.

Decentralized clock frequency generation is not the only possibility for bit and character synchronization. If a clock line is available beside the data transmission line, the transmitter clock frequency can be sent on it directly to the receiver, which excludes the clock generator on the side of the receiver. In this case, the clock frequency signal has to be delayed by half a period for data acquisition.

5.4.4 Asynchronous Serial Interface Module

In the following, we will discuss an asynchronous serial interface module equipped with one 8-bit interface for the system data bus and two 1-bit interfaces for the peripheral. It manages the parallel-to-serial and the serial-to-parallel conversion of the characters to be transmitted, parity generating and checking, and bit and character synchronization. Moreover, it allows eight different data formats. - A market survey on asynchronous serial components is included in [22].

Block Structure. Figure 5.18 shows the structure of the asynchronous serial interface module with one transmitter and one receiver component on the side of the peripheral (Universal Asynchronous

Receiver/Transmitter - UART). Beside the central registers TDR and RDR to store data and the two shift registers for parallel-to-serial and serial-to-parallel conversion, the module has a control unit with several registers, an interrupt device with self-identification of the module as interrupt source, and a daisy-chain logic for the priority assignment of the module according to the daisy-chain principle. (Simple module versions lack the self-identification and the chain logic.) An additional communications control unit manages three control signals for signal exchange with the peripheral.

The interface with the system bus is implemented as in a parallel interface module; i.e., data transfer between the microprocessor and the interface as well as within the interface module takes place in a bit-parallel way in byte format, where the eight data signals are alternatively connected to the lower or higher half of the system bus.

The interface with the peripheral requires a Transmitted Data signal (TD) for the transmitter and a Received Data signal (RD) for the receiver for bit-serial data transmission. Sender and receiver also have the clock frequency inputs Transmitter Clock (TCLK) and Receiver Clock (RCLK) respectively. The module generates the internal clock pulses from the input clock signals as indicated by the frequency division ratio (1:1, 1:16 or 1:64).

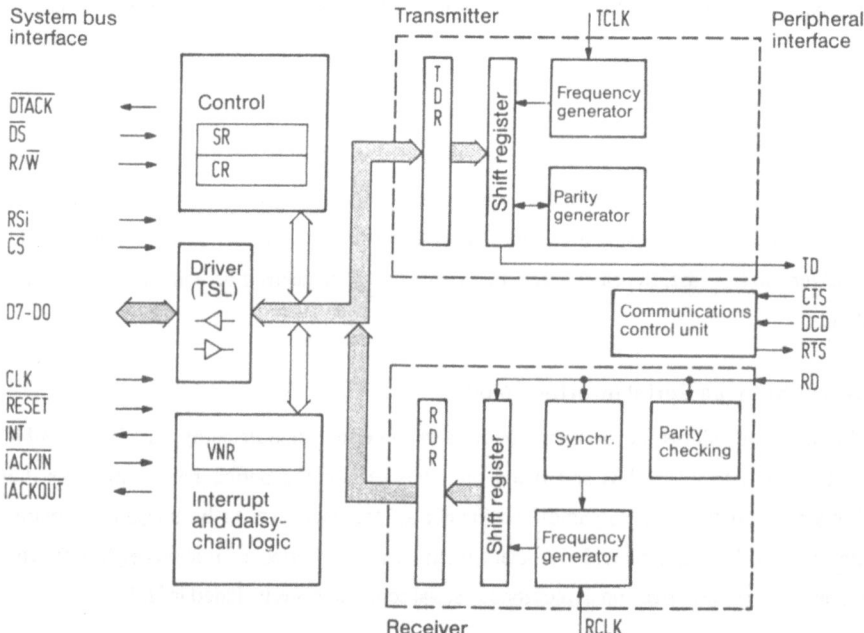

Fig. 5.18. Structure of an asynchronous serial interface module

For data transmission with the peripheral, there are two control signal inputs Clear To Send ($\overline{\text{CTS}}$) and Data Carrier Detect ($\overline{\text{DCD}}$) and one control signal output Request To Send ($\overline{\text{RTS}}$). These three signals are designed as elements of the V.24 and the RS-232-C interface for connection with a modem, but they can also be used directly for transmission synchronization with the peripheral (see also Fig. 5.8). $\overline{\text{RTS}}=0$ causes the modem to activate its transmission device; $\overline{\text{CTS}}=0$ indicates its availability and $\overline{\text{DCD}}=0$ indicates that the signal level received by the modem is within the specified tolerance range.

Behavior. A character is sent at the end of the write instruction with which the microprocessor loads the character into the 8-bit Transmitter Data Register (TDR). The character is buffered in an 8-bit shift register and is then sent bitwise at the transmission clock frequency to the transmitter data line (parallel-to-serial conversion). The data bits are completed with start, parity and stop bits to satisfy the data format requirements included in the 8-bit Control Register (CR). The end of the transmission is indicated in the 7-bit Status Register (SR) and can be either checked by the microprocessor or it can cause an interrupt request.

The acquisition of a character that arrives bitwise on the receiver data line is started by its start bit edge (character synchronization). Starting from the start bit edge, the receiver delays its clock by a half period and acquires the data bits in an 8-bit shift register. The character, without start and stop bits, is transferred from there to the 8-bit Receiver Data Register (RDR), whose content can be read by the microprocessor (serial-to-parallel conversion). The end of the transmission is indicated in the status register. During character acquisition, the receiver evaluates the parity bit and the stop bits according to the data formats included in the control register. Possible transmission errors are indicated in the status register. Status information can be examined by the microprocessor or can cause an interrupt request.

Figure 5.19 shows the control register that can be loaded with a control byte by the microprocessor. FT0=FT1=1 (reset control byte \$03) resets the component, the other registers are loaded with zero. The remaining three combinations of the two control bits determine the frequency division ratio of the external clock signal and the transmission frequency. If the division ratio is 1:1, the clock synchronization has to be performed externally, otherwise it is done internally. Bits DF0 through DF2 describe the data format. The value of the $\overline{\text{RTS}}$ bit is given as signal level to the $\overline{\text{RTS}}$ output. Bits RIRE and TIRE (Receiver or Transmitter Interrupt Enable) enable or disable the interrupt requests of the receiver or of the transmitter. The requests themselves are stored in the status register.

Figure 5.20 shows the status register that can be read but not written by the microprocessor to evaluate the transmission status of the transmitter and the receiver. If allowed by the control

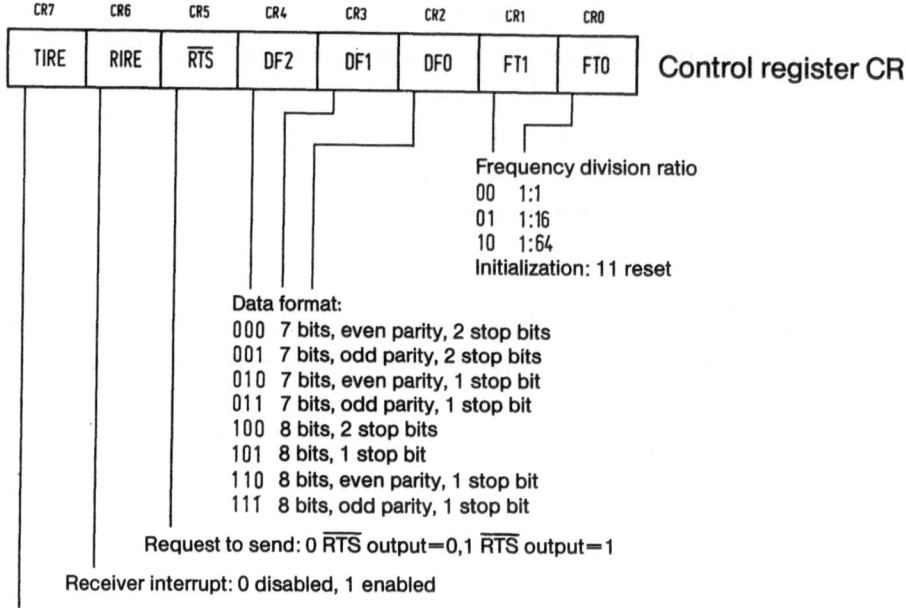

Fig. 5.19. Control register of the asynchronous serial interface module

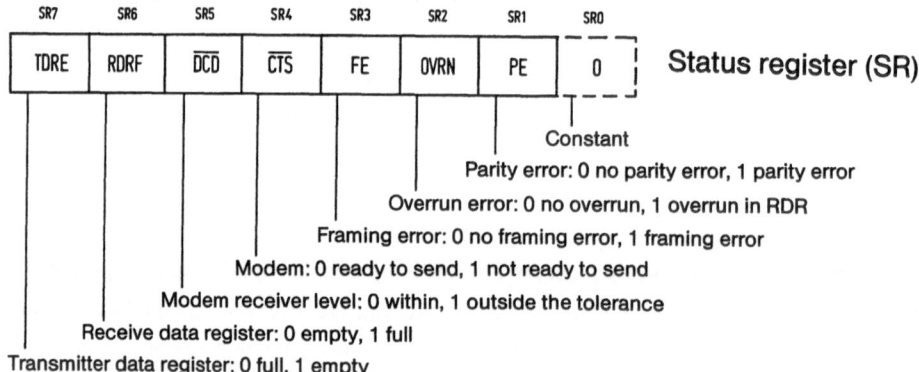

Fig. 5.20. Status register of the asynchronous serial interface module

register, some bits can become interrupt requests and interrupt the processor. Since the status register only comprises seven bits, bit 0 in the status word is set to zero during the reading of the register.

The Transmit Data Register Empty bit (TDRE) is used when the character contained in the Transmitter Data Register (TDR) is sent and the module is thus available again; this bit is reset when the register is loaded. This bit is also set when the control register is loaded in order to indicate that the module can send the first byte (exception: TDRE is not set when the reset control byte $03 is loaded). The Receive Data Register Full bit (RDRF) is set when a character is available for acquisition in the Receiver Data Register (RDR); it is reset when the receiver data register is read. $\overline{DCD}=1$ indicates that the signal level received by the modem is outside the tolerance range. Simultaneously, the RDRF bit is set to 0 (input is impossible). Later, if the $\overline{DCD}$ input becomes zero, the $\overline{DCD}$ bit can be reset by loading the reset control byte. $\overline{CTS}=0$ shows the availability of the modem to transmit. As long as $\overline{CTS}=1$, the TDRE bit has value 0 (output is impossible).

FE, OVRN and PE bits are used in the case of certain transmission errors. The Framing Error bit (FE) indicates faulty start or stop bits in a received character. The Overrun Error bit (OVRN) is used when a character arrives in the receiver data register and the RDRF bit is still set. The previous register content, which was not yet acquired by the processor, is overwritten. The Parity Error bit (PE) is set, when the received character does not correspond to the parity indicated in the data format. All three error bits are reset by the reading of the receiver data register.

Both the receiver and the transmitter can trigger interrupts, as long as the corresponding interrupt enable bits RIRE and TIRE are set in the control register. Causes of interrupts are character acquisition (RDRF=1) as well as both time critical error reports $\overline{DCD}=1$ and OVRN=1 in the receiver and the output of a character (TDRE=1) in the transmitter. Data transfer between microprocessor and peripheral can be synchronized through program interrupts produced by RDRF=1 and TDRE=1. On the other hand, if the synchronization has to occur through busy waiting, the interrupts have to be prevented by the enable bits in the control register and the two status bits have to be read in a program loop.

Note: Interface modules like the one described above can also be equipped with a 16-bit data bus connection, so that the processor can process two bytes for each read/write access. In this case, interface data registers are expanded to 16 bits. During bytewise output to the peripheral they are disassembly registers for the two bytes, during bytewise input from the peripheral they are assembly registers.

Example 5.4. Data input and data output through an asynchronous serial interface module. An alphanumeric video terminal with keyboard is connected to the microprocessor system bus through an asynchronous serial interface module (Figure 5.21). The ASCII characters originated in the keyboard are transferred by the receiver data line, and the ASCII characters output on the display are transmitted through the transmitter data line of the interface. The $\overline{RTS}$ line can either release the keyboard ($\overline{RTS}=1$) or block it ($\overline{RTS}=0$). A program is needed to read a typed character sequence into a buffer area with address LINE and to output each character immediately as an echo on the display for notification. The character sequence is to be closed by the carriage return character ($0D) and may have a maximum size of 80 characters. The keyboard is to be free before input and to be blocked right afterwards. The input should be synchronized by program interrupt (CR6=1) and the output by busy waiting (CR7=0). The interface is initialized with a frequency division

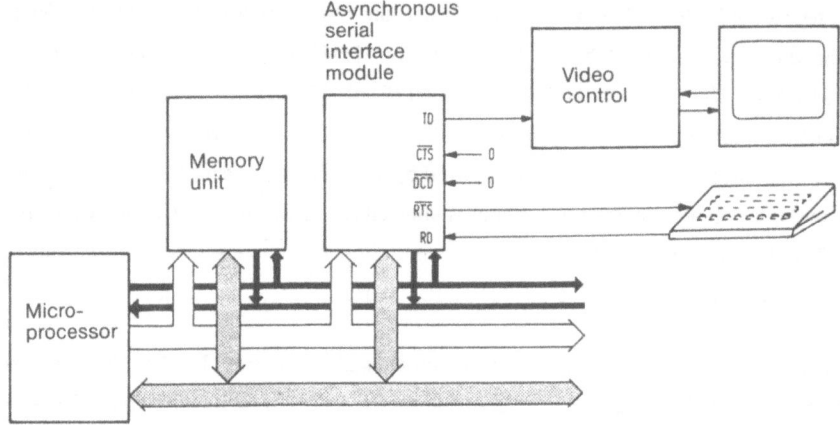

Fig. 5.21. Connection of a video terminal with an asynchronous serial interface module

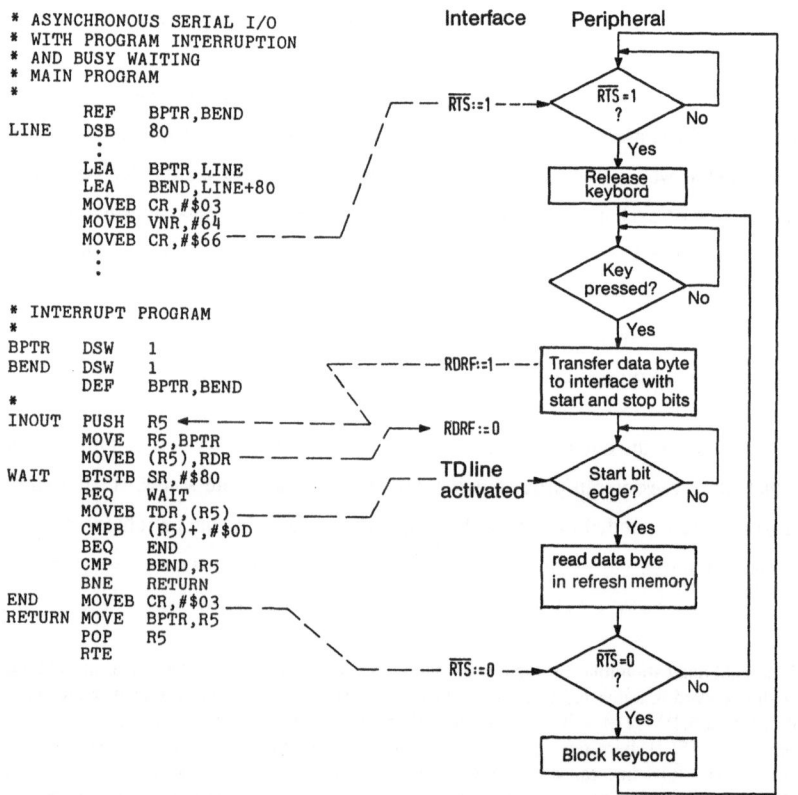

ratio of 1:64 (CR1 = 1, CR0 = 0) and a data format of 7 data bits, odd parity and 2 stop bits (CR4 = CR3 = 0, CR2 = 1). Signal inputs $\overline{\text{CTS}}$ and $\overline{\text{DCD}}$ are set to 0.

In order to initialize the interface (see program), it first has to be reset to its starting condition by the reset byte $03. Then, the vector number 64 is loaded in the Vector Number Register (VNR) and the control byte $66 is loaded in the Control Register (CR). The control byte corresponds to the synchronization conditions specified in the task, to the data format and to the frequency division ratio. Moreover, with CR5 = 1 it releases the keyboard for input of the character sequence ($\overline{\text{RTS}}$ = 1). When the control byte is loaded, also the TDRE bit in the status register is set to one, and the interface module indicates its transmission availability.

When a key of the keyboard is pressed, one character is transferred bit-serially to the interface and the interface status bit RDRF is set to one. This starts an interrupt program, in which the character is read from the Receiver Data Register (RDR) of the interface into a buffer area LINE that is addressed indirectly through register R5. The following output of this character to the Transmitter Data Register (TDR) for echo on the display occurs as soon as the interface shows its transmission availability with TDRE = 1 in the Status Register (SR). The program requests the TDRE bit in the waiting loop WAIT. An I/O procedure is terminated after the reception of a carriage return character or when the buffer is full. The control register is loaded with the reset control byte $03, the keyboard is locked ($\overline{\text{RTS}}$ = 0), the RDRF interrupt is blocked and the TDRE bit in the status register is set.

5.5 Synchronous Serial Data Transmission

As already discussed before, during serial data transmission character bits are transferred one after the other on a single data line. They are sent at a fixed clock frequency that will be used by the receiver during data acquisition. Contrary to asynchronous serial transmission, the characters of a data transmission block are lined up tightly in synchronous serial data transmission so that a continuous bit flow is achieved (Figure 5.22). The synchronization of transmitter and receiver frequency is thus not performed for each single character, it has to be constantly available throughout the entire transmission.

Synchronous serial data transmission is used for those transmission devices that are able to transfer a continuous character flow. Such a transmission device could be a microprocessor system and its corresponding peripheral, e.g. a display terminal with blockwise transmission or two connected microprocessor systems.

Synchronous serial data transmission is mainly important for remote data transmission, because it guarantees good line utilization. Another possible field of application are the so-called distributed systems, in which several autonomous working units (e.g. several microprocessor systems) are

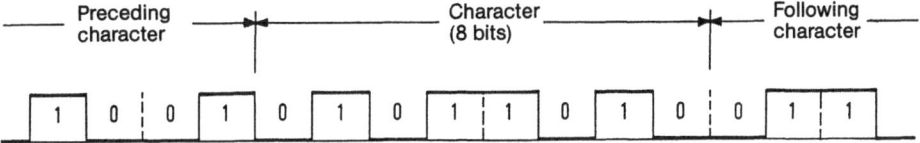

Fig. 5.22. Synchronous serial transmission of 8-bit characters

connected through data transmission networks and exchange information. Here as well, high data throughput is important.

5.5.1 Bit Synchronization and Character Synchronization

There are several ways to perform bit synchronization between transmitter and receiver. For instance, the transmitter clock frequency can be sent to the receiver over its own clock frequency line, which is only economically possible over short distances because it requires an additional line. Clock frequency lines are not available for remote data transmission for economical reasons, so that the receiver has to be equipped with its own clock frequency generator. Similarly to what happened in asynchronous serial data transmission, the synchronization of the receiver clock frequency with the transmitter clock frequency is obtained here with the signal transitions on the data line. To this purpose, either special synchronization characters are introduced in the data flow at large intervals, about every 100 characters, or the synchronization is performed with the level transitions of the data signal. In the first case, the frequencies of both generators have to be very stabile due to the large synchronization interval. In the second case, it is necessary that level transitions in the data signal are certain to appear at specific intervals by means of the appropriate information encoding. If these intervals are less than 100 characters, the demands for frequency stability of the clock generators decrease accordingly. Due to the continuity of the bit flow, an additional character synchronization is needed along with the bit synchronization, so that the beginning of the first valid character is indicated to the receiver. For this reason, one or two 8-bit synchronization characters, e.g. the ASCII characters SYN, are transferred to the beginning of the data transmission block. The receiver, that is in hunt mode, starts with the actual data acquisition only when it recognizes 8 or 16 consecutive bits as synchronization characters. These characters are also used for bit synchronization.

5.5.2 Communications Protocols

Bisync Protocol. As is the case with asynchronous serial data transmission, in synchronous serial data transmission the rules necessary for unambiguous transmission are contained in protocols [35, 36, 33]. Such protocols are recommended by industry and standardization institutes. One of their

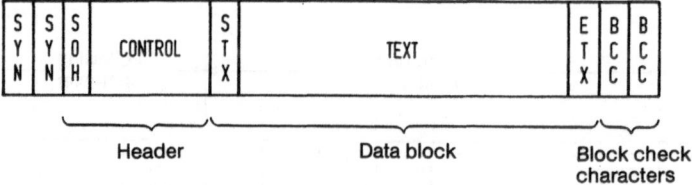

Fig. 5.23. Transmission format in Bisync protocol

characteristics is the transmission format of a transmission block. The example in Figure 5.23 shows the basic structure of a transmission format for Bisync protocol (Binary Synchronous Communications - BSC, IBM [37]). The control characters used in the example are defined as ASCII characters, but other character codes can also be used.

A Bisync transmission block begins with two Synchronization characters SYN (synchronous idle) followed by either a header or the data block itself. The header is identified by Start Of Heading (SOH). It contains one or more characters for block transmission CONTROL (e.g. it is used to define the source or destination address of the block or to identify the content of the block as data or as control information). The actual data block (TEXT) begins with Start of Text (STX) and ends with End of Text (ETX). The transmission block is terminated by two Block Check Characters (BCC) for error checking. A sender, unable to manage an uninterrupted character flow, inserts additional SYN characters into the character flow. These are then removed by the receiver and used as post-synchronization at the same time. Both SYN characters at the beginning of the block can be dropped if a separate synchronization line is used for the synchronization. In abstraction, a transmission block consists of text, i.e. needed information that has to be transferred, and of the frame surrounding this text to control transmission.

With the help of these and other conventions, transmission formats with different combinations can be generated as well as formats which contain only one or two control characters in addition to the synchronization characters. Such formats with no text are used to exchange control information between sender and receiver and to control the data transmission. Figure 5.24 illustrates an example of such a transmission protocol with initiation, execution and termination of a data transmission. In a handshaking procedure, the sender and the receiver exchange transmission blocks which are shown from left to right in the illustration according to their time sequence. The transmission is carried out in half-duplex operation, i.e. sender and receiver alternate when using the communications channel. The blocks that are sent by the transmitter are in the upper half of the illustration, and the receiver blocks are in the lower half. Due to space limitations, the SYN characters do not appear in front of the blocks. In order to improve data checking, the data to be transferred are divided into two transmission blocks. In the first block, this is indicated by the use of End of Transmission Block (ETB) instead of ETX for the receiver.

Protocols like the Bisync protocol, in which the fields of transmission format are defined by control characters of a specific character code, are called Character-Oriented Protocols (COPs). Their implementation requires a lot of effort for the interpretation of these control characters. Furthermore, the data of the text field also have to be encoded in the character code used. This kind of data representation, in which specific data bit configurations are not allowed because they are read as control characters, is called non-transparent. Additional measures are required to obtain

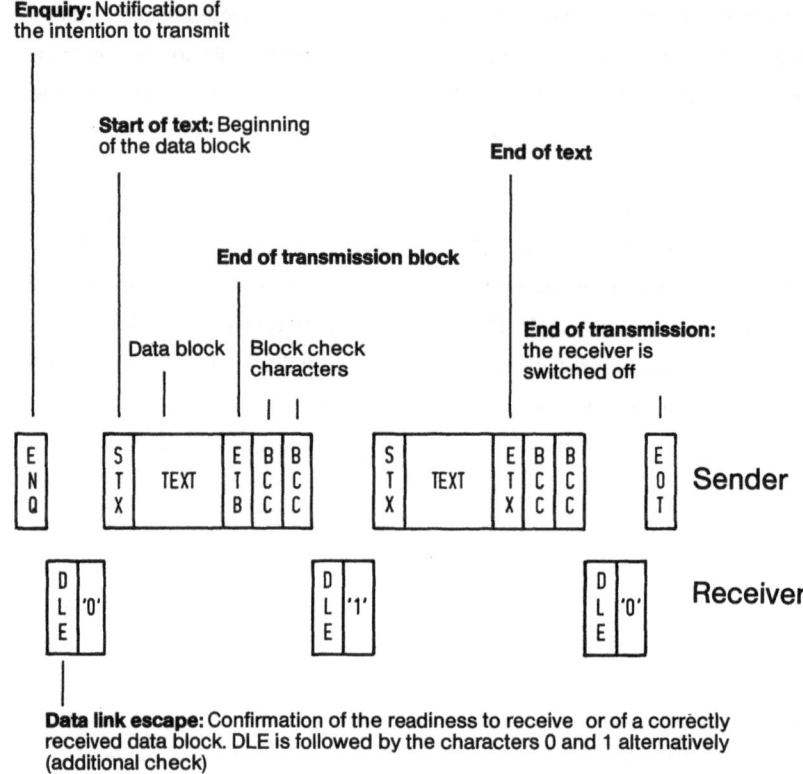

Fig. 5.24. Transmission control in Bisync protocol

a transparent data representation. In the Bisync protocol, control characters STX and ETX, that delimit data blocks, are preceded by a DLE character which identifies them. In order to avoid mistakes in the interpretation of the possible combination DLE ETX in the data block by the receiver, the sender completes each data bit configuration identical to DLE with an additional DLE character. This is detected by the receiver which removes this character.

An additional drawback of character-oriented protocols is the availability of several different transmission formats for data, control and acknowledge information (see Figure 5.24). These drawbacks are not found in Bit-Oriented Protocols (BOPs).

SDLC/HDLC Protocol. A bit-oriented protocol has a uniform transmission format in which the single fields are defined by their bit positions in the transmission block. Besides being easy to interpret, this definition also has the advantage of transparent data representation; i.e., arbitrary bit configurations can be transferred as data, for example BCD characters in packed representation, control or text characters of any character code or a program's machine code.

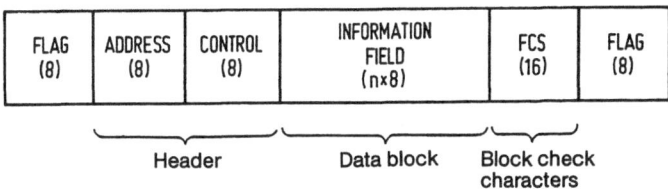

| FLAG (8) | ADDRESS (8) | CONTROL (8) | INFORMATION FIELD (nx8) | FCS (16) | FLAG (8) |

Header Data block Block check characters

Fig. 5.25. Transmission format in SDLC protocol

Figure 5.25 shows the transmission format of an SDLC protocol (Synchronous Data Link Control, IBM) [35]. As is the case with all bit-oriented protocols, the transmission block is framed by two so-called FLAG bytes with code 01111110. They are used to delimit the block and to synchronize characters. The first flag byte is followed by the header with an 8-bit ADDRESS field and an 8-bit CONTROL field. By indicating an address, the transmission block can be sent to several receivers simultaneously (broadcasting). Each one of the addressed receivers can determine, through the address, if the block is directed to it or not. The control field characterizes the content of the transmission block as data or control information, it indicates the number of the transferred or of the correctly received data blocks, and it contains control commands. The header is followed by the actual data field (INFORMATION FIELD) which can contain an arbitrary number of 8-bit information units in the SDLC protocol. The block is closed by a 16-bit Frame Check Sequence (FS) and by the second flag byte. A gap between two transmission blocks is filled by additional flag bytes that maintain the working condition of the connection.

The HDLC protocol (High Level Data Link Control, ISO - International Standards Organization) has a format similar to that of the SDLC protocol. Its address and control fields can be expanded to several bytes and its data field allows any amount of data bits, so that it is not bound to the 8-bit units of the SDLC protocol any longer [35]

In bit-oriented protocols there are only three different bit configurations with a specific function that appear outside a transmission block and that have to be recognized by the receiver: the flag byte 01111110, the bit sequence ABORT 01111111... (from 7 to 14 ones) and the bit sequence IDLE 111111111111111... (15 or more ones). ABORT ends the transmission of a block prematurely, and IDLE indicates that the connection is not being used. Due to the composition of these three bit configurations with their sequences of ones, the transparency of the information representation can be easily obtained. Within the transmission block and independently from the value of the following bit, the sender inserts a zero bit in the bit flow after every five consecutive ones. Thus, there will be no bit sequences that can be interpreted like any of the three mentioned bit configurations by the receiver. The receiver counts the consecutive ones and every time removes the bit following five ones as long as its value is zero. If it has value 1, it is one of the bit configurations FLAG, ABORT or IDLE. The hardware handles the insertion and removal of the zero bits so that the software is not involved.

If the insertion of zero is connected with the NRZI signal encoding (Non Return to Zero with Interchange), an additional advantage of bit-oriented protocols is that signal transitions in the bit flow can be used to synchronize the receiver clock frequency generator. In NRZI encoding, a one is represented by constant polarity and a zero by a change in the polarity of the signal. When a zero is inserted, such changes occur after each fifth bit at the most.

5.5.3 Protocol Layers

For information transmission in network structured information or computation systems, the so-called layer models are recommended by different standardization institutes like CCITT and ISO to clearly describe data transmission specifications. These layer models consist of up to seven protocol layers of different abstraction that are hierarchically constructed upon each other. Each layer is defined so that its behavior is independent from the surrounding layers, but it assumes the operational ability of the preceding layer. A transmission block information consisting of frame and text on one protocol layer is considered as text in the next lower layer and will be completed with a frame. Finally, the frame on the lowest layer contains the control information needed to

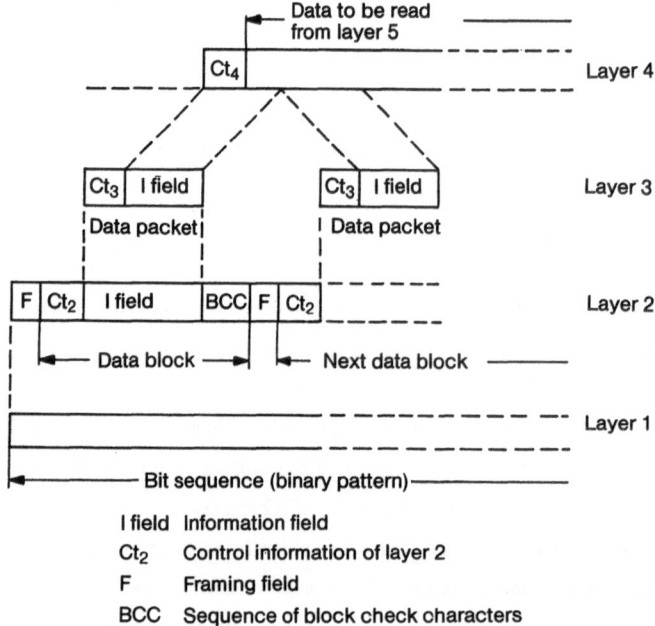

I field   Information field
Ct_2 Control information of layer 2
F   Framing field
BCC   Sequence of block check characters

Fig. 5.26. Creation and transmission of data packets at the X.25 interface [38]

transfer the information, consisting of the frame of higher protocol layers and of the text to be transmitted, through electrical signals.

Taking the ISO layer model [38] as a basis, whose lowest three layers are defined in CCITT Recommendation X.25 [39] for data package transmission in public data networks, the above considerations refer to layers 1 and 2 (Figure 5.26).

Level 1 (physical layer) is the lowest layer and describes the electrical, physical and functional characteristics of establishing, maintaining and breaking the connection between one data terminal equipment and one data communications equipment or between two data terminal devices. It contains interface agreements, similar to what is determined in the V.24/V.28 Recommendations, it includes the transmission of bit sequences and it indicates whether the transmission is synchronous or asynchronous.

Layer 2 (data link layer) is the next layer and describes the transmission of information as transmission blocks between two connection points (nodes) of a network. It includes the Bisync, SDLC and HDLC protocols mentioned above with the indication of transmission formats, character synchronization, data checking, half-duplex/full-duplex operation, establishing and breaking and the transmission control of a data connection.

Layer 3 (network layer) describes the transmission of data packages in a data network. It includes the connection structure of several nodes through receiver addressing, the path selection in the network as well as the transmission control and error handling in this layer. The data packages contain the information of layer 2 as data and also the control information required for layer 3. - With each additional layer, the level of abstraction is more and more detached from the technical facts and will finally allow pure application-oriented considerations on data transmission.

5.5.4 Synchronous Serial Interface Module

In the following paragraph, we describe a synchronous serial interface module, whose function is limited to parallel-to-serial conversion, to serial-to-parallel conversion and to bit and character synchronization. For data transmission on the basis of the layer 2 protocols described above there are more efficient modules, so-called protocol support chips, which accordingly reduce the use of software for transmission control. - A market survey on synchronous serial interface modules including protocol modules is given in [22].

Block Structure. Figure 5.27 shows the structure of the synchronous serial interface module for character-oriented data transmission (Universal Synchronous Receiver/Transmitter - USRT). Similar to the asynchronous serial module, it has a Transmit Data Register (TDR) and a Receive

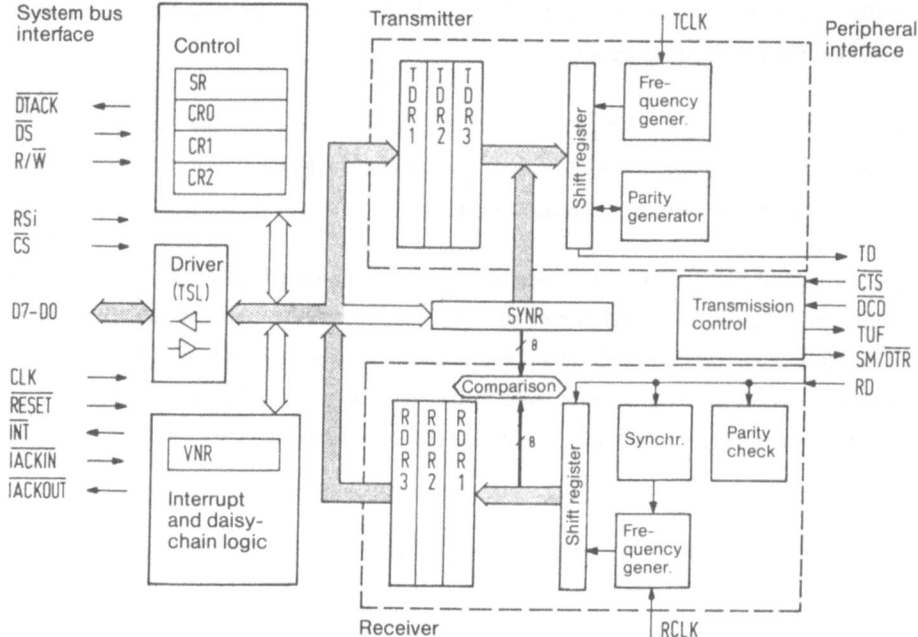

Fig. 5.27. Structure of a synchronous serial interface module

Data Register (RDR), expanded for buffer storage, with a shift register after for parallel-to-serial output conversion (sender) and a shift register before for serial-to-parallel input conversion (receiver). In addition, it is equipped with a transmission control device for control signal exchange with the peripheral, with interrupt equipment with self-identification of the module as interrupt source and with a chain logic for assigning a priority to the module according to the daisy-chain principle. (Self-identification and chain logic are missing in simpler module versions.)

The system bus interface is identical to the one in the asynchronous serial module, but there are differences in the interface to the peripheral because of both control signal outputs TUF and SM/DTR. The Transmitter Underflow output (TUF) is activated if the sender does not have a data byte to output and is sending synchronization characters instead. The SM/DTR output indicates the identification of the synchronization character (Sync Match) or the availability (Data Terminal Ready) of the interface module. The determination of the function occurs through a control register bit.

Behavior. In order to provide support for an uninterrupted character transmission, both the sender and the receiver are equipped with a buffer memory with three 8-bit data registers TDR1 through TDR3 and RDR1 through RDR3 that are managed according to the queue waiting principle: the first character input into the buffer memory is the first to be output (FIFO principle: First-In-First-

Out). During data output, an 8-bit shift register of the sender reads one byte from the data register TDR3 and transfers it bitwise to the Transmitter Data line (TD) (parallel/serial conversion). At this point, the contents of data registers TDR2 and TDR1 are respectively shifted into the next register. (Accordingly, one byte that was written by the microprocessor in the data register TDR1 is shifted into the next free data register.) If the buffer memory is empty, the content of the 8-bit Synchronization Register (SYNR), which was loaded with the synchronization character during the initialization of the module, is read by the shift register. This happens also at the beginning of a data transmission for the synchronization of the receiver.

At the beginning of the data input, after each bit is read by the Receiver Data line (RD) into the 8-bit shift register, the content of the register is compared with the content of the synchronization register (character synchronization). Depending on the programming of the module, one or two consecutive synchronization characters have to be identified before data can be read into the data buffer of the receiver. During the actual data transmission, this comparison is only performed characterwise, so that the synchronization characters, that fill the gaps in the data flow, can be removed . The byte that was read by the shift register, is transferred to the input data register RDR1 (serial-to-parallel conversion). According to the FIFO principle, it moves up to data register RDR3, where it is read by the microprocessor.

As already mentioned in Figure 5.27, the programming of single functions of the interface module occurs through control registers CR0 through CR2, and the indication of the transmission state is carried out over the Status Register (SR). The description of these registers' function is beyond the purpose of this book because of the excessive details involved. To this purpose see the data sheets of module suppliers.

6 Input/Output Controllers and Input/Output Computers

In the last Chapter we assumed that both the transmission of data between memory and interfaces and the management of the transfer, e.g. address generation and byte counting, are managed by the microprocessor. This can be very time consuming in relation to the processor's central processing tasks, in particular during data transmission with busy waiting. Even when the transmission of a single datum is synchronized by interrupts, saving the status, executing the interrupt program and finally restoring the status still use much more than the actual data transmission time. This is a drawback especially in the case of high transmission speed, e.g. during data transmission with a floppy disk or during communication between several microprocessor systems. However, this bottleneck can be removed with hardware support in form of additional I/O controllers or I/O computers.

Two basic possibilities for processor independent I/O are described in Sections 6.1 and 6.2: in particular, 6.1 will deal with I/O with direct memory access through a DMA controller, and 6.2 will discuss I/O by means of an I/O computer. Section 6.3 will describe the behavior of two particular controller units, which support the connection of floppy disk units and of video terminals.

6.1 Input/Output with Direct Memory Access

During I/O with direct memory access (DMA), a special control unit, the DMA Controller (DMAC), manages the data transmission between interface and memory. Depending on the design of the controller, the transmission to the system bus occurs either directly between the interface module and the memory or indirectly, where the DMA controller, as an intermediary, stores a byte or a word (Figure 6.1). The microprocessor is not used. The microprocessor's processing tasks are limited only when the DMA controller needs the system bus to access the interface and the memory.

The tasks of the DMA controller include requesting the system bus, addressing the interface module and the memory, controlling the read/write protocol and counting the bytes that are transferred to obtain the termination condition. The DMA controller is programmed by loading its control register before starting the data transmission. The transmission can be monitored and also influenced, e.g. interrupted, by the microprocessor which checks the contents of the status register of the controller. This is only possible when the microprocessor has access to the system bus.

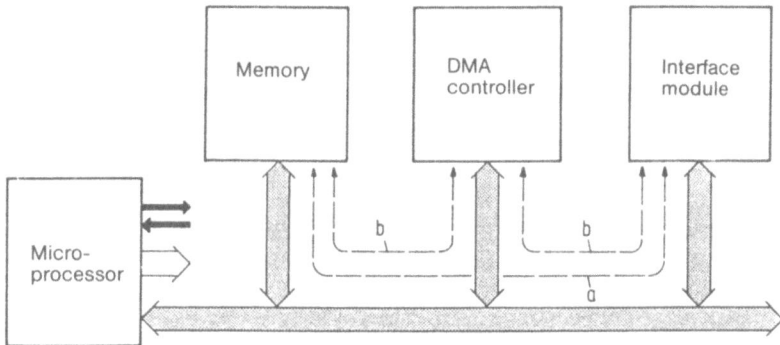

Fig. 6.1. Direct memory access. a) direct transmission, b) indirect transmission

6.1.1 Types of Accesses

Depending on the time in which the microprocessor cannot access the system bus because of a DMA operation, there are several types of direct memory access:

- cycle stealing mode: The DMA controller uses the system bus during the transmission time of a single byte or word by stealing a bus cycle from the microprocessor. In reality, the time is some machine clock frequencies longer, so that the bus request and the bus release are synchronized with the microprocessor. Cycle stealing mode is used for relatively slow data transmission.

- burst mode: The DMA controller uses the system bus for the whole transmission time of a data block, so that the microprocessor will be prevented from using the system bus for a longer period of time. Burst mode is used for very fast data transmission.

- transparent mode: The DMA controller uses the system bus only during those clock cycles in the machine instruction cycle, when the microprocessor does not need the system bus; i.e., the microprocessor and the DMA controller use the system bus and the memory at different times without interfering with each other. A relatively short memory access time is a prerequisite for this kind of access, so that the bus slots that are not needed by the processor can be used. Transparent mode is used for both slow and fast data transmission.

6.1.2 DMA Controller Module

In the following, we will discuss the basic structure and behavior of a DMA controller module, which performs data transmission indirectly, i.e. with intermediate storage of data in a data register of the controller. It is equipped with two so-called DMA channels to process two independent DMA procedures at the same time.

Block Structure. Figure 6.2 shows a block diagram of the DMA controller module with its two channels A and B. Each channel has a Control Register (CR), a Status Register (SR) and a Vector Number Register (VNR), plus two address registers IAR (Interface Address Register) and MAR

System bus interface   Peripheral
                                                                            interface

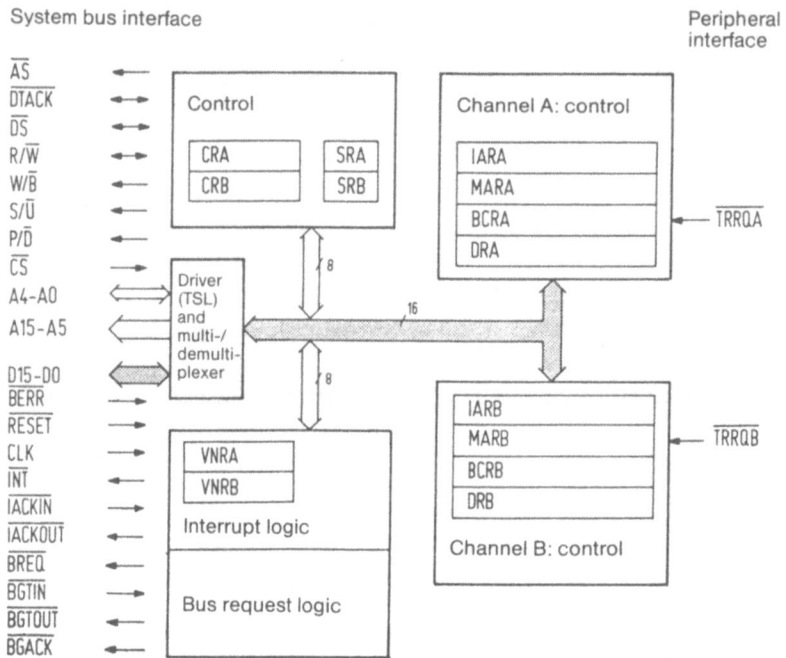

Fig. 6.2. DMA controller module with two channels

(Memory Address Register) to address the interface or the memory, one Byte Count Register (BCR) for block management and one Data Register (DR) for intermediate storage of a byte or a word. Both channels have a common interrupt device with daisy-chain control and self-identification with one vector number each. Moreover, they have a device for bus request and a daisy-chain control to propagate the bus grant signal. By internal determination, channel A has priority over channel B.

The system bus interface is equipped with a bidirectional 16-bit data bus connection, 16 address outputs, control signal outputs $\overline{AS}$, $\overline{DS}$ and R/$\overline{W}$ as well as control signal input $\overline{DTACK}$ for the transmission of data with the memory and the interface module. Furthermore, memory addressing is supported by output signals W/$\overline{B}$, S/$\overline{U}$ and P/$\overline{D}$. Thus, the DMA controller can execute read/write operations autonomously. In order to allow the selection of the DMA controller registers by the microprocessor, connections $\overline{DS}$, R/$\overline{W}$, $\overline{DTACK}$ and A4 through A0 (register selection inputs) are bidirectional. Besides, the interface includes an interrupt output $\overline{INT}$, that is shared by both channels, and the daisy-chain connections $\overline{IACKIN}$ and $\overline{IACKOUT}$. It is also equipped with a Bus Request output ($\overline{BREQ}$), that is shared by both channels, two Bus Grant connections ($\overline{BGTIN}$ and $\overline{BGTOUT}$) to build a daisy-chain for the bus arbitration signal $\overline{BGT}$, and one output for the acknowledge signal $\overline{BGACK}$.

The peripheral interfaces of both channels have only one Transfer Request input ($\overline{\text{TRRQ}}$) each that is used to accept transmission requests by the interface modules.

Behavior. The DMA controller can execute I/O either in cycle stealing mode or in block mode. In both cases, data transmission is started with the Transfer Request input ($\overline{\text{TRRQ}}$). Then the DMA controller requests the system bus, executes a read cycle, and reads the datum into the data register of the appropriate DMA channel. In the write cycle that follows, it transfers the datum to its destination. The source address and the destination address are indicated by address registers IAR and MAR, and the transfer direction is defined by a status bit.

Data transmission between DMA controller and memory occurs either bytewise or wordwise, data transmission between DMA controller and interface occurs on the most significant or least significant data bus half. During each byte access, the memory address register is either incremented or decremented by one; whereas, during each word access, it is incremented or decremented by two. Byte counting occurs in the byte counting register which is loaded during initialization with the number of bytes to be transferred, and whose content is decremented by either one or two for each memory access. If the byte counter reaches value zero (end of the block), a status bit is set. This bit has either the effect of an interrupt signal, or it is checked by the microprocessor.

The multiplexing of the module internal 16-bit data bus and therefore of the internal registers with the address and data lines of the system bus interface are managed by a multiplexer/demultiplexer circuit. During byte transfer with the memory or with an interface module, this circuit also switches the connection between the data register half, that was used for intermediate storage, and the higher or lower data bus half of the interface that is indicated by address bit A0 in the Memory Address Register (MAR) or in the Interface Address Register (IAR). During word transmission with the memory, the multiplexer/demultiplexer circuit also performs the connection of both data register halves to the data bus.

Figure 6.3a shows the interconnection of the data register for input through interface/DMA controller/memory, and Figure 6.3b for output through memory/DMA controller/interface during byte and word data transfer with the memory. For better understanding, the bidirectional data bus is represented by unidirectional bus lines as register inputs and register outputs. The continuous line to the left of the data register shows the connection of the interface module to the lower data bus half, the dotted line shows its connection to the higher data bus half. During word input, two bytes are collected in the Data Register (DR) and are transferred to the memory as one word; DR operates like an assembly register. During word output, DR works as a disassembly register. When two bytes are assembled and disassembled, the system bus for either read or write cycles is requested and released every time, so that the bus usage by the DMA controller is optimized.

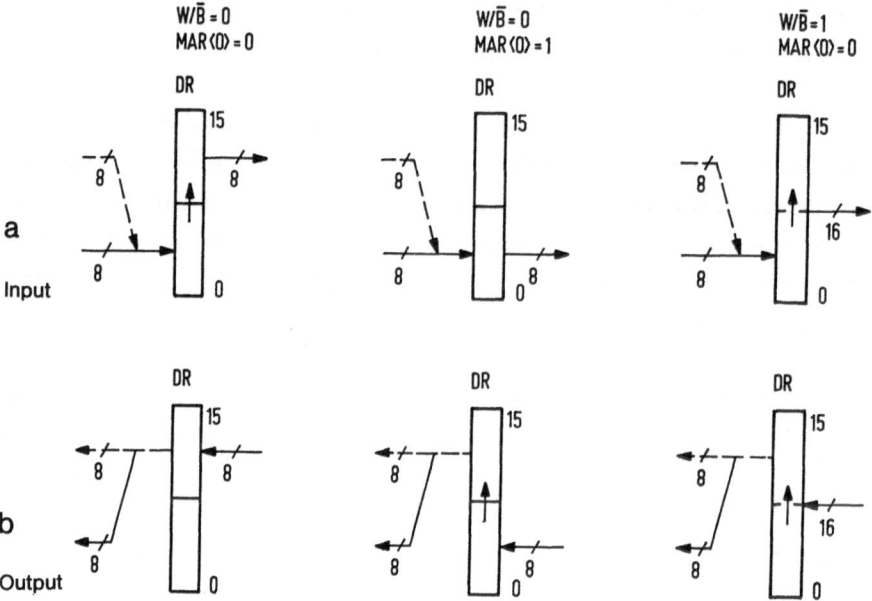

Fig. 6.3. Behavior of the multiplexer/demultiplexer in the DMA controller during bytewise and wordwise data transmission with the memory. a) input, b) output

Figure 6.4. shows the 8-bit control register with the functions of the single bits. Control bit $R/\overline{W}$ indicates the level of the Read/Write signal ($R/\overline{W}$) for memory control; the complement of this bit value produces the read/write signal that controls the interface. The $C/\overline{B}$ bit determines the mode, either cycle stealing mode or burst mode. The $U/\overline{D}$ bit determines whether memory addressing is counting upwards or downwards. The $W/\overline{B}$ bit indicates whether the data transmission with the memory will occur wordwise or bytewise. This bit influences the $W/\overline{B}$ output and is used together with bit 0 of the Memory Address Register (MAR) to address bytes and words in the memory. Bits $P/\overline{D}$ and $S/\overline{U}$ control the signal levels of the control lines with the same name and are used for memory management. The control bit RQE is the enable bit for the Transfer Request input ($\overline{TRRQ}$); it can activate the DMA channel. The IRE bit is the enable bit for the end-of-block interrupt and the error interrupt that are indicated by the bits BE and ERR of the status register.

Figure 6.5 shows the 8-bit status register, in which only three bits are used; the remaining bits are fixed at zero when the status byte is read. The End-of-Block bit (BE) is set when the byte counting register, that is loaded with the byte count at the beginning of the block transmission and that is decremented by one or two for each byte or word transfer, reaches value zero. The Error Status bit (ERR) is set either by a transfer error, e.g. when the $\overline{DTACK}$ signal is lost (bus error trap), or by an incorrectly programmed DMA controller, e.g. when accessing a word operand with an odd memory address. Both bits BE and ERR act as interrupt requests, as long as the interrupt enable bit in the

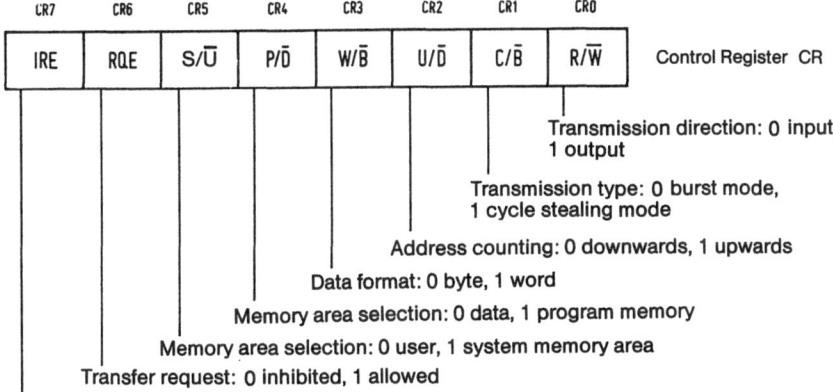

Fig. 6.4. Control register of the DMA controller

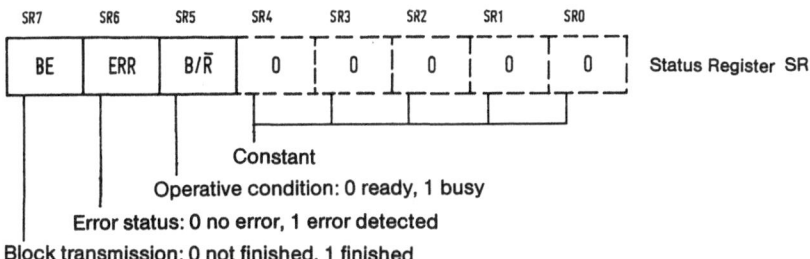

Fig. 6.5. Status register of the DMA controller

status register is set. The Busy/Ready bit (B/$\overline{R}$) shows whether the DMA channel is executing a block transmission (busy) or is ready for a new block transmission (ready).

Note: There are several versions of DMA controllers for existing microprocessor systems and they mainly differ in the number of channels they have. Due to the internal necessity to assign a priority between the channels, the one with the highest priority obtains access to the system bus, and this is not always desirable. A remedy is offered by some components that cyclicly exchange priority after each channel activation, so that the last active channel has lowest priority (rotating priority).

Furthermore, search operations can be executed by DMA controllers, which act as intermediaries and store data during the transmission, so that bytes, words or specific bit fields of a datum can be analyzed. The available operations are: only transmitting, only searching, searching and transmitting. A status bit is set as the result of a successful comparison and an interrupt can be triggered; in this case, for example, the search operation is interrupted. - [22] gives an overview of DMA controllers.

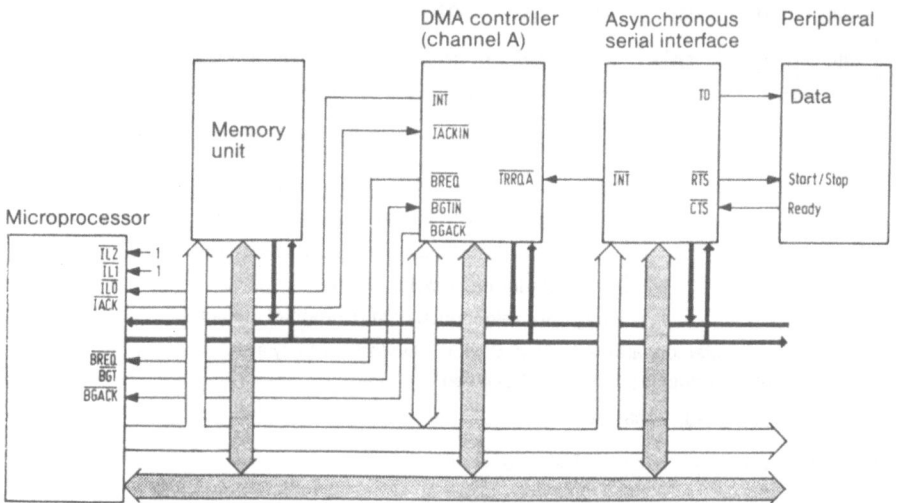

Fig. 6.6. Cicuit structure for data transmission with DMA controller

In order to illustrate the behavior of the DMA controller, the following example describes the DMA procedure during the output of a data byte block in cycle stealing mode.

Example 6.1. Data output with direct memory access. By using an asynchronous serial interface, 128 data bytes have to be transferred in direct memory access with cycle stealing from a memory area BUFFER to a peripheral. The peripheral is started by means of the $\overline{\text{RTS}}$ line of the interface ($\overline{\text{RTS}}$ = 1): the availability of the device is indicated by the $\overline{\text{CTS}}$ input of the interface in its status register ($\overline{\text{CTS}}$ = 0) and has to be checked through busy waiting. Then, control of the data output goes to the DMA controller. At the end of the data output, the DMA controller should trigger a program interrupt to stop the peripheral ($\overline{\text{RTS}}$ = 0) and to disable the interrupt outputs from interface and DMA controller.

Figure 6.6 shows the logical structure with the DMA controller described above and an asynchronous serial interface module described in Subsection 5.4.4, but without any chain and self-identification mechanism for interrupt handling. The DMA control is performed by the controller's channel A.

In order to initialize data transmission (see program), the microprocessor loads the registers of DMA channel A: the memory address register (MARDMA) with the data address BUFFER, the interface address register (IARDMA) with the address of the interface data register (TDRI), the byte counting register (BCRDMA) with the byte number 128, the vector number register (VNRDMA) with the vector number 65 and the control register (CRDMA) with the control byte $C7 for the byte output cycle stealing mode. The control byte also sets the transfer Request Enable bit (RQE) to one, so that the DMA controller can be activated from the peripheral by the $\overline{\text{INT}}$ line of the interface. Furthermore, the Interrupt Enable bit (IRE) is set to enable the end-of-block and error interrupt.

After the initialization of the DMA controller, the data output begins by starting the peripheral. The processor loads the Interface Control Register (CRI) with the control byte $26 and thus sets $\overline{\text{RTS}}$ = 1. (The data format indicated in the control byte and the frequency division ratio correspond to the specifications in Example 5.4.) The test of the peripheral's ready signal takes place in a waiting loop WAIT (busy waiting), in which the processor checks the $\overline{\text{CTS}}$ bit of the Interface Status Register (SRI). Finally the processor sets the transmitter interrupt enable bit of the interface with control byte $A6 and thus forwards the transmission requests to the DMA controller. From this point on, the data transmission is managed by the DMA controller.

```
* DATA OUTPUT OF 128 BYTES WITH DIRECT MEMORY ACCESS
* PROGRAM INTERRUPTION AT END OF BLOCK
* MAIN PROGRAM
*
BUFFER DSB    128
*
* INITIALIZATION OF THE DMA CONTROLLER
        MOVE   MARDMA,#BUFFER    MEMORY ADDRESS
        MOVE   IARDMA,#TDRI      INTERFACE ADDRESS
        MOVE   BCRDMA,#128       BYTE COUNT
        MOVEB  VNRDMA,#65        VECTOR NUMBER
        MOVEB  CRDMA,#$C7        CONTROL BYTE
*
* INITIALIZATION OF THE INTERFACE AND START OF THE
* PERIPHERAL
        MOVEB  CRI,#$26          START PERIPHERAL
WAIT    BTSTB  SRI,#$10          PERIPHERAL READY?
        BNE    WAIT
        MOVEB  CRI,#$A6          ENABLE INTERRUPT
          .
          .
          .


* DATA OUTPUT ENDED OR INTERRUPTED
* INTERRUPT PROGRAM
*
IOEND   MOVEB  CRI,#$30          STOP PERIPHERAL, DISABLE INTERRUPT
        MOVEB  CRDMA,#$00        DISABLE INTERRUPT IN DMAC
        BTSTB  SRDMA,#$06        READ ERROR STATUS
        BEQ    RETURN
* ERROR HANDLING
          .
          .
RETURN  RTE
```

A transfer request of the interface is indicated by the status bit TDRE (TDR empty) being at 1. This bit is set for the first byte output through initialization of the interface control register, then it is set after each output of a byte from the interface data register to the peripheral. The TDRE bit works as interrupt signal and activates the DMA controller by its $\overline{\text{TRRQA}}$ input. This requests the system bus from the microprocessor through the controller's $\overline{\text{BREQ}}$ output. The microprocessor first finishes its present bus cycle, then switches its three-state outputs to high impedance state and indicates the bus release by setting the $\overline{\text{BGT}}$ signal at the $\overline{\text{BGTIN}}$ input of the DMA controller (see also Subsection 4.5.1). The DMA controller takes control of the bus and confirms this by setting the $\overline{\text{BGACK}}$ signal; at the same time, it resets its $\overline{\text{BREQ}}$ signal. Then, it executes a read cycle with the memory, stores the data byte in its data register and transfers it in the following write cycle in the data register of the interface. Memory and interface are addressed with the address register contents of channel A.

After the write procedure, the DMA controller resets its $\overline{\text{BGACK}}$ signal, and the microprocessor can access the system bus again. At the same time, the DMA controller increases the content of its memory address register by one and decreases the byte counter by one. If value zero is reached in the byte counting register, the DMA controller sets the BE bit in its status register and thus triggers the end-of-block interrupt. The data transfer is completed in the interrupt program. The processor loads the interface control register with the reset control byte $03, so that the peripheral is stopped ($\overline{\text{RTS}}$=0), the transmission requests of the interface are inhibited (TIRE-0) and the request bit TDRE is reset in the interface status register. Besides, it loads the DMA control register with $00, which locks the interrupts in the DMA controller. Since also the error state bit ERR can lead to a program interruption, it has to be checked in the interrupt program and, if necessary, an error handling procedure should be executed.

As long as the system bus is available, the microprocessor can influence the DMA controller throughout the block transmission. It can request its status, which includes the status bits as well as the contents of the memory address and byte counting register. Furthermore, it can terminate the transmission prematurely by resetting the transfer request enable bit. ∎

6.2 Input/Output Computers

As already mentioned in Section 6.1, control modules like the DMA controller provide a large portion of the transmission management required for I/O, for instance they manage address counting, byte counting, byte assembly and disassembly and control of the direct memory access. However, other tasks, that can vary depending on the need, have to be programmed and thus they overload the microprocessor. These tasks include starting and stopping peripherals, polling, data encoding, data preprocessing and file management. I/O processors and computers are used to unburden the microprocessor, they can be regarded as very complex control modules and can be programmed like microprocessors. Such an expanded microprocessor system becomes a multiprocessor or multicomputer system with different processor types.

I/O processors are 8-bit or 16-bit microprocessors with an instruction set tailored for I/O and mostly with several I/O channels with DMA functionality. They communicate with the microprocessor that is responsible for central processing by means of control signals and memory areas, whose access they share. These memory areas are loaded by the central microprocessor in order to initialize the I/O processor with control information and with I/O programs. They are also used to exchange commands and status for the execution of single I/O procedures.

The structure of I/O computers, on the other hand, is more complex. They include a programmable processor and several components that are connected to the microprocessor by means of an internal system bus. Such components are for instance ROMs and RAMs for the storage of I/O programs, data, control and status information, or I/O interfaces for serial and parallel data transmission as well as DMA channels. Communication with the central microprocessor occurs by means of control signals and through information and data exchange with shared access memory areas. In the following, we will further examine the applications and the structure of such an I/O computer unit. As an example, we will use a less complex I/O computer, which does not contain DMA channels; thus, if necessary, the DMA channels must be provided externally.

6.2.1 Multicomputer System with Input/Output Computer

Figure 6.7 shows the design of a multicomputer system including a 16-bit traditional microprocessor system and an 8-bit I/O computer system. The I/O computer itself is equipped with an asynchronous serial and two parallel interfaces, that are used to connect a printer and to create a local I/O bus (8-bit data bus, 16-bit address bus) in our example. A program and a data memory are connected to this bus to expand the internal small memory of the I/O computer which is tailored for simple systems; in addition, an interface unit for data transmission with a peripheral (e.g. a disk drive) is connected to this bus. Furthermore, by means of this bus, the processor of the I/O computer controls a DMA unit, which executes the actual data transfer between the memory

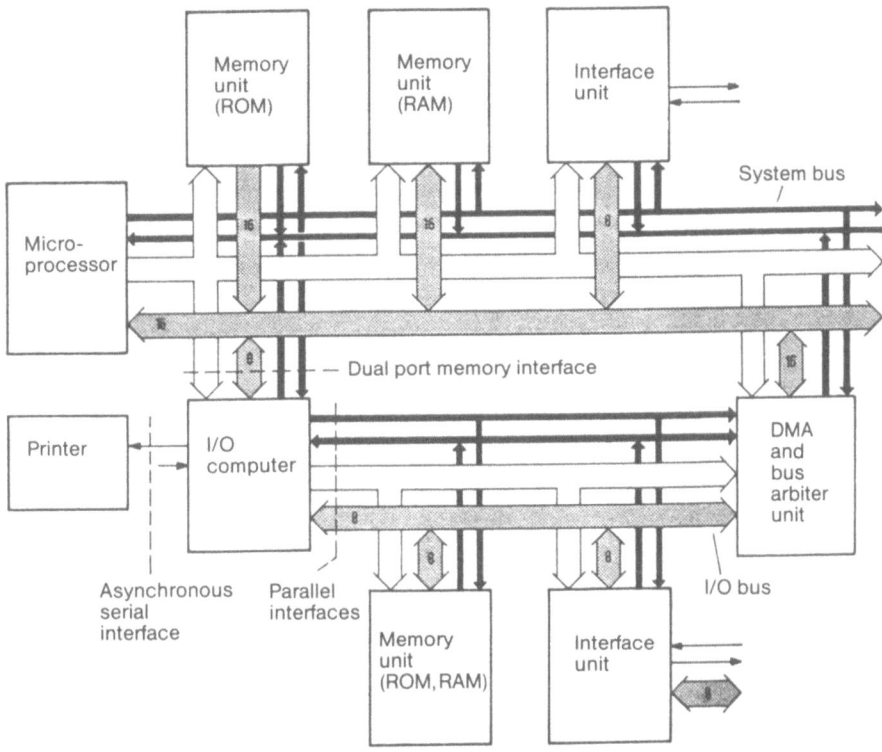

Fig. 6.7. Multicomputer system with central processor and I/O computer

unit of the system bus and the interface unit of the I/O bus. It can access both busses through a multiplexer and is thus involved in the bus arbitration of both systems. The DMA unit with its assembly/disassembly data register manages the conversion of the data formats between the 16-bit system data bus and the 8-bit I/O data bus (see Subsection 6.1.2).

The I/O computer, that is tailored to the I/O processing of the I/O devices connected to its bus and also manages the DMA unit, receives its tasks from the central microprocessor system in form of commands (e.g. input, output, type of preprocessing) and parameters (e.g. device and area addresses, type of address counting), which it evaluates with its own software. When a task is completed, it sends status information back to the central microprocessor (e.g. correct transmission, premature interruption). The transmission of commands, parameters and status information is carried out through a dual port memory located in the I/O computer and several so-called semaphore registers that can be accessed from both the main microprocessor and the processor in the I/O computer. Thus, the I/O processor does not have direct access to the components connected to the system bus. With the structure chosen here (similar to the Motorola MC68120 [41]), the I/O processor is a passive system component for the main microprocessor.

Dual port memory interface

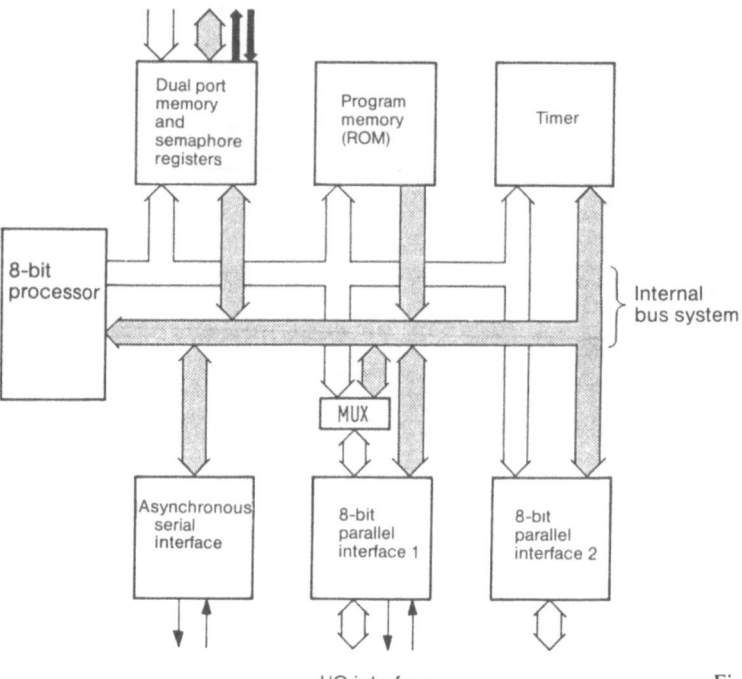

I/O interfaces   Fig. 6.8. I/O computer

6.2.2 Structure of the Input/Output Computer

Components. Figure 6.8 shows the structure of the I/O computer presented in Figure 6.7 which can be regarded as a complete microprocessor system condensed on one component (single-chip computer). The most important part of the component is a programmable processor with an 8-bit word length, which is connected with the other module components through an internal bus system consisting of an 8-bit data bus, an address bus and a control bus that is not represented in Figure 6.8.

The dual port memory mentioned above forms the interface to the system bus. A dual port memory is a random access memory, equipped with two decoders and read circuits. It can be addressed through both the internal bus system and the system bus, and it is used to exchange data and information between the I/O processor and the microprocessor. Here it has a 128-byte capacity. The sharing of this memory as well as the use of other shared equipment is regulated with 6 semaphore registers, which also have dual port access. Access priorities to these registers and the dual port memory are determined in favor of the I/O processor by fixed priorities. A 2-K byte ROM is used to store I/O programs. The programmable timer allows the setting of timing specifications for I/O control.

Input/Output Interfaces. Data transmission with the peripheral occurs over three I/O interfaces. One of them is designed as an asynchronous serial interface and the other two are designed as 8-bit parallel interfaces, one of which has two additional control lines. Each interface is equipped with special registers to control data transmission. There are three different operations that can be performed in this component when parallel interfaces are used:

1. Both interfaces are used for parallel data input and output; the two control lines of interface 1 are used to synchronize handshaking.

2. Interface 1 is used as 8-bit data bus and interface 2 as 8-bit address bus when an I/O bus system is built; the two control lines form the control bus.

3. In multiplex mode, interface 1 is used as 8-bit data bus and as 8-bit address bus (lower address byte), interface 2 is used as 8-bit address bus (higher address byte) for the composition of an I/O bus system. The two control lines constitute the control bus (see Figure 6.7).

The use of an additional I/O bus beside the system bus makes it possible to construct a microprocessor system, that is tailored to I/O, with the I/O computer module as the central processing unit. I/O programs and data can be kept in the connected memories and I/O can be executed through the connected interface modules.

Semaphore Registers. Semaphore registers are actually designed as 8-bit registers, but only the two higher-value bits are used (Figure 6.9). Bit 7 has the function of a semaphore bit. If it is set, the equipment that is dependent on the semaphore bit, for example a memory area or an I/O program, is being used. Otherwise, the equipment is available. Bit 6 can be used to indicate which device is using this equipment at the time or used it last: either the I/O computer or another processor that is connected to the system bus.

Semaphore bits are read with the Test And Set instruction (TAS) which compares the content of the semaphore register with the value zero and influences condition bits N and Z with the result; the N bit is given the same value of the semaphore bit. Finally, this instruction sets the semaphore bit to one, independently from its previous condition, i.e. the equipment is then considered busy. The

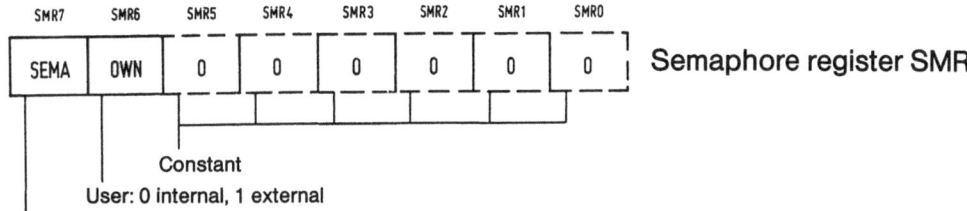

Fig. 6.9. I/O computer Semaphore Register

evaluation of bits N and Z can supply an indication of the equipment's condition at the time. If the equipment is free, it can be used by the inquirer. In order to make the equipment available again, bit 7 in the semaphore register has to be loaded with zero.

Example 6.2. Synchronizing the microprocessor and the input/output computer. In a system like the one described in Figure 6.7, that is expanded by a second central microprocessor as additional bus master, a data block has to be loaded into the memory unit of the system bus through the local interface unit of the I/O computer. The procedure has to be started and terminated by the first microprocessor. - The microprocessor enters the input command and the input parameters (source and destination, addresses, block length, address counting direction) into the dual port memory of the I/O computer. The I/O computer reads the information, initializes the DMA unit and switches it on for data transmission. At completion, the I/O computer, using the dual port memory, sends the status (ready message, error code) to the starting processor and is then once again available to the two central microprocessors for the execution of additional I/O procedures. (For simplicity's sake, the intermediate storage and the preprocessing in the I/O computer system are avoided.)

The synchronization of the information exchange through the dual port memory and the mutual exclusion during access to this memory occur in handshaking mode through two of the six semaphore registers. A third semaphore register is used to prevent the second central microprocessor from accessing the I/O computer for the duration of the I/O procedure.

In order to synchronize and implement the mutual exclusion, we define the two operations lock X and unlock X. The variable X corresponds to the symbolic address of a semaphore register. Unlock X sets bits 7 in the semaphore register to zero and thus releases the access that was controlled by the register (dual port memory area, I/O computer). Lock X examines the semaphore bit: if it has value one (access disabled), the request is repeated; if the value is zero (access enabled), the access for other requests is blocked by setting the semaphore bit to one. A requirement for the execution of the lock operation in mutual exclusion is that the test and set of the semaphore bit be carried out in an uninterrupted sequence. At the machine level this is guaranteed by the TAS instruction (Figure 6.10).

Figure 6.11 shows the input procedure in form of a flow chart. The mutual exclusion of the two microprocessors when accessing the dual port memory of the I/O computer occurs through the semaphore variable EXCL. This variable is set by the first microprocessor at the beginning of the input process, and it is reset at its completion. The two variables SYN1 and SYN2 are used for the synchronization of the dual port memory access of the central microprocessor and of the I/O computer. Unlock SYN1 indicates that the central microprocessor has written its memory area and has then released the access. With unlock SYN2, the I/O computer indicates that the status is ready and the access is possible. Unlike what happens with EXCL, the necessary lock operations are executed by the respective transmission partner. Thus, a mutual dependency is created, which defines the sequence of the write and read accesses (synchronization through handshaking).

The test symbol is used in Figure 6.11 to represent the lock operation. Note that the operation also contains the setting of semaphore bits along with the test.

```
unlock X:               CLRB   X               X⟨7⟩:=0


lock X:        WAIT    TAS    X         WAIT: if X⟨7⟩=1 then N:=1
                       BMI    WAIT            else N:=0; X⟨7⟩:=1;
                                             if N=1 then goto WAIT
```

Fig. 6.10. Assembler representation and effect of the semaphore operations unlock X and lock X

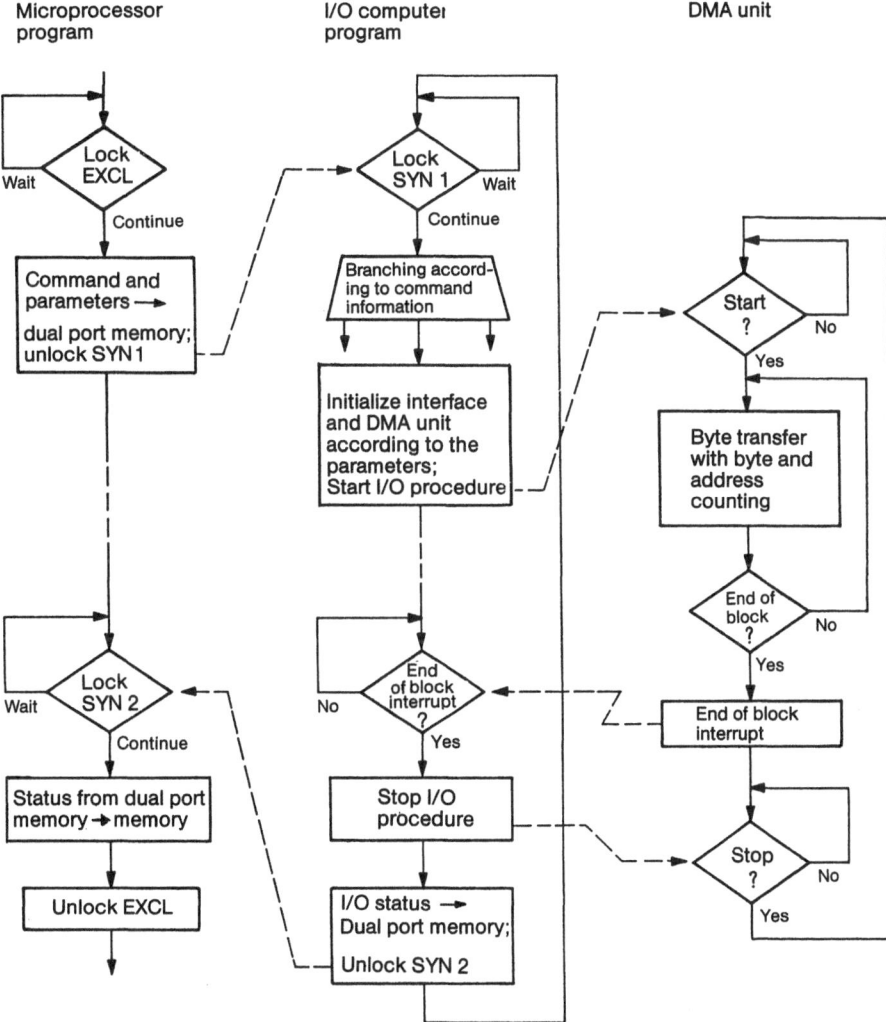

Microprocessor program

I/O computer program

DMA unit

Fig. 6.11. Procedure for the control of the main microprocessor, the Input/Output computer and the DMA unit for the start, the execution and the termination of a data transmission procedure

6.3 Controller Modules for Special Functions

Sections 5.3 through 5.5 described interface modules that could be used to connect very different peripheral devices to a microprocessor system. A prerequisite for this is that the interfaces of the interface module and peripheral be adapted to each other. This requirement is usually met during parallel data transmission because of the universality of parallel interfaces; during serial data transmission this is accomplished through interface standardization. In the case of peripherals with very complicated interfaces, the described interface modules are not sufficient. These devices have to be supplied with special control modules whose interfaces are adapted to each other and which manage part of the device control. Two of these control modules, a floppy disk controller and a cathode ray tube controller, are described below. The emphasis of the descriptions is on the behavior of these modules rather than on their internal structure.

6.3.1 Floppy Disk

A floppy disk is a cost effective, relatively small magnetic disk memory which is often put in a microprocessor system as a memory unit for larger quantities of data. Its memory medium is a rotating flexible plastic disk (diskette) with a surface film that can be magnetized. So-called microfloppies have diameters of 3 to 4 inches, minifloppies have a 5.25-inch diameter, and regular floppies have an 8-inch diameter. Their memory capacity is up to 1,6M bytes (unformatted), depending on the type of disk and the writing density, medium access times are between 100 and 300 ms. The basic components of a floppy disk are the drive mechanics with a read/write head that can be positioned electrically, and the electronics that translates control signals into motion actions and generates status information. The connection to a microprocessor system occurs through a Floppy Disk controller module (FD controller), which mainly handles control signal generation, status signal evaluation and management of information blocks. Data transfer between this interface and the primary memory can be supported by a DMA controller.

Diskette Formatting. Data storage occurs in concentrical tracks which are addressed by the position of a radial moving read/write head. The tracks are divided into sectors of the same size. Usually, the values for an 8-inch diskette are 76 data tracks and an additional index track to store diskette specific indications. The number of sectors per track depends on the type of sector addressing. For so-called hardsectoring, the diskette contains 32 equidistant holes which are scanned photoelectrically. Each hole marks the beginning of a sector. Sector 0 is characterized by an additional perforation. The so-called softsectoring is more common; it has only one perforation, which indicates the position of sector 0. Sector subdivision is carried out by the software with the help of identification fields in the tracks. Each track of the current IBM 3740 format is divided into 26 sectors. Figure 6.12 shows the format of a sector.

The identification field is used to search a sector. It contains an identification byte, which is also used for character synchronization, one byte each for the track and the sector address and the 2-byte block check of the identification field as Cyclic Redundancy Code (CRC bytes). The data field also begins with an identification byte, followed by the actual 128-byte data block and by two block check bytes. Between the two fields, as well as between the single sectors, there are gaps of several bytes, so that smaller shiftings of the field limits, depending on the variation in timing of the motor drive, can be accomodated when a single field is re-written. Each track has an additional track

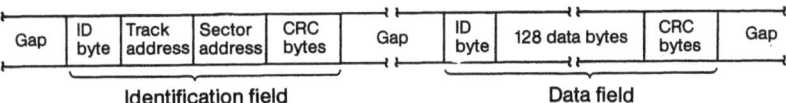

Fig. 6.12. Sector format

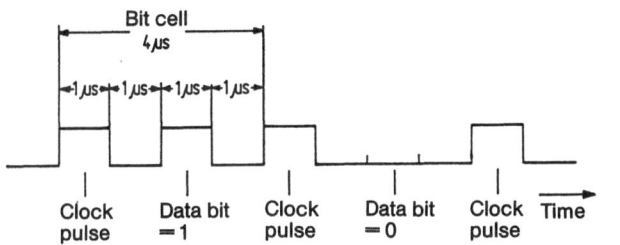

Fig. 6.13. Diagram with single writing density

identification field at the beginning of the track which is separated by the first and the last sector by gaps.

Before a diskette can be used for data storage, it has to be formatted. All tracks are described with their identification fields. When data access occurs later, a sector is localized by comparing the established track address and the sector address with the contents of the identification fields. The actual data transmission is carried out in 128-byte blocks (for example IBM 3740 format), i.e. by sector.

Information Representation. Data recording is bit-serial; the values of the single bits are represented by two opposing magnetization directions on the diskette surface. The data signal that is recorded is modulated with the write clock frequency; different modulation techniques are used for single and double writing density. Figure 6.13 shows signal representation with single writing density (3268 bit/inch), which is also used in IBM 3740 format. The modulation frequency is 1 MHz, which corresponds to a frequency period of 1 μs. Data bits and frequency impulses alternate; every time they are separated by a modulation cycle with level 0. Therefore, a time slot of 4 μs is available for recording the data bit, which corresponds to a transmission speed of 250 K bit/s. When the recorded signal is read, data and frequency information are separated from each other. The frequency signal, reconstructed by what is called a Phased Locked Loop circuit (PLL), is used to sample the data bit signal.

6.3.2 Floppy Disk Controller Module

Behavior. The information exchange between microprocessor system and floppy disk requires a large amount of control, which is managed by the floppy disk controller. Its basic tasks are:

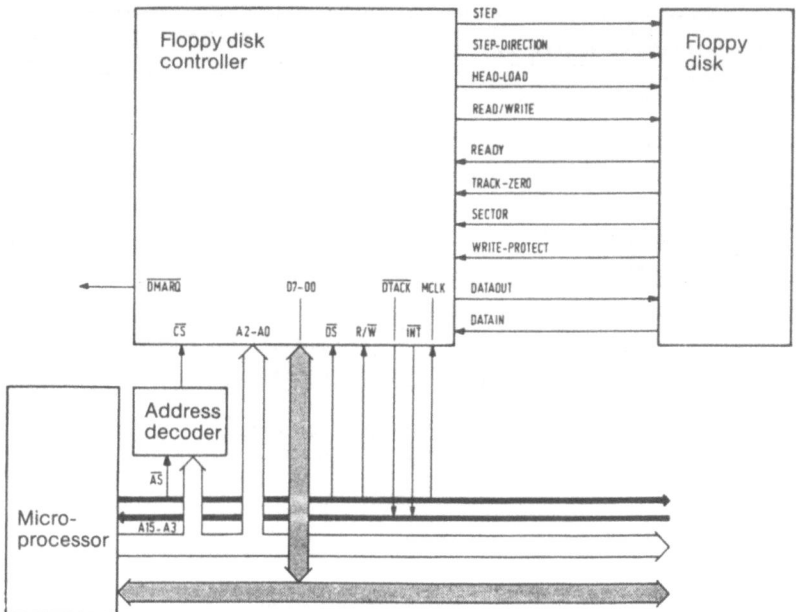

Fig. 6.14. Connection of a floppy disk to a system bus

- exchange of control signals with the floppy disk, e.g. to position the read/write head during track selection and to synchronize data transmission

- sector search through address comparison,

- writing and reading of data blocks with parallel-to-serial or serial-to-parallel data byte conversion,

- modulation of the data write signal and demodulation of the data read signal, and

- generation and evaluation of block check information.

Figure 6.14 shows the connection of a floppy disk with a microprocessor system with data, address and principal control lines between the units involved. Data transmission is either program controlled by the microprocessor, or it is in direct memory access if a DMA controller is used.

Write data are stored in parallel in an 8-bit output data register of the FD controller and are transmitted bit-serially in modulated form to the floppy disk (DATAOUT connection). Read data are acquired by the FD controller bit-serially as a modulated input signal (DATAIN connection). The sampling frequency is obtained from the read signal by means of demodulation; it samples the data bits and gathers them in an 8-bit input register. (Often frequency restoration already occurs in the floppy disk control electronics.) The smallest unit for a read/write procedure is a 128-byte data block, i.e. one sector of one track.

In microprocessor controlled I/O, data transfer requests to the microprocessor are indicated by a status bit in the FD controller which can also be used to trigger an interrupt signal. In the case of I/O with direct memory access, this task is performed by a DMA request signal $\overline{\text{DMARQ}}$, which will be transmitted to the DMA controller input $\overline{\text{TRRQ}}$.

Interfaces. The system bus interface is used to either write or read both data registers and the control, address and status registers; to a great extent it is identical to the interfaces of the interface modules described in Section 5. In addition, it includes a clock frequency input MCLK for the modulation clock from which the control timing for the read/write head is also internally derived. It also comprises an additional signal connection $\overline{\text{DMARQ}}$, which is used to send a transmission request to a DMA controller.

The most important interface control outputs to the floppy disk are:

- STEP: to move the read/write head by one track,

- STEP DIRECTION: to indicate the STEP's direction of movement,

- HEAD LOAD: to lower the read/write head to read or write on the diskette surface, and

- READ/WRITE: to indicate data flow direction read or write.

Some floppy disk controllers are also equipped with additional address outputs (DRIVE SELECT) with which one of several connected mechanisms can be selected.

The most important interface control inputs to the floppy disk are:

- READY: to indicate readiness of the floppy disk for a transmission,

- TRACK ZERO: to indicate whether the read/write head is at track 0,

- SECTOR: to indicate sector perforation, and

- WRITE PROTECT: to indicate whether the diskette is write protected.

Commands. Several commands, which are loaded into a special control register through the system data bus, activate certain control functions of the FD controller. Some of these commands are:

- FREE FORMAT WRITE. The diskette is formatted; either the IBM 3740 format or any other format defined by the user can be employed.

- SEEK TRACK ZERO. The read/write head is positioned over track 0.

- SEEK TRACK. The read/write head is positioned on the track whose address is in the track address register of the FD controller.

- STEP IN, STEP OUT. The read/write head is moved inwards by one track in direction of track 76 or it is moved outwards by one track in direction of track 0.

- SINGLE SECTOR READ. The 128 data bytes of the sector, whose address is in the sector address register of the FD controller, are read and the block check test is executed.

- SINGLE SECTOR WRITE. 128 data bytes are written in the sector whose sector address is in the sector address register of the FD controller; block check characters are generated and concatenated with the data block.

- READ FOR CRC. The 128 data bytes of the sector whose address is in the sector address register of the FD controller, are read and the block check test is executed; the data bytes are not delivered to the microprocessor system. Thus, it is possible to verify if a previous write operation is error-free and repeat it if it is not.

Additional commands allow the writing or reading of several consecutive sectors, the address of the first sector is indicated in the sector address register, and the sector number is given in a counter.

All commands influence the corresponding control lines of the peripheral interface of the FD controller, partly depending on its control register contents. Furthermore, they influence the status register bits in order to indicate the condition of specific operations or possible errors.

See also [17] for a supplement to this brief description; [22] provides an overview on floppy disk controller modules.

6.3.3 Video Terminals

Video terminals (for short "displays") are used for the temporary representation of text. A display consists of a keyboard for the input and of a video for the output of information. Usually a cathode ray tube is used as video, it works like a TV tube according to the raster-scan principle. A beam of electrons is deflected on the video from left to right one line after the other, and it is modulated light or dark depending on the dots that have to appear on the video. At the end of the line, there is an invisible movement of the beam to the beginning of the next line, and at the end of the figure the beam is invisibly sent back to the beginning.

Cathode Ray Tube controllers (CRT controllers) are used to manage such cathode ray tubes. These controllers can be used to easily connect commercial TV monitors for text representation in microprocessor systems. In order to determine which tasks pertain to a CRT controller, we have to discuss some details on picture generation.

Picture Generation. 625 (US: 525) video lines are available to represent a picture. In so-called non-interlaced mode, a half picture of 312 (262) lines is written with picture refresh frequency of 50 (60) Hz, i.e. only every other video line is used for picture representation. In the so-called interlaced mode, two half pictures are always written consecutively in order to obtain a better resolution of picture representation, the lines of the second half picture lie between those of the first. With a picture refresh frequency of 50 (60) Hz each for the two half pictures, i.e. 25 (30) Hz for the total picture, the representation is sometimes flickering. Thus, interlaced mode is not very common in the construction of displays with TV monitors as opposed to the transmission of moving pictures in commercial TV.

The dots are drawn on the video by a beam of electrons that is controlled by a video signal. The video signal consists of impulses for light/dark control of the single dots and impulses for the synchronization of horizontal and vertical beam retrace (Figure 6.15). Characters are produced with a character generator as dots in a grid of usually 5 x 7 or 7 x 9 dots. In the case of a 5 x 7 matrix, 5 successive dots are drawn in 7 consecutive picture lines (Figure 6.16).

A ROM is used to generate characters by storing the lines of the dot matrixes of each character in 0/1 values. When a line of the matrix has to be selected, the ROM is addressed with the 7-bit or 8-bit code of the character (e.g. in ASCII code) and with the line index of the character matrix (Figure 6.17). The matrix line, containing between 5 and 7 bits according to the 5 x 7 or 7 x 9 dot

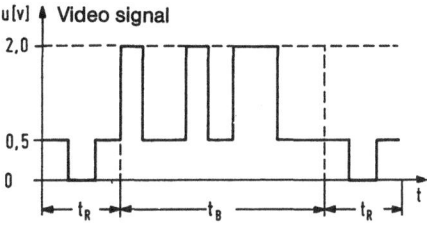

Fig. 6.15. Video signal, t_R time for beam return, t_B time for picture line generation

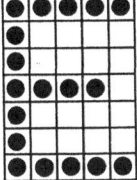

Fig. 6.16. 5 x 7 dot matrix
for the representation of character E

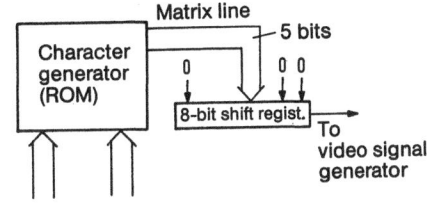

Fig. 6.17. Character generation

matrix, is read in a shift register and sent bitwise to the video signal generator; this generator then generates light/dark signals from it. In order to obtain character separation within one line, the shift register is extended by the necessary number of bits and is filled with zeroes in the outer bit positions.

Refresh Memory. The complete picture content is stored in a refresh memory (RAM). In order to write a line of text, the refresh memory is addressed so that the characters of this line are read repeatedly the same number of times as the number of matrix lines of the dot matrix. Each time, the line index for the character generator is increased by one starting from zero. When two text lines have to be separated, the video signal is forced to light or darkness, depending on the type of chosen background, during several electron beam deflections.

When a video is connected to a microprocessor system, one part of the primary memory can be used as refresh memory. As shown below, this requires a DMA connection for the refresh hardware and a relatively fast primary memory. With a half picture of 312 (US: 262) lines and a picture refresh frequency of 50 (60) Hz, about 64 μs are available to write a picture line and for beam deflection. With the typical number of 64 characters per line with 8 dots each (5 x 7 matrix, 3 blank dots each for character separation) and a dot clock frequency of 10 MHz we obtain 512 dots per line and a writing time of 51,2μs. Thus, 0,8μs are available for reading a character from the refresh memory.

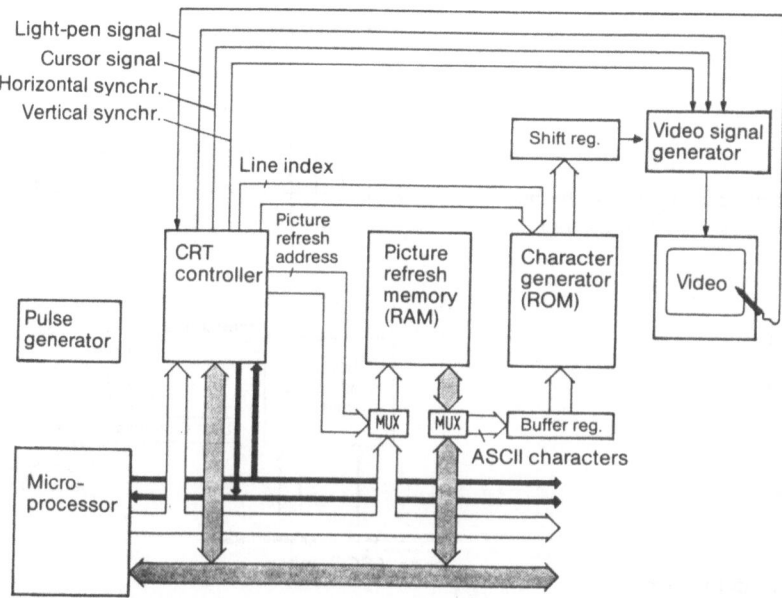

Fig. 6.18. Video control with direct access to the picture refresh memory

In order to avoid a DMA access and the related degradation of the program processing in the microprocessor, the video is usually equipped with its own refresh memory and with direct memory access for picture generation (Figure 6.18). The microprocessor access to this memory, that is necessary for picture alteration, is controlled by a multiplexer circuit and is limited by a hardware control to the interval of the beam deflection outside the 512 line picture points, so that access conflicts during picture production and alteration can be avoided. The refresh memory occupies one part of the microprocessor addressing space with time-limited access through the system bus.

Picture alteration through the processor can occur for instance when a character is read from the display keyboard, which can be connected to the microprocessor system through an asynchronous serial interface (not represented in Figure 6.18; see Subsection 5.4.4, Example 5.4). Alterations can also take place due to different video operations, like the scrolling up or the scrolling down of the video content or through the exchange of a video content (previous page, next page). In order to allow the picture refresh memory to handle such operations, its capacity is designed to hold the content of several video screens.

6.3.4 CRT Controller Modules

Tasks. Figure 6.18 shows the structure of a video control using a CRT controller. This control module, that can be programmed through its system bus connection, basically performs these tasks:

- addressing of the picture refresh memory depending on picture generation (interlaced/non-interlaced mode), on the number of characters per line and on the number of text lines per picture;

- generation of the line index for the character generator depending on number of lines of the dot matrix;

- generation of the instants of time and pulse widths for horizontal and vertical synchronization;

- generation of a cursor signal (shape of the cursor, blink/no blink); and

- reaction to the light pen signal.

Cursor and Light Pen. The cursor is a marking character that indicates the place where a typed character will be written on the screen. The cursor can be shaped as a dotted area with a different number of matrix lines and arbitrary vertical position within one text line. To this purpose, two registers are loaded with the beginning line index and the end line index in the CRT controller. The position of the cursor on the video is controlled through the keyboard; in the CRT controller, this is done by storing the corresponding address of the refresh memory in an additional control register. When the register content matches the actual picture refresh address, the CRT controller transmits the cursor signal which overlaps the actual video signal. The cursor can be emphasized by blinking.

A light pen is an input device in form of a pen with a light sensor at the tip. If it is positioned like a pencil on an arbitrary place on the video, it transmits a signal at the passage of the electron beam through that point. This signal is sent to the CRT controller, which then stores the picture refresh address at that instant of time in a register. The register content can be read by a program.

For further information on this subject see [17]; and for a general overview on CRT controller modules see [22].

7 16-Bit Microprocessors by Motorola, Zilog and Intel

The microprocessor market today is basically controlled by three producers, whose 16-bit processors will be briefly described in this chapter. Section 7.1 will deal with Motorola's MC68000, Section 7.2 will describe Zilog's Z8000 and Section 7.3 will introduce Intel's 8086. The short descriptions will include programming models, data formats, addressing types, instruction sets, trap and interrupt mechanisms as well as microprocessor signals. Moreover, a review will be given of the different structures of the new machines based on these processors. - For more details, see the producers' manuals (Motorola [4, 49-51], Zilog [3, 48, 52, 53], Intel [2, 54-56]). Comparative considerations regarding the three processors mentioned above can be found in [42-47].

7.1 Motorola MC68000

Motorola Inc. offers a 16-bit microprocessor, whose internal structure is already designed for 32-bit processing. It is characterized by the regular structure of its register set, its instruction set and its addressing types. The processor offers elementary functions to support the implementation of high-level programming languages and operating systems, for instance a general register set, large 16M byte address space, stacks, special instructions to chain stack data areas, two operation modes, privileged instructions, a multiple-level interrupt system with priorization and vectorization, a trap system, and the possibility of memory management through memory management modules. Furthermore, it supports multiprocessor structures by means of a special instruction for the implementation of semaphores. The processor is packaged in a 64-pin package.

7.1.1 The Programming Model

Figure 7.1 shows the set of programmable registers. It consists of eight 32-bit data registers D0 through D7, seven 32-bit address registers A0 through A6, two 32-bit stack pointer registers A7, that are assigned to the address registers, one 16-bit status register and one 32-bit program counter register. Data registers are used as source and destination registers for byte, word and double word operations, where every byte and word access refers to the lowest byte or word in the register. Address registers are used as base address registers, as stack pointer registers and for register indirect operand addressing. Both stack pointer registers A7 are implicitly used to manage the stack during subprogram calls, trap and interrupt processing and special stack instructions; they are differentiated by the two operational conditions: user state and supervisor state. All 17 data and

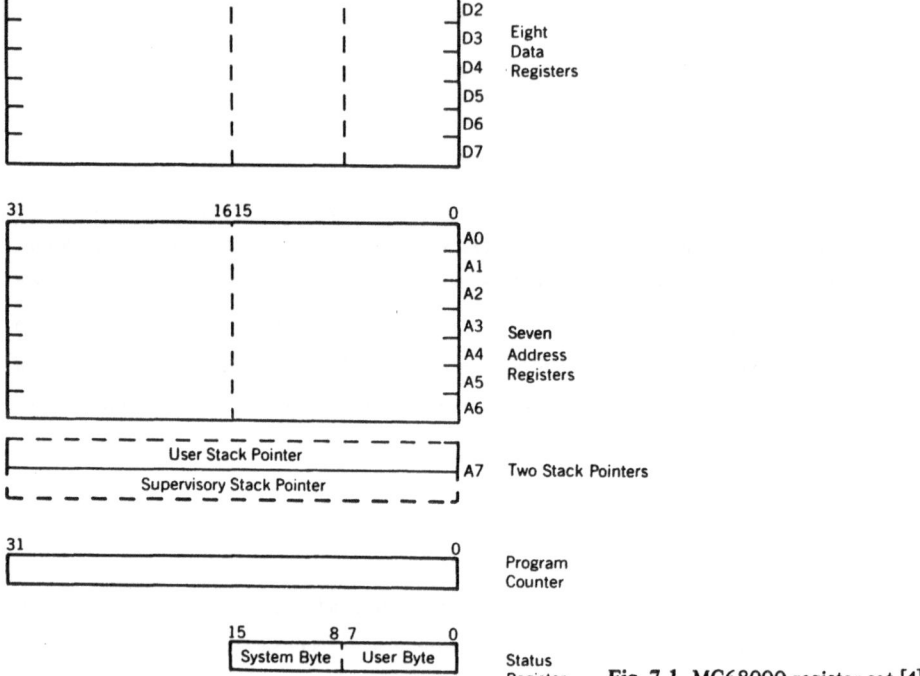

Fig. 7.1. MC68000 register set [4]

address registers can also be used as index registers. Address values in registers A0 through A7 and in the program counter register use the 24 lower register bits. Thus, a directly addressable 16M byte area is generated.

The mode bits in the status register are combined in a system byte and the condition bits are collected in a user byte (Figure 7.2). Mode bits determine the trace mode, the user state and supervisor state, and the interrupt mask. Beside the usual condition bits Negative (N), Zero (Z), Overflow (O) and Carry (C), the user byte includes an extend bit X, which indicates binary number overflow like the Carry bit (C). C and X are used differently: the C bit is used as a branching condition; the X bit represents the carry bit for the ADD and SUBTRACT instructions, that are extended by using this bit. Separating the two functions simplifies the programming of arithmetic operations for operands with a word length exceeding 32 bits.

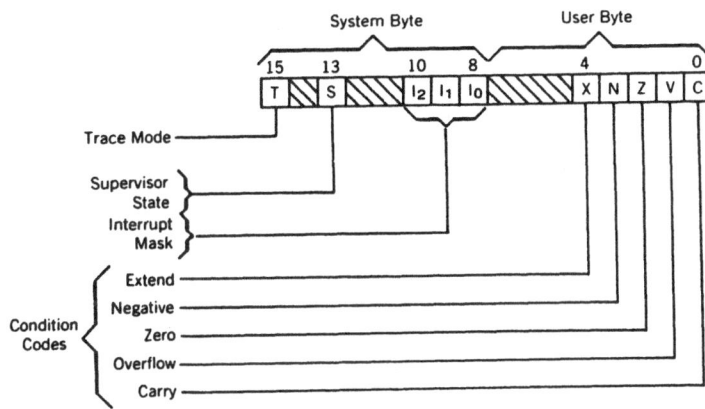

Fig. 7.2. MC68000 status register [4]

7.1.2 Data Formats

The three traditional data formats are: byte, word and double word (long word). These formats are allowed in most arithmetic and logical operations. Moreover, the instruction set allows the processing of single bits and BCD digits.

The operands are stored inside the processor in 32-bit data and address registers. The external memory is organized wordwise according to the 16-bit data bus and can be addressed bytewise or wordwise. Double word transfers require two consecutive memory accesses. Words and double words have to be stored at word boundaries with even addresses.

7.1.3 Addressing Modes

The MC68000 has over 14 addressing modes, which can be used in almost the whole instruction set, with the exception of *quick immediate* and *implied register* (Table 7.1). The addressing modes *postincrement register indirect* and *predecrement register indirect* both simplify the processing of operands that were stored consecutively (block and string processing). In connection with the MOVE instruction, they can also be used for an easy implementation of stacks (LIFO principle) and queues (FIFO principle). The relative to the program counter mode and the register indirect addressing mode allow a dynamic relocation of program and data areas with the possibility of indexed addressing in these areas. Index register contents and offset values in the instructions are interpreted as two's complement numbers, i.e. offsets can be either positive or negative.

7.1.4 Instruction Formats and Instruction Set

The MC68000 instruction set includes 77 instructions, which consist of one to five 16-bit words altogether depending on the instruction type and addressing mode. Standard instructions for dyadic operations are two-address instructions. Figure 7.3 shows the instruction format of the ADD

Table 7.1. MC68000 addressing modes [4]

Mode	Generation
Register Direct Addressing	
Data Register Direct	EA = Dn
Address Register Direct	EA = An
Absolute Data Addressing	
Absolute Short	EA = (Next Word)
Absolute Long	EA = (Next Two Words)
Program Counter Relative Addressing	
Relative with Offset	EA = (PC) + d_{16}
Relative with Index and Offset	EA = (PC) + (Xn) + d_8
Register Indirect Addressing	
Register Indirect	EA = (An)
Postincrement Register Indirect	EA = (An), An ← An + N
Predecrement Register Indirect	An ← An − N, EA = (An)
Register Indirect With Offset	EA = (An) + d_{16}
Indexed Register Indirect With Offset	EA = (An) + (Xn) + d_8
Immediate Data Addressing	
Immediate	DATA = Next Word(s)
Quick Immediate	Inherent Data
Implied Addressing	
Implied Register	EA = SR, USP, SP, PC

NOTES:

EA = Effective Address
An = Address Register
Dn = Data Register
Xn = Address or Data Register used as Index Register
SR = Status Register
PC = Program Counter

d_8 = Eight-bit Offset (displacement)
d_{16} = Sixteen-bit Offset (displacement)
N = 1 for Byte, 2 for Words and 4 for Long Words
( ) = Contents of
← = Replaces

15	14	13	12	11	10	9	8	7	6	5	4	3	2	1	0
1	1	0	1	Register			Op-Mode			Effective Address					

Fig. 7.3. Instruction format for the ADD instruction

instruction as an example of instruction structure. The register field indicates the address of a register operand with a 3-bit address. The second operand is defined as register, memory or direct operand through the effective address field. It describes the addressing mode either through 3 mode bits and one 3-bit register address or through 6 mode bits. The selection of the addressing mode also determines the number of instruction words. The data format (byte, word or double word) and the indication of which address will be the source or the destination address are in the op mode field. Memory addresses occupy either a word (16-bit absolute short address) or two words (24-bit absolute long address) within one instruction.

The instruction set is divided into eight instruction groups to perform the following operations:

- Data Movement,

- Integer Arithmetic,

- Binary Coded Decimal,

- Logical,

- Shifts and Rotates,

- Bit Manipulation,

- Program Control,

- System Control.

Data Movement Operations. Data transfers with 8-bit, 16-bit and 32-bit operands are performed by the instruction MOVE, while source and destination can be either a general register or the memory. The MOVE instruction and the addressing modes *postincrement register indirect* and *predecrement register indirect* can create stacks and queues with registers A0 through A7. The quick loading of the data registers with 8-bit operands is performed by the instruction Move Quick (MOVEQ). The instruction Move Multiple (MOVEM) saves and loads the general registers; the involved registers can be indicated separately and in arbitrary sequence in the assembler representation. Address operands are loaded on the stack or in an address register by the instructions Push Effective Address (PEA) and Load Effective Address (LEA), and the indicated address modification is executed.

Two instructions that are typical of the MC68000 are the instruction Link and Allocate (LINK) and instruction Unlink (UNLK). They are used to allocate and deallocate subprogram data areas on the user stack or on the supervisor stack (LIFO principle). They are used to manage the base addresses of the data areas (frame pointer) and to perform area chaining. When LINK is the first instruction of a subprogram, it writes the content of the address register specified in the instruction as the main program frame pointer on the stack (chaining) and loads the address register with the content of the stack pointer register A7 (actual frame pointer). Finally, it increments the stack pointer by the number of memory words of the subprogram data area indicated in the LINK instruction (memory area allocation). When UNLK is the last instruction before the subprogram return, it loads the stack pointer register A7 with the content of the address register indicated in the instruction, i.e. with the actual frame pointer (memory area deallocation), and then in a stack access it reads the frame pointer of the main program into the address register, so that the data area of the main program is again active.

Integer Arithmetic Operations. The group of arithmetic instructions includes a complete set of add, subtract and compare instructions for 8-bit, 16-bit and 32-bit operands. The operand accesses take place in memory-to-register, register-to-memory or register-to-register mode. The source operand can also be a direct operand. Two multiply and divide instructions each execute operations with 16-bit binary numbers and with 16-bit two's complement numbers. Instruction Negate (NEG) creates the two's complement of an operand, instruction Sign Extend (EXT) expands an operand in a double length two's complement. Instruction Test (TST) for a comparison with zero and instruction Test And Set an operand (TAS), for the generation of semaphores, complete this instruction group. TAS tests a byte operand and affects the condition bits N and Z. Finally it sets the most significant bit of the operand to one. The two memory cycles (read-modify-write) needed by the instruction cannot be interrupted.

Binary Coded Decimal Operations. The available BCD operations are addition, subtraction and negation, always including the extend bit X. The negation forms the ten's complement (X=0) or the nine's complement (X=1) depending on X. 8-bit units consisting of two BCD digits are processed as operands.

Logical Operations. Logical instructions AND, OR, EXOR and NOT (negation, one's complement) work with 8-bit, 16-bit and 32-bit operands in memory-to-register or in register-to-register mode, where only data registers are accepted as registers.

Shift and Rotate Operations. The group of shift and rotate instructions comprises a complete set of logical and arithmetic shift instructions as well as rotate instructions for 8-bit, 16-bit and 32-bit register operands and for 16-bit memory operands. All instructions are one-word instructions. In the case of register operands, the number of shifts n is either in the instruction as a constant ($n=0$ through 7) or in one of the data registers as a variable ($n=0$ through 63). In the case of memory operands, the shift number is fixed at $n=1$.

Bit Manipulation Operations. Bit manipulation is general-purpose. It includes the instructions Bit Test (BTST), Bit Test and Set (BSET), Bit Test and Clear (BCLR) and Bit Test and Exchange (BCHG). The test is the result of one single bit in an 8-bit memory operand or in a 32-bit data register operand, and it influences the Z bit. Then, depending on the instruction, the tested bit is either left unchanged, or it is set, reset or complemented. The bit number is indicated either as a constant in the instruction or as a variable in one of the data registers.

Program Control Operations. The set of program control instructions includes 14 conditional branch instructions (Bcc), one unconditional Branch instruction (BRA) as well as a Subprogram Branch (BSR) with relative to the program counter addressing of the branch destination. The branch distances are between ± 128 bytes (one-word instructions) and ± 32K bytes (two-word instructions). An unconditional Jump instruction (JMP) and the instruction Jump to Subroutine (JSR) allow full memory addressing. Subprogram instructions are also completed with two Return instructions (RTS, RTR), one of which also restores both the program counter and the original status of the condition bits in the status register.

The instruction Set Byte Conditionally (Scc), which sets or resets the eight bits of a byte operand in connection with condition cc, and the instruction Test Condition Decrement and Branch (DBcc) complete the program control instructions. Instruction DBcc simplifies the generation of inductive and iterative program loops, while it makes leaving a loop dependent on a condition cc indicated in the instruction or on the content of a data register (counting register) specified in the instruction. For each loop execution, the data register content is also decremented by one by the DBcc instruction and it is compared with -1.

System Control Operations. The group of system control instructions includes several logical instructions as well as transfer instructions to influence the condition bits or the status word. The instructions that affect the whole status word are privileged. Other privileged instructions are RESET, for the initialization of external functional units through the reset control line; STOP, which stops the program execution; and Return from Exception (RTE), which is used to terminate interrupt and trap programs, and restores the original processor status. Moreover, there are three non-privileged instructions in form of software traps: Trap on Overflow (TRAPV), which triggers a trap when the overflow bit V is set; TRAP, which can be used to call 16 different trap programs; and Check Register against Bounds (CHK). The latter checks if an index stored in a data register is within an area, whose limits are defined by the value zero and by an operand addressed by the instruction. In case of boundary violation, the instruction transfers to a trap program.

The MC68000 instruction set does not include I/O instructions; I/O addressing is memory mapped. Furthermore, it does not include block or string instructions. Block and string processing is supported by the addressing modes *postincrement register indirect* and *predecrement register indirect* in connection with the DBcc instruction.

7.1.5 Trap and Interrupt System

The MC68000 includes 227 possibilities of program interruption to be executed through traps and interrupts as listed in Table 7.2. Interrupt requests are carried out in coded form by means of the three interrupt inputs. There are seven interrupt levels with different priorities in connection with a 3-bit mask in the status register. Level 7 interrupts are non-maskable because of their high priority. The selection of an interrupt program is either carried out through an autovector assigned to the level or through one of 192 user interrupt vectors, which is selected with a vector number input

Table 7.2. MC68000 interrupt vectors [4]

Vector Number(s)	Address Dec	Address Hex	Space	Assignment
0	0	000	SP	Reset: Initial SSP
	4	004	SP	Reset: Initial PC
2	8	008	SD	Bus Error
3	12	00C	SD	Address Error
4	16	010	SD	Illegal Instruction
5	20	014	SD	Zero Divide
6	24	018	SD	CHK Instruction
7	28	01C	SD	TRAPV Instruction
8	32	020	SD	Privilege Violation
9	36	024	SD	Trace
10	40	028	SD	Line 1010 Emulator
11	44	02C	SD	Line 1111 Emulator
12	48	030	SD	(Unassigned, reserved)
13	52	034	SD	(Unassigned, reserved)
14	56	038	SD	(Unassigned, reserved)
15	60	03C	SD	(Unassigned, reserved)
16-23	64	040	SD	(Unassigned, reserved)
	95	05F		—
24	96	060	SD	Spurious Interrupt
25	100	064	SD	Level 1 Interrupt Auto-Vector
26	104	068	SD	Level 2 Interrupt Auto-Vector
27	108	06C	SD	Level 3 Interrupt Auto-Vector
28	112	070	SD	Level 4 Interrupt Auto-Vector
29	116	074	SD	Level 5 Interrupt Auto-Vector
30	120	078	SD	Level 6 Interrupt Auto-Vector
31	124	07C	SD	Level 7 Interrupt Auto-Vector
32-47	128	080	SD	TRAP Instruction Vectors
	191	0BF		—
48-63	192	0C0	SD	(Unassigned, reserved)
	255	0FF		—
64-255	256	100	SD	User Interrupt Vectors
	1023	3FF		—

through the data bus. The differentiation between the two possibilities occurs through a control signal that is produced outside the processor. Special interrupts *reset* and *bus error* have two separate signal inputs.

A program interruption transfers the processor in supervisor mode and causes it to write the processor status (program counter content and status register content) in the system stack. Finally, the interrupt mask in the status register is set equal to the interrupt code, so that the following interrupts of equal or lower priority are blocked. The branching to the interrupt program occurs through the vector table storing the start addresses of all interrupt and trap programs. A reset interrupt triggers processor and system initialization because it is an interrupt condition with the highest priority. During this process, not only the program counter but also the system stack pointer is loaded through the vector table.

7.1.6 Processor Signals

Figure 7.4 shows the 64 MC68000 signal connections grouped by their functions. The data bus includes 16 bits; the address bus is designed for 23-bit word addresses. Byte selection as well as word/byte differentiation occurs through the two data strobe signals $\overline{\text{LDS}}$ and $\overline{\text{UDS}}$. Together with

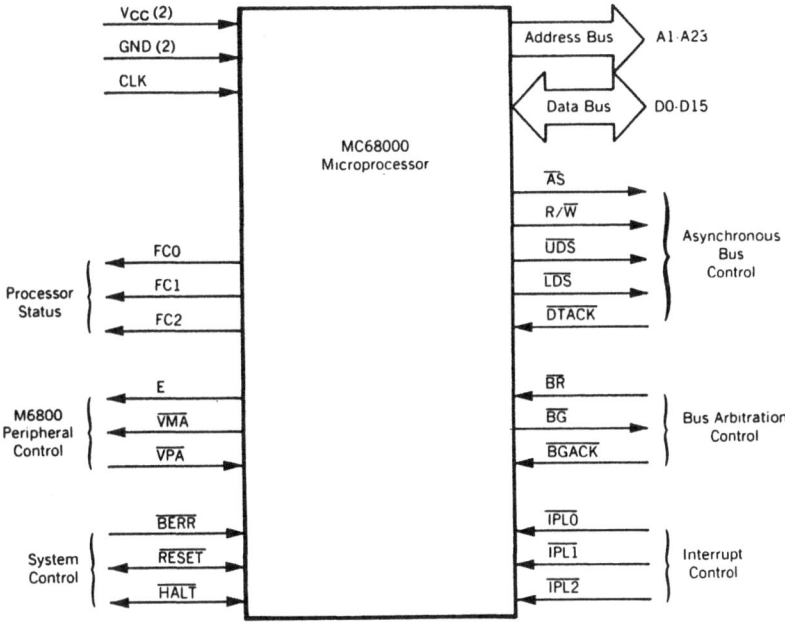

Mnemonic	Signal name
V_{cc}	Power input
GND	Ground
CLK	Clock
FC0 FC1 FC2	Function code output
E	Enable
$\overline{\text{VMA}}$	Valid memory address
$\overline{\text{VPA}}$	Valid peripheral address
$\overline{\text{BERR}}$	Bus error
$\overline{\text{RESET}}$	Reset
$\overline{\text{HALT}}$	Halt

Mnemonic	Signal name
A1–A23	Address bus
D0–D15	Data bus
$\overline{\text{AS}}$	Address strobe
$R/\overline{W}$	Read/Write
$\overline{\text{UDS}}$, $\overline{\text{LDS}}$	Upper and lower data strobes
$\overline{\text{DTACK}}$	Data transfer acknowledge
$\overline{\text{BR}}$	Bus request
$\overline{\text{BG}}$	Bus grant
$\overline{\text{BGACK}}$	Bus grant acknowledge
IPL0 IPL1 IPL2	Interrupt priority level

Fig. 7.4. MC68000 processor signals [4]

the $\overline{\text{DTACK}}$ input as a transfer acknowledge signal, they control the asynchronous data transfer (asynchronous bus control). These signals are completed by three signals for synchronous data transfer (M6800 peripheral control), e.g. as it is done with the interface modules of the M6800 8-bit microprocessor family. The selection between the two transfer modes is performed by the $\overline{\text{VPA}}$ signal.

Bus allocation, for example in a DMA environment, is managed by three control signals (bus arbitration control). Three additional signals (interrupt control) allow interrupt requests in seven priority levels, where autovector and user vector interrupts are also differentiated by the $\overline{\text{VPA}}$ signal. Three status signals (processor status) characterize the four conditions user/supervisor data access and user/supervisor program access. Furthermore, the interrupt acknowledge is coded in these signals. Three system control signals are used as special interrupt, stop and initialization signals.

7.1.7 Successors of the MC68000

Motorola offers at present (1984) three successors of the MC68000 processor: the MC68008, the MC68010 and the MC68020. They have the same internal 32-bit structure of the MC68000 and are software compatible with it. The enhancement shared by these three variations consists in an instruction buffer which can store a minimum of two instruction words, so that the actual instruction fetching time is shortened (instruction prefetch). In particular, this buffer allows the efficient execution of a number of string operations that are structured as 3-word program loops from the conditional jump instruction DBcc and from a preceding operation. Thus, since the whole loop can be contained in the buffer, a repeated reading of the instructions from the memory can be avoided.

MC68008. The MC68008 (16-bit microprocessor with 8-bit data bus) was designed for the construction of systems with an 8-bit data bus and thus has only eight connections for the data bus. The reduction of its connections to a total of 48 leads to some functional limitations:

- The logical address space with 20 address lines is reduced to 1M byte.

- Instead of the usual three interrupt inputs there are only two inputs and therefore only three interrupt levels.

- The processor does not provide the $\overline{\text{VMA}}$ signal (Valid Memory Access) that is necessary for the control of a synchronous bus. This operation must be dealt with outside the processor.

- The $\overline{\text{BGACK}}$ signal of the bus arbitration is missing, so that there is no possibility of overlapping during bus allocation.

MC68010. The MC68010 (16-bit virtual memory microprocessor) supports systems which work with virtual memory or which are used as virtual machines for the creation of new operative systems. The most important improvement with respect to the MC68000 is the possibility of interruption when accessing virtual segments that are not loaded in the main memory (page faults). In this case, the execution of the corresponding instruction is stopped by a Bus Error signal ($\overline{\text{BERR}}$) generated by the memory management module, and a trap routine for exception handling is started in which, for example, the missing segment is loaded. The status needed for the continuation of the instruction execution is saved on the supervisor stack during the interruption and is reloaded at the end of the trap routine by means of the Return from Exception instruction (RTE). The status comprises 29 words.

In order to allow generation of new operative systems, reading the status byte of the processor status register is a privileged operation. Thus, an operative system, that has to be tested and that is forced to run in user mode under the existing operative system, generates a trap when it requests its own status. The trap program (which runs in supervisor mode) then returns the real supervisor mode status. Virtual devices of the new operative system, i.e. devices that are not physically present in the existing system, are simulated for the test by means of program interruptions.

Additional characteristics are:

- The supervisor program can access all address areas that are differentiated by status lines FC2 through FC0 by means of an instruction MOVES (Move Alternate Address Space). To this purpose, there are two 3-bit function code registers in the processor which can be loaded by the supervisor program and whose contents are output on the status lines during source or destination addressing.

- Software breakpoints can be notified by external hardware through the function code.

- The 1K byte vector table can be moved in the whole address space by adding a vector base register.

MC68020. The MC68020 is a complete 32-bit processor with a 32-bit data bus connection. It is software compatible with the MC68008, the MC68000 and the MC68010; its register set contains the MC68010 register set. The most important improvements over the mentioned processors are:

- additional instructions (e.g. a block transfer instruction with access to all address areas that are differentiated by the function code), efficient enter and leave instructions for procedure calls and conversion instructions for ASCII and BCD representations;

- additional addressing modes (e.g. memory indirect addressing) and expansion of the existing addressing modes to 32-bit addresses and displacements;

- an expanded instruction buffer (cache memory);

- better execution times for instructions and bus cycles; and

- support of the connection with additional processors (e.g. floating point co-processor MC68881).

7.2 Zilog Z8000

With the Z8000, Zilog Inc. offers two 16-bit microprocessor versions, whose basic difference is in the width of their address bus. The so-called segmented version Z8001 is equipped with a 23-bit address bus and thus permits the addressing of 8M bytes. It allows the connection of memory management modules (Z8010); the seven high address bits have the function of a segment number. The 7-bit segment number is missing in the non-segmented version Z8002, so that the address space is limited to 64K bytes and no memory management modules can be attached.

Both processor versions exhibit a regular structure of their register sets, their instruction sets and their addressing modes. They offer elementary functions to support the implementation of high-level programming languages and operating systems, e.g. a general register set, a big 8M byte address space in the Z8001, stacks, two processing states, privileged instructions, and a trap and interrupt system with vectored interrupts. They also support the operation of multiprocessor systems through bus control signals, called multimicrosignals, together with instructions for the management of these signals, and through a special instruction for semaphore management. Moreover, they are equipped with a large instruction set for block transfer, for string processing and for I/O. There is also the possibility to include special processors (Extended Processing Units EPUs) in the system, which execute the so-called EPU instructions in co-operation with the central processor. Both processor versions are in 48-pin or in 40-pin packages and part of the signal lines are operated in time multiplex mode. We will use the Z8001 as a basis for the following description.

7.2.1 The Programming Model

The general register set of the Z8001 includes sixteen 16-bit registers R0 through R15, which can be used as data registers, address registers and, with the exception of R0, as index registers (Figure 7.5). The register pair R14/R15 is implicitly used as stack pointer register; since the processor has two op modes (user and system mode), the pair is double.

The first eight registers can also be used as sixteen 8-bit registers RH0, RL0 through RH7, RL7. Furthermore, in the whole register set, every two 16-bit registers can be combined into up to eight 32-bit registers RR0 through RR14, or four 16-bit registers can be combined into four 64-bit registers RQ0 through RQ12. Address values in the registers are represented as 23-bit byte addresses; they occupy one register pair with a 7-bit segment number and a 16-bit offset.

Additional registers, that are accessible to the user (Figure 7.6), are the 16-bit status register (flag and control word), the 32-bit program counter register (program counter), the 32-bit base address

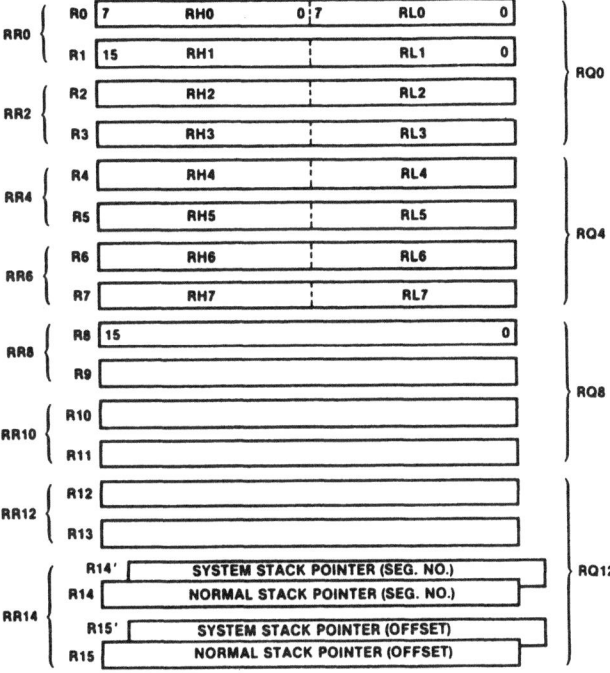

Fig. 7.5. Z8001 general register set [48]

register of the program status area (program status area pointer) and the 16-bit counting register (refresh counter).

The status register contains six condition bits in the low-order register byte: bits Carry (C), Zero (Z), Sign (S) and Parity or Overflow (P/V) for program branching and bits Decimal Adjust (DA) and Half Carry (H) to correct the results during BCD operations. The high-order register byte contains five mode bits. With bits Non-Vectored Interrupt Enable (NVIE) and Vectored Interrupt Enable (VIE), two interrupt inputs for vectored or non-vectored interrupts can be masked. The Extended Processor Architecture bit (EPA) indicates, when set, that there are special processors (EPUs) in the system. If it is not set, the EPU instructions trigger a trap. The System/User bit (S/Ū) indicates the processor's mode. The Z8001 processor can be put in non-segmented state through the Segmentation enable bit (SEG); then it works like the Z8002 processor with 16-bit addresses.

The program status area pointer generates the vector table base address, which contains the information for calling interrupt and trap programs. Thus, the position of the vector table in the address space can be chosen. When the RATE counter (which is decremented by one at each fourth processor clock cycle) reaches zero, the refresh counter register starts a so-called refresh cycle, in which the contents of the system's dynamic RAMs are refreshed. The value of the 9-bit

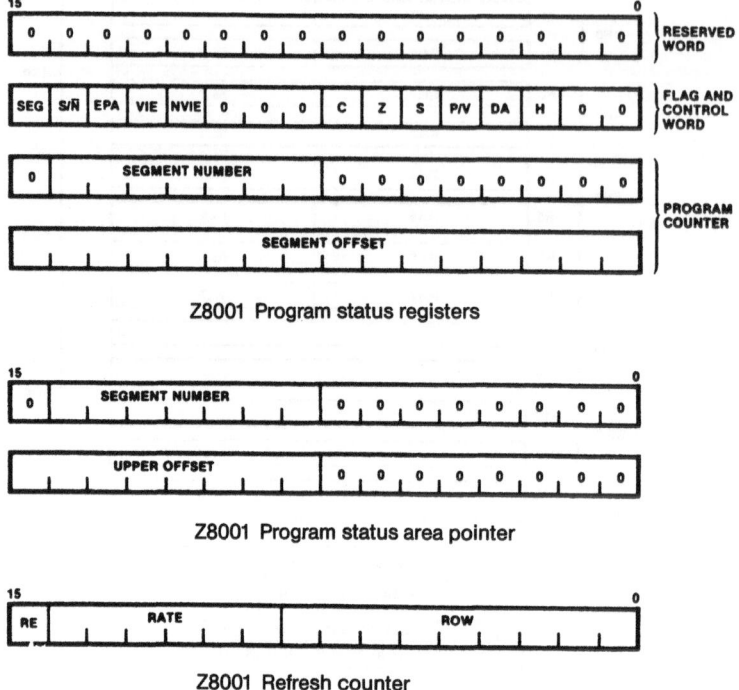

Z8001 Program status registers

Z8001 Program status area pointer

Z8001 Refresh counter

Fig. 7.6. Z8001 special register set[48]

COUNTER is used as the address of the RAM line to be refreshed. The refresh procedure can be prevented by the Refresh Enable bit (RE).

7.2.2 Data Formats

The arithmetic and logical operations in Z8000 processors are designed for byte, word and double word operands. In addition, the instruction set is equipped for the processing of single bits, BCD digits and byte and word strings of up to 64K bytes. Strings can only be in the primary memory, while all other operands can also be in the register file.

The primary memory has a wordwise structure corresponding to the 16-bit data bus and can be addressed bytewise and wordwise. Double word transfers require two consecutive memory accesses. Words and double words have to be stored at word boundaries with even addresses.

7.2.3 Addressing Modes

Z8000 processors include eight addressing modes that are listed in Table 7.3. The first five modes (IM, R, IR, DA and X) are used for standard instructions with operand access, while the remaining three modes (RA,BA and BX) can only be used for some jump and some data transfer instructions.

Table 7.3. Z8001 addressing modes

addressing mode		effective address
immediate	IM	DATA = operand
register	R	EA = Rm or RRn or RQp
indirect register	IR	EA = (RRn)
direct address	DA	EA = address
index	X	EA = (Rm) + address
relative address	RA	EA = (PC) + offset
base address	BA	EA = (RRn) + displacement
base index	BX	EA = (RRn) + (Rm)

The addressing modes autoincrement and autodecrement are not explicitly provided; they are implicitly included in the block transfer and string manipulation instructions. Since Z8001 addresses are 23 bits long, in the register file, they use one register pair each (RRn); index values are represented with 16 bits (Rm). The expressions *operand, address, offset* and *displacement* refer to the operands and address fields in the instruction.

7.2.4 Instruction Formats and Instruction Set

The Z8000 instruction set includes 110 instructions altogether; each includes one to four 16-bit words depending on the instruction and on the addressing mode. Standard instructions for binary operations are two-address instructions. Figure 7.7 shows the general instruction format through the example of the ADD instruction. The source address is specified by the mode field and the source field, where the latter includes one of the 4-bit register addresses 1 through 15 or the value zero. The content of the source field leads to two different interpretations of the mode field. The destination address is indicated in the destination field as a 4-bit register address. The respective data format (byte, word or double word) is defined in the op code, which results in the two different instruction representations in Figure 7.7. Memory addresses use either one word (7-bit segment number, 8-bit short offset) or two words (7-bit segment number, 16-bit long offset) in the instruction.

The instruction set is divided into nine groups of operations:

- Load and Exchange,
- Arithmetic,
- Logical,

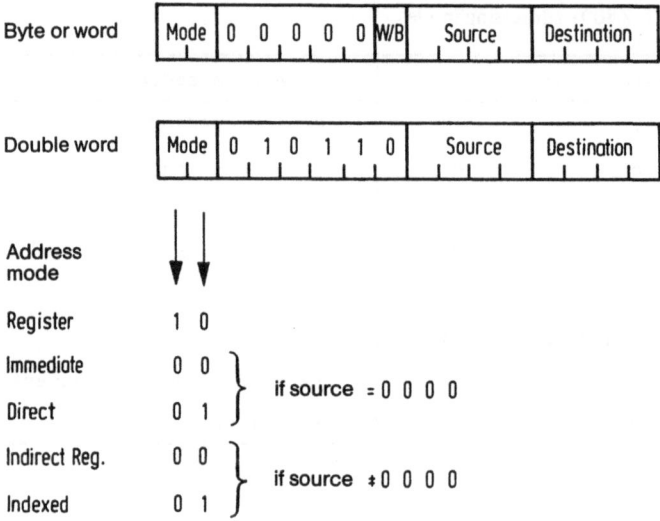

Fig. 7.7. Instruction formats for the ADD instruction

- Rotate and Shift,

- Bit Manipulation,

- Block Transfer and String Manipulation,

- Input / Output

- Program Control,

- CPU Control.

Load and Exchange Operations. Data transfers with 8-bit, 16-bit and 32-bit operands are carried out by the instruction Load (LD) in memory-to-register, register-to-memory or register-to-register mode; the source operand can also be an immediate operand. Content saving and loading of 1 through 16 consecutive general registers is made possible by the instruction Load Multiple (LDM). The instructions PUSH and POP are designed for stack operations; with the exception of RR0, they allow each register pair to be used as stack pointer register. Address operands are loaded into the register file by means of the Load Address instruction (LDA) and the Load Address Relative instruction (LDAR), which executes address modifications.

Arithmetic Operations. The set of arithmetic instructions includes a complete set of add, subtract and compare instructions for 8-bit, 16-bit and 32-bit operands. Operand accesses are executed in memory-to-register or register-to-register mode. The source operand can also be an immediate operand. Instructions Increment (INC) and Decrement (DEC) are available for the addition and subtraction of 4-bit immediate operands. Decimal operands in BCD representation are added and subtracted by using binary arithmetic instructions. whose results have to be corrected by instruction Decimal Adjust (DAB). Multiplication and division are designed for 16-bit and 32-bit two's complement numbers. Instruction Negate (NEG) generates the two's complement of an operand, instruction Extend Sign (EXTS) doubles the length of an operand in two's complement.

Logical Operations. Logical instructions AND, OR, XOR and COM (negation, one's complement) work with 8-bit, 16-bit and 32-bit operands in memory-to-register or register-to-register mode. Instruction TEST executes the OR function of an operand with zero, so that the condition bits are influenced depending on the operand, but does not change it. When condition CC, which is indicated in the instruction, is satisfied, the instruction Test Condition (TCC) sets the lowest bit of the register operand addressed in the instruction.

Rotate and Shift Operations. The group of shift and rotate instructions includes a complete set of logical and arithmetic shift instructions as well as rotate instructions. In the shift instructions, which are all designed as two-word instructions, the shift number n can be indicated either as a constant in the instruction or as a variable in one of the registers ($n=0$ through 31). In the rotate instructions, the shift number is a constant in the instruction with $n=1$ or with $n=2$. Two special rotate instructions allow the shifting of half bytes.

Bit Manipulation Operations. The instructions for bit processing include the testing (BIT), setting (SET) and resetting (RES) of one bit in 8-bit and 16-bit operands. In register operands, the bit number can be indicated as a constant in the instruction or as a variable; in memory operands it can only be a constant. Instruction Test and Set (TSET), that is used to generate semaphores, sets first the S bit equal to the highest bit of the register or memory operand it is addressing, then all operand bits are set to one. During the execution of the instruction, the processor's bus request input is blocked, so that the two cycles needed by TSET cannot be interrupted by an external bus request.

Block Transfer and String Manipulation Operations. This instruction group contains a large set of transfer. compare and translation instructions for the processing of byte and word strings. The translation instructions change byte strings from one code to the other. The destination operand is evaluated as 8-bit index in a code table, whose base is indicated by the source address. The 8-bit table entry substitutes the original destination operand. For all three instruction types there are several alternatives through implicit incrementing or decrementing of the destination address or through single or repeated execution of the respective operations. In case of repeated execution, the termination is either due to a counting condition in one of the general registers or to a condition indication related to the condition bits of the status register.

Input/Output Operations. I/O instructions are divided into two similar instruction groups for data transfer with the peripheral and for data transfer with memory management units (MMUs). The I/O addresses include 16 bits, the differentiation of the two address areas outside the processor is carried out by the processor's status signals. 8-bit and 16-bit operands are transferred. As was the case with block and string instructions, variants result from implicit incrementing or decrementing of the operand address and from single or repeated execution of the transfer. All I/O instructions are privileged.

Program Control Operations. Two conditional jump instructions (JP, JR) and two subprogram jumps (CALL, CALR) belong to the set of program control instructions. Instructions JR and CALR only work with relative to the program counter addressing, where JR's jump range is ± 256 bytes and CALR's is ± 4K bytes. Conditional jump instructions distinguish between 15 jump conditions; if no jump condition is indicated in the instruction, there is an unconditional jump. An additional instruction Decrement and Jump if Non Zero (DJNZ) supports the generation of inductive loops by counting the loop executions in one of the general registers and by interrupting the loop if the count is zero.

Program control instructions are integrated by a conditional subprogram Return (RET), by the privileged instruction Interrupt Return (IRET) and by the instruction System Call (SC), as a software trap, which allows the programmed passage from user to system mode.

CPU Control Operations. There is a special load instruction for loading and reading the status register, the program status area pointer register, the user/stack pointer register (in system mode) and the refresh counter. An additional instruction loads the status register as well as the program counter and thus sets the processor status. Moreover, there are two instructions for setting and resetting the interrupt mask bits VIE and NVIE. Since they change the status, all four instructions are privileged. Furthermore, the processor can use several non-privileged instructions, with which only the condition bits can be changed. The privileged instruction HALT sets the processor to a standstill that can only be left by means of an external interrupt request. Instruction No Operation (NOP) causes a time delay of several clock cycles in the execution of the program.

A special characteristic of these two Z8000 processors is the fact that they are equipped with four privileged instructions for the management of operational devices that are shared by several processors. These instructions test and influence the two multimicrosignal connections $\overline{MI}$ and $\overline{MO}$.

Apart from the instructions described above, there are several special op codes, which can cause an instruction execution in one of several special processors (Extended Processing Units EPUs). In these cases, the main processor only performs address computation and data transfer. Typical tasks of special processors are floating point operations, data bank operations and supporting graphic systems.

7.2.5 Trap and Interrupt System

As shown in Figure 7.8, Z8000 processors are equipped with four traps, one non-maskable interrupt, one non-vectored interrupt, and 256 vectored interrupts. During the decoding of EPU instructions when the EPU mode bit is not set, the extended instruction trap leads to a trap program

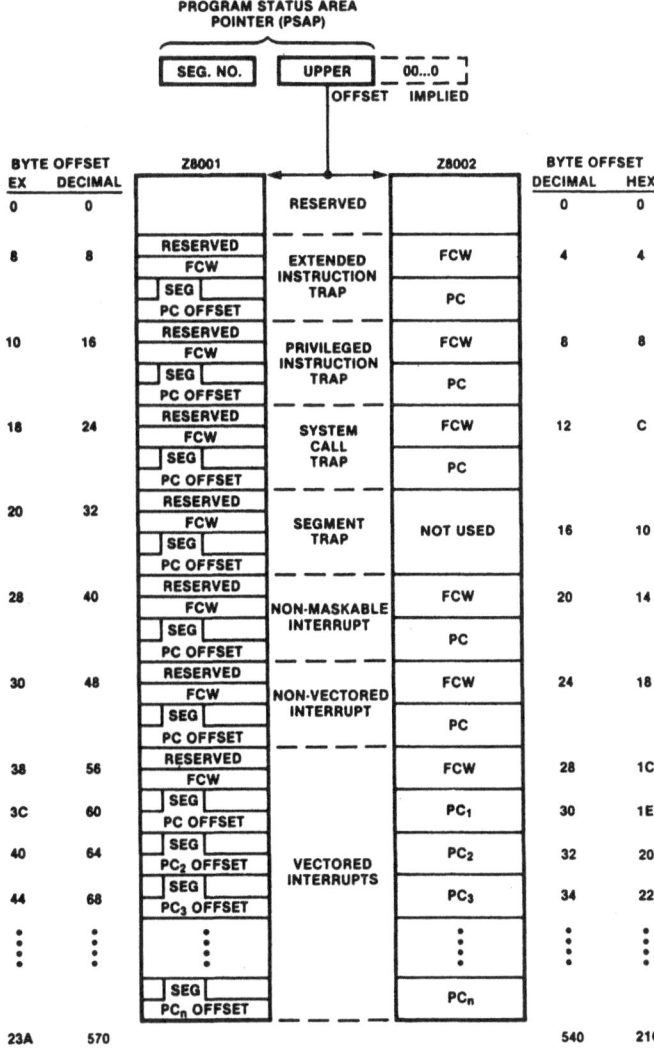

Fig. 7.8. Program status area of the Z8001 and the Z8002 [48]

for the simulation of the function of the missing special processor. Other internal program interruptions are generated by the privileged instruction trap and the system call trap. The segment trap as an external interruption is triggered by memory management units. For each of the three external interrupt types there is an individual signal input. The differentiation between the vectored interrupts is done through an 8-bit vector number which is input by the interrupt source through the data bus. Beside the program address, trap and interrupt vectors also include the status word (FCW). The status word is common for rectored interrupts and is thus only stored once in the vector table.

During program interruptions, the processor switches to system mode and writes the processor status (program counter and status register content) to the system stack together with an interrupt identificator. Finally it loads these two registers with the processor status assigned to the interrupt which is taken from the vector table (program status area). The position of the vector table in the memory is indicated by the program status area pointer register.

Processor and system initialization occurs through a reset signal, which has highest priority over all interrupt requests. The connected interrupt vector in stored from address zero independently from the position of the vector table.

7.2.6 Processor Signals

Figure 7.9 shows the 48 signal connections of the Z8001 combined into function groups. The 16 data bus lines and the 16 low address bus lines are operated in time multiplex mode. Seven segment number outputs complete the address bus to 23 bits. Memory addresses are distributed with 23 bits. I/O addresses are distributed with 16 bits. The low address bit is used for byte selection; word/byte differentiation is carried out by the BYTE/$\overline{\text{WORD}}$ signal. Memory and I/O addresses are identified through control signal $\overline{\text{MREQ}}$; the two I/O address spaces of the peripheral and of the memory management units are differentiated through status signals ST3 through ST0. The three processor's activities data access, stack access and program access are also coded in the four status signals; they can be used as additional address indications to expand memory address space. Data transfer is asynchronous and is controlled by the two strobe signals $\overline{\text{AS}}$ and $\overline{\text{DS}}$ and by the acknowledge signal $\overline{\text{WAIT}}$.

Three interrupt inputs, Non-Maskable Interrupt ($\overline{\text{NMI}}$), Vectored Interrupt ($\overline{\text{VI}}$) and Non-Vectored Interrupt ($\overline{\text{NVI}}$), control interrupt requests; moreover, there is the segmentation trap input $\overline{\text{SEGT}}$. For each of the four interrupt inputs there is an acknowledge signal that is coded in status signals ST3 through ST0.

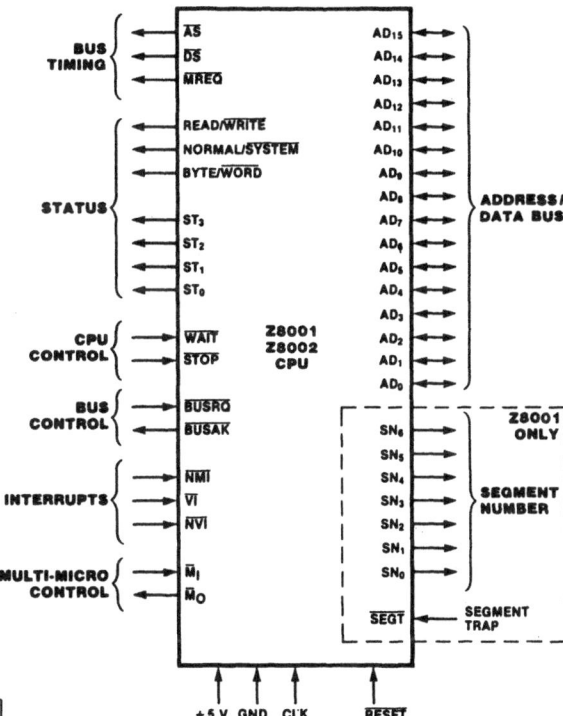

Fig. 7.9. Z8001 processor signals [48]

Bus allocation, by a DMA controller for example, occurs by means of two bus control signals $\overline{BUSRQ}$ and $\overline{BUSAK}$. The management of shared operational devices in a multiprocessor system is supported by two multimicro signals $\overline{MI}$ (Multimicro In) and $\overline{MO}$ (Multimicro Out) in co-operation with four CPU control instructions. Priority chains in form of daisy-chains can be created with these signals.

Additional connections are the USER/$\overline{SYSTEM}$ output for an external distinction between the programming modes (e.g. as a memory protection condition), the $\overline{STOP}$ input for single-step control of the program execution (e.g. for test purposes), and the interrupt input $\overline{RESET}$ for the processor's initialization.

7.2.7 Successors of the Z8001 and Z8002

Zilog offers at present (1984) two 16-bit processors, Z8003 and Z8004, as well as a 32-bit processor, Z80000, as additions to the Z8000 family.

Z8003/Z8004. The Z8003 (segmented version) and the Z8004 (non-segmented version) are identical to their predecessors Z8001 and Z8002 as far as the structure is concerned, but are different in their support of systems with virtual memory and in the management of semaphores. A memory access instruction leads to a program interruption during the addressing of a virtual segment that is not loaded in main memory, and can be restarted after the missing segment is loaded. A pre-condition is for the interrupt program to reconstruct the processor status needed for the new start, e.g. the original instruction counter content. The nine status bytes that are required in this case have to be prepared outside the processor, and this task is carried out by the Paged Memory Management Unit (PMMU) Z8015. - Furthermore, during the execution of the semaphore instruction Test and Set (TSET), a specific 4-bit status code is generated, which can be employed by the processor external hardware to block the access to other segments by the corresponding memory segment during this time.

Z80000. The basic structure of the Z80000 represents an expansion of the Z8000 processor. The register set and the address and data paths are now 32 (address space of 32 Gbytes) and the addressing modes are now completed with the relative to the program counter addressing with indexing. The instruction set was enlarged, but it still includes the Z8000 instructions as a subset, so that it is compatible with the Z8000 machine code. It is furthermore compatible with the additional components designed for 16-bit systems when the Z bus is used as system bus. Other changes are:

- an instruction buffer of 256 bytes (cache memory);

- an integrated Memory Management Unit (MMU) that can be switched off; and

- an interface for the connection of so-called Extended Processing Units (EPU's) like, for example, the Z8070 arithmetic processing unit for floating point, integer and BCD operations.

7.3 Intel 8086

The 8086 is a 16-bit microprocessor by Intel Corporation, that favors byte processing beside 16-bit processing and thus does not implement 32-bit operations. Its instruction set and its register set are subsets of the two 8-bit microprocessors 8080 and 8085, with which it is completely compatible.

The 8086 offers elementary functions to support the implementation of high-level programming languages and operating systems, in particular through implicit segmented memory addressing. This allows dynamic relocation of program, data and stack areas, and the addressing of 1M bytes altogether. Also, the 8086 has a set of I/O instructions with their own 64K byte address space as well as a trap and interrupt system with vectored interrupts. Furthermore, it offers the possibility to expand the instruction set with operations that are executed in additional special processors in co-operation with the 8086 processor. Multiprocessor systems design is supported by bus control signals for two independent bus requests and by two synchronization signals $\overline{\text{TEST}}$ and $\overline{\text{LOCK}}$ with their related control instructions. The 8086 is contained in a 40-pin package and most of the signal lines are operated in time multiplex mode.

7.3.1 The Programming Model

The 8086 registers that can be programmed are divided into several groups of 16-bit registers with different functions: four general registers, four pointer and index registers, four segment registers, the program counter and the status register (Figure 7.10). The general registers can be addressed both as 16-bit registers and as 8-bit registers. They are mainly used as operand registers for arithmetic and logical operations. Furthermore, they are used implicitly by some instructions and some addressing modes, e.g. as source or destination registers for I/O operations, as counter registers in string operations and as base address registers with the transfer instruction XLAT. The pointer and index registers include one stack pointer register, one base address register and two index registers, whose contents represent offsets in memory segments. Memory segments are created with the help of the four segment registers. They contain the 16 most significant address bits of the 20-bit segment base addresses. The four low bits of the segment base addresses are set to zero by the processor during address computation. The segment register selection occurs implicitly during program, data and stack accesses. One extra segment register describes a second data segment that is addressed during string operations. A segment comprises up to 64K bytes.

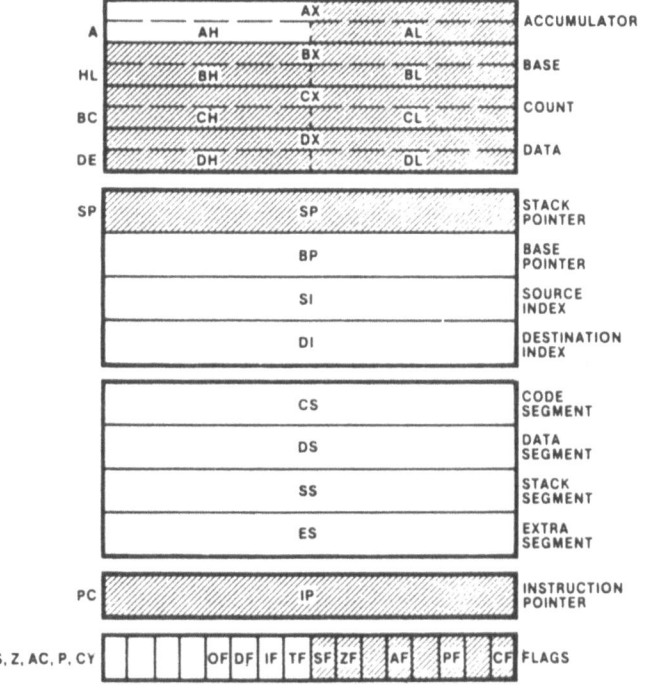

Fig. 7.10. 8086 register set [2]; the subset of the 8080/8085 register and of the 8080/8085 status bits is shaded

The content of the 16-bit program counter register indicates the offset of the actual instruction to the program segment base. Beside the usual condition bits (flags) Overflow Flag (OF), Sign Flag (SF), Zero Flag (ZF), Parity Flag (PF) and Carry Flag (CF), the status register contains an auxiliary carry flag as half byte carry for BCD processing. The mode bits include the Direction Flag (DF), which indicates address counting direction during string operations (autoincrement or autodecrement addressing), the Interrupt Enable Flag (IF) to mask an interrupt input and the Trap Flag (TF), which puts the processor in single-step mode.

7.3.2 Data Formats

Byte and word are the standard data formats for arithmetic and logic operations. In addition, the instruction set includes operations with decimal operands in BCD representation (packed data) and in ASCII representation (unpacked data) as well as operations with byte and word strings.

The memory is organized wordwise, like the 16-bit data bus, and can be addressed bytewise and wordwise. Independently from this, word operands can be at both even and odd address boundaries, so that a continuous memory assignment with byte and word operands is possible. During access to a word operand with odd address, the processor executes two consecutive memory cycles.

7.3.3 Addressing Modes

The 8086 has over 24 addressing modes which are based on four address generation principles:

1. direct addressing with a 16-bit offset,

2. indirect addressing through a base address register (BX or BP) and either an 8-bit or a 16-bit offset,

3. indirect addressing through an index register (SI or DI) and either an 8-bit or a 16-bit offset,

4. indirect addressing through a base address register (BX or BP) and an index register (SI or DI) and either an 8-bit or a 16-bit offset.

The resulting effective addresses generate offsets within the memory segments defined by the segment register. The selection of the segment registers is implicit for address calculation; on the other hand, it can be bypassed in some instances by a so-called segment override prefix. Table 7.4 shows all 24 addressing modes and their encoding in the instruction word through a Register/Memory field (R/M) and a Mode field (MOD). It also shows byte and word selection of the general registers and of the pointer and index registers. The selection is indicated by one bit in the instruction Word (W).

Table 7.4. 8086 addressing modes [2]; for abbreviations see Fig. 7.10

MOD = 11			EFFECTIVE ADDRESS CALCULATION			
R/M	W = 0	W = 1	R/M	MOD = 00	MOD = 01	MOD = 10
000	AL	AX	000	(BX) + (SI)	(BX) + (SI) + D8	(BX) + (SI) + D16
001	CL	CX	001	(BX) + (DI)	(BX) + (DI) + D8	(BX) + (DI) + D16
010	DL	DX	010	(BP) + (SI)	(BP) + (SI) + D8	(BP) + (SI) + D16
011	BL	BX	011	(BP) + (DI)	(BP) + (DI) + D8	(BP) + (DI) + D16
100	AH	SP	100	(SI)	(SI) + D8	(SI) + D16
101	CH	BP	101	(DI)	(DI) + D8	(DI) + D16
110	DH	SI	110	DIRECT ADDRESS	(BP) + D8	(BP) + D16
111	BH	DI	111	(BX)	(BX) + D8	(BX) + D16

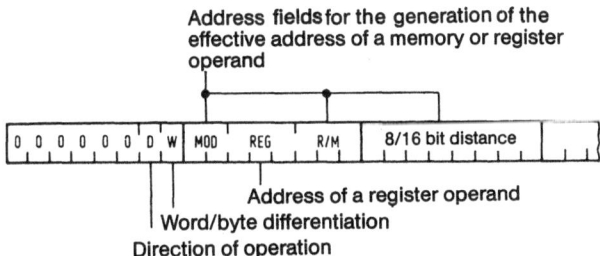

Fig. 7.11. Instruction format of the ADD instruction; for the function of the address fields see also Table 7.4

7.3.4 Instruction Formats and Instruction Sets

The 8086 instruction set includes 77 instructions altogether. Depending on the type of instruction, the addressing mode and the length of an immediate operand, they use from one to six bytes. Standard instructions for dyadic operations are two-address instructions. Figure 7.11 shows the ADD instruction format as an example of instruction structure. One of the two operands is a register operand, the other is a memory or a register operand. They are specified either through the Register field (REG) or through the Mode field (MOD) and the Register/Memory field (R/M) according to Table 7.4. The definition of source and destination addresses occurs through the Direction bit (D), the word/byte differentiation takes place through the Word bit (W). An 8-bit or 16-bit offset required for the generation of the memory address is stored in one or two additional instruction bytes. The ADD instruction includes two additional instruction formats for the use of an immediate operand as source in case of different destination addresses.

The instruction set is divided into six instruction groups for the following operations:

- Data Transfer,

- Arithmetic,

- Logic,

- String Manipulation,

- Control Transfer,

- Processor Control.

Data Transfer Operations. This instruction group includes data transfer and I/O instructions. The general data transfer with 8-bit or 16-bit operands is executed by the instruction Move (MOV) in memory-to-register, register-to-memory or register-to-register mode; the source operand can also be an immediate operand. The instruction Exchange (XCHG) exchanges two operands. The instructions PUSH and POP are available for data transfer with the stack, and the stack pointer is in register SP. SP is the only register for stack management. Two I/O instructions allow byte and word transfers between the peripheral and the accumulator registers AL (8 bits) and AX (16 bits). The peripheral is addressed either directly with an 8-bit address or indirectly with a 16-bit address.

Additional instructions allow addresses to be loaded into the pointer, index and segment registers, as well as data transfers between the status register and the accumulator or the stack. A translate instruction (XLAT) is designed as a special transfer instruction for code conversion. The base address of the code table is indicated in register BX and the table index is indicated in register AL. XLAT replaces the content of AL with the corresponding table entry. - Data transfer instructions have no effect on condition bits.

Arithmetic Operations. Arithmetic instructions include the four basic arithmetic operations with 8-bit and 16-bit operands as binary numbers and as two's complement numbers. Operand accesses occur in memory-to-register, register-to-memory or register-to-register mode. The source operand can also be an immediate operand. The instructions of the four basic arithmetic types can also be used with unpacked decimal operands (ASCII representation) and with packed decimal operands (BCD representation); in this case the results have to be corrected with decimal adjust instructions. Additional arithmetic instructions are: Increment (INC), Decrement (DEC) and Negate (NEG) for counting and generating the two's complement, as well as instruction Compare (CMP) as a comparison instruction.

Logical Operations. This instruction group includes a complete set of logical instructions and of shift and rotate instructions. The logical instructions are AND, OR, XOR and NOT (negation, one's complement). They work with 8-bit and 16-bit operands. Instruction TEST is used as AND instruction; it influences the condition bits, without changing the destination operand. Shift and rotate operations are carried out with register and memory operands in byte and word format. The shift number n is either in the instruction as a constant ($n=1$) or is indicated in the general register CL as a variable ($n=0$ through 255).

String Manipulation Operations. The processing of byte and word strings is based on some primitive string instructions, which can be executed repeatedly through a one-byte instruction prefix (Repeat Prefix REP). Operand addressing occurs through the two index registers SI and DI. Operations are counted in the general register CX; the direction flag in the status register indicates the address counting direction. Transfer, compare and subtract instructions are designed as primitive string instructions.

Control Transfer Operations. Jump instructions, instructions for loop generation and for calling subprograms and interrupt programs belong to the control transfer instructions. Instruction JMP allows unconditional jumps both within the actual code segment as well as outside the boundaries of the segment. In the case of conditional jump instructions, for which there are 16 different jump conditions altogether, the jump area is limited to $\pm$ 128 bytes by the relative to the program counter addressing. The generation of inductive and iterative program loops is supported by four loop instructions. They perform the counting of loop executions and terminate the loop depending on the counter value or on the zero flag in the status register.

Two subprogram jump instructions CALL and RET control the execution of subprograms. Occasionally, the stack pointer can be actualized with RET by a constant indicated in the instruction, e.g. in order to deallocate a parameter field in the stack. Instructions INT and INTO allow the calling of interrupt programs by means of the software (software traps). INT contains an 8-bit vector number for the selection of one out of 256 interrupt programs. INTO branches to an interrupt program for handling arithmetic overflow if the overflow flag is set in the status register (trap on overflow). Both instructions cause the status to be saved on the stack and the masking of additional interrupts, similarly to what is executed by the processor in case of an external interrupt request. The return from an interrupt program is performed by instruction IRET which restores the original status.

Processor Control Operations. Seven instructions are designed for setting, resetting and inverting the condition and mode bits *carry*, *direction* and *interrupt enable*. The instruction Halt (HLT) puts the processor in a halt state, which can only be left through an interrupt or through the reset signal. The instruction WAIT puts the processor in a wait condition until the input signal $\overline{\text{TEST}}$ is set. The wait condition can be interrupted by an interrupt request. At the end of the interrupt program, the program is again under the control of the wait instruction. The wait instruction is used to synchronize programs with external events.

The instruction Bus Lock (LOCK) used as a prefix sets the $\overline{\text{LOCK}}$ output during the execution time of the instruction following LOCK. The LOCK instruction is used in multiprocessor systems to synchronize accesses, it is also used for example with the instruction Exchange (EXCHG) to generate semaphores. The instruction Escape (ESC) allows the introduction of op codes, that will be evaluated by an additional processor, in the 8086 instruction flow. In this case, the 8086 performs the address calculation and the memory access of the memory operand indicated in the instruction.

The 8086 instruction set does not contain bit-processing instructions. furthermore, there are no privileged instructions, since the processor has only one programming mode.

7.3.5 Trap and Interrupt System

In the 8086 there are 256 possibilities of program interruption altogether, whose vectors are in the memory starting from address zero. Each vector consists of a 16-bit segment base address and a 16-bit offset for the generation of the starting address for the trap or interrupt program. The first 32 vectors are reserved for special interrupt conditions, the first five are defined according to Figure 7.12. Interrupts type 0 and 1 are hardware traps which can be triggered by a division by zero or by the trap flag in the status register (single-step mode). A type 2 interrupt is generated through a Non-Masked Interrupt input (NMI). Interrupts type 3 and 4 are generated as software traps through the INT instruction, which is used as breakpoint instruction in its one-byte version, and through the INTO instruction as a reaction to an overflow during arithmetic operations with two's complement numbers. Interruptions type 32 through 255 are triggered by a masked Interrupt input (INTR); vector selection is managed by an 8-bit vector number prepared by the interrupt source. All interrupts can also be triggered by the INT instruction which is used for testing.

During a program interruption, the processor status (program counter value, code segment register contents and status register contents) is written on the stack. In addition, the mode bits trap flag and interrupt enable flag are reset, which turns off the single-step mode and disables the interrupt input INTR. Finally, the appropriate interrupt program, whose starting address is taken from the vector table, is called.

The initialization of the processor and of the system is done by means of a reset interrupt signal through the RESET input. This signal has highest priority over all interrupt conditions. It causes the processor to start an initialization program, for which the last 16 bytes in the memory are reserved.

227

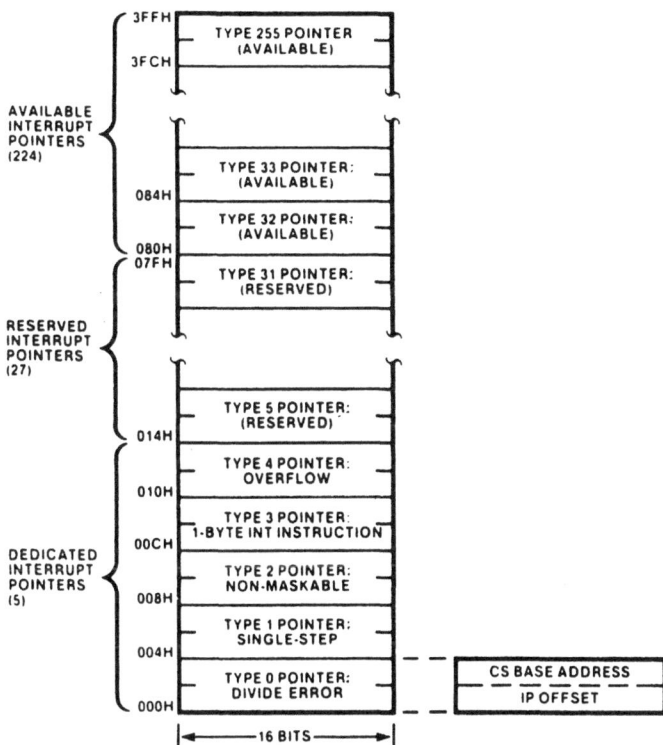

Fig. 7.12. 8086 interrupt pointer table [2]

7.3.6 Processor Signals

Figure 7.13 shows the 40 signal connections of the 8086. A large portion of these is operated in time multiplex mode, thus the number of pins is small for a 16-bit microprocessor. The data bus includes 16 bits, the address bus includes 20 bits. Byte selection and word/byte selection occur through the least significant address bit and the control signal Bus High Enable (BHE).

The generation of control signals for addressing and data transfer depends on either minimum mode or maximum mode, which is indicated through the MN/MX input. In minimum mode, which is used for small system configurations, the processor generates the signals necessary at connections 24 through 31. In maximum mode, which is designed for larger system configurations, a bus control component manages signal generation. Control signals S0 through S2 are read into this module; they indicate the different conditions read, write, I/O and memory access, instruction and data access. Furthermore, the interrupt acknowledge signal is coded in them. Independently from the op mode, the data transfer is asynchronous with a READY input for transmission acknowledgement. During a memory access, two additional control signals S3 and S4 show which one of the four segment registers is used for memory addressing.

Common Signals		
Name	**Function**	**Type**
AD15–AD0	Address/Data Bus	Bidirectional, 3-State
A19/S6–A16/S3	Address/Status	Output, 3-State
$\overline{BHE}$/S7	Bus High Enable/Status	Output, 3-State
MN/$\overline{MX}$	Minimum/Maximum Mode Control	Input
$\overline{RD}$	Read Control	Output, 3-State
$\overline{TEST}$	Wait On Test Control	Input
READY	Wait State Control	Input
RESET	System Reset	Input
NMI	Non-Maskable Interrupt Request	Input
INTR	Interrupt Request	Input
CLK	System Clock	Input
Vcc	+5V	Input
GND	Ground	

Minimum Mode Signals (MN/MX = Vcc)		
Name	**Function**	**Type**
HOLD	Hold Request	Input
HLDA	Hold Acknowledge	Output
$\overline{WR}$	Write Control	Output, 3-State
M/$\overline{IO}$	Memory/IO Control	Output, 3-State
DT/$\overline{R}$	Data Transmit/Receive	Output, 3-State
$\overline{DEN}$	Data Enable	Output, 3-State
ALE	Address Latch Enable	Output
$\overline{INTA}$	Interrupt Acknowledge	Output

Maximum Mode Signals (MN/MX = GND)		
Name	**Function**	**Type**
$\overline{RQ/GT1,0}$	Request/Grant Bus Access Control	Bidirectional
$\overline{LOCK}$	Bus Priority Lock Control	Output, 3-State
$\overline{S2}$–$\overline{S0}$	Bus Cycle Status	Output, 3-State
QS1, QS0	Instruction Queue Status	Output

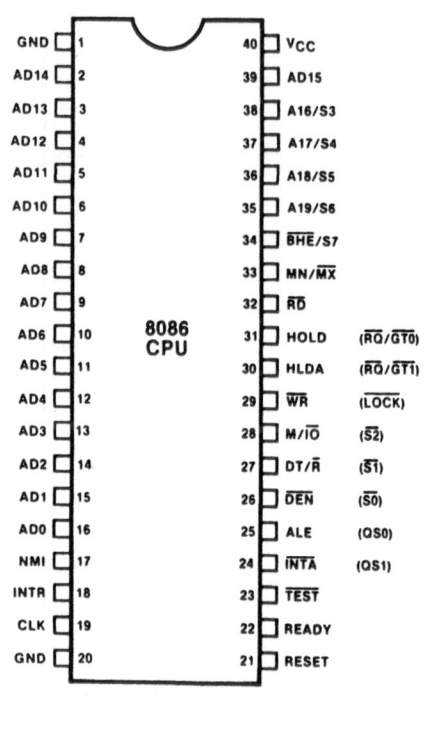

MAXIMUM MODE PIN FUNCTIONS (e.g., $\overline{LOCK}$) ARE SHOWN IN PARENTHESES

Fig. 7.13. 8086 processor signals [2]

NMI is used as interrupt input for non-maskable interrupts and INTR is used for masked vectored interrupts; the RESET input is used to initialize the processor. For bus allocation to additional bus masters, e.g. in a DMA environment, there are two bidirectional Request/Grant connections ($\overline{RQ/GT}$) with different priorities. Multiprocessor systems are supported by the $\overline{LOCK}$ output, which prevents bus components from being accessed by other processors for the duration of an instruction execution. The program execution can be synchronized with external events through the $\overline{TEST}$ input and the WAIT instruction.

7.3.7 Successors of the 8086

Intel offers at present (1984) three new 16-bit processors: the iAPX186, the iAPX188 and the iAPX286. They all developed differently from the 8086 and can also handle 8086 machine programs. Furthermore, Intel offers a 32-bit processor, the iAPX432, which is heavily tailored for the support of operative system functions and for the use of ADA as high-level programming language. Since this processor is substantially different in its structure from the processors described in this book, it will not be further discussed.

iAPX186/iAPX188. The iAPX186 is based on the register structure, the addressing modes and the instruction set of the 8086, but its structural characteristics substantially increase its efficiency with respect to the 8086. The most important characteristics are:

- shorter instruction execution times and expansion of the instruction set in relation to the Input/Output, to the interrupt handling and to the support of higher-level programming languages;

- an overlapping, working bus control unit with a 6-byte instruction buffer for the execution of all memory accesses (as in the 8086), that is expanded by its own address computation device;

- two integrated DMA channels, which share the bus control unit;

- three timer/counters that are independent from each other;

- an integrated interrupt controller with 10 levels altogether for the two DMA channels, the three timer/counters and five external interrupt sources;

- an integrated clock frequency generator; and

- 13 internal address decoders with one chip select output each for selection of six memory areas and seven peripheral units.

On the whole, the processor allows a very compact system structure by means of the integration of functional units which are usually to be managed outside the processor. - The same processor, with an 8-bit data bus connection, is offered as iAPX188.

iAPX286. The iAPX286 is also based on the 8086 in its basic structure. Part of its increased efficiency results from the expanded instruction set; from the enlargement of the bus control unit that works in parallel, including an address computation device and an instruction decoder; as well as from the reduction and overlapping of bus cycles. Its main feature, though, is the support of systems with virtual memory, whereby we must consider the following characteristics:

- an integrated Memory Management Unit (MMU) with address conversion based on segments, where the segment descriptors are stored in tables in the memory and are loaded in the buffer register during access;

- the expansion of the virtual (internal) address word to 30 bits and of the physical (external) address word to 24 bits;

- multiple access control by means of the segment descriptors and of four processor operation modes that are differently privileged;

- an extensive early recognition of accesses to non-loaded segments, so that the interruption of memory access instructions and their new start is limited to a small instruction group.

In so-called Read Address Mode, the memory management unit is switched off, so that the processor works with 20-bit segment addresses like the 8086.

Bibliography

1. 9900 family systems design and data book. Texas Instruments 1978

2. SAB 8086 family user's manual. Siemens 1979

3. Microcomputer components data book. Zilog 1980

4. MC68000 16-Bit microprocessor user's manual, 3rd ed. Motorola 1982

5. Steinbuch, K.; Weber, W.: Taschenbuch der Informatik, Vol. 2, Struktur und Programmierung von EDV-Systemen. Berlin, Heidelberg, New York: Springer 1974

6. Hoffmann, R.: Rechenwerke und Mikroprogrammierung, 2nd ed. München, Wien: Oldenbourg 1983

7. Stein, M. L.; Munro, W. D.: Introduction to machine arithmetic. Reading, Menlo Park, London, Don Mills: Addison-Wesley 1971

8. Mead, C.; Conway, L.: Introduction to VLSI systems, 2nd printing. Reading, Menlo Park, London, Don Mills: Addison-Wesley 1980

9. Kraft, G. D.; Toy, W. N.: Mini/Microcomputer hardware design. Englewood Cliffs: Prentice Hall 1979

10. Barron, D. W.: Assemblers and loaders. Macdonald: London and American Elsevier: New York 1969

11. Hemenway, J. (Associate editor): Software systems design course. EDN 23 (1978) H.21, 252-311

12. Eckhouse Jr., R.H.; Morris, L.R.: Minicomputer systems - organization, programming and applications (PDP-11), 2nd. ed. Englewood Cliffs: Prentice Hall 1979

13. Knuth, D. E.: The art of computer programming, Vol.1. Reading, Menlo Park, London, Don Mills: Addison-Wesley 1961

14. Nassi, I.; Shneiderman, B.: Flowchart techniques for structured programming. SIGPLAN Notices 8 (1973) H.8, 12-26

15. DIN 66001: Informationsverarbeitung, Sinnbilder für Datenfluss- und Programmablaufpläne. Berlin, Köln: Beuth 1978

16. Schnupp, P.; Floyd, C.: Software, Programmentwicklung und Projektorganisation, 2nd ed. Berlin, New York: de Gruyter 1979

17. Lesea, A.; Zaks, R.: Microprocessor interfacing techniques, 3rd ed. Berkeley, Paris: Sybex 1979

18. VERSAbus. preliminary specification. Motorola 1979

19. VME bus, specification manual, Motorola

20. Johnson, R.C.: Microsystems exploit mainframe methods. Electronics 54 (1981) H.16, 119-127

21. MC68451, Memory management unit, advance information. Motorola 1981

22. Burskey, D.: Support circuits - the 'power' behind powerful processors. Electronic Design 28 (1980) H.24,123-139

23. Designing 8086, 8088, 8089 multiprocessing systems with the 8289 bus arbiter, application note 51. Intel 1979

24. EL-Ayat, K.A.: The Intel 8089: an integrated i/o processor. Computer 12 (1979) H.6, 67-78

25. Bocker, P.: Datenübertragung, Vol. 1, Grundlagen. Berlin, Heidelberg, New York: Springer 1976

26. Bocker, P.: Datenübertragung, Vol. 2, Einrichtungen und Systeme. Berlin, Heidelberg, New York: Springer 1977

27. Hofer, H.: Datenfernverarbeitung. Berlin, Heidelberg, New York: Springer 1973

28. Planungshilfe für die Datenfernverarbeitung. Deutsche Bundespost 1980

29. Gabler, H.; Tietz, W.: Datenkommunikation in den Fernmeldenetzen der Deutschen Bundespost. Informatik Spektrum 4 (1981) H.1, 11-30

30. DIN 66020: Datenübertragung, Anforderungen an die Schnittstelle bei Ubergabe bipolarer Datensignale. Berlin, Köln: Beuth 1978

31. Haas, J.; Hofmann, W.: Die V.- und X.-Empfehlungen des CCITT. Elektronik 28 (1979) H.21, 87-90

32. Gibson, R.D.: Designer's guide to: data modems. EDN 25 (1980) H.5, 96-102

33. Goldberger, A.: A designer's review of data communications. Computer Design 20 (1981) H.5, 103-112

34. Münchrath, R.: Datensicherung auf Ubertragungswegen mit zyklischen Codes. Elektronik 25 (1976) H.8, 55-59

35. Weissberger, A.J.: Orient your data-link protocols toward bits, though characters still count. Electronic Design 27 (1979) H.15, 86-92

36. Goldberger. A.; Lau, S.Y.: Understand datacomm protocols by examining their structures. EDN 28 (1983) H.5, 109-118

37. Binary synchronous communications, 3rd ed. IBM systems reference library. 1970

38. Hegenbarth, M.: Stand der Normung im CCITT, Ebenen 2-6. GI-Fachtagung Kommunikation in verteilten Systemen. Berlin, Heidelberg, New York: Springer 1981

39. Tietz, W.: Daten-Paketvermittlung - Internationale Standards, Übersetzung der Empfehlungen X.3, X.25, X.28, X.29. Heidelberg, Hamburg: Decker's Verlag G. Schenck 1978

40. Parker, Y.: Multi-microprocessor systems. London, New York: Academic Press 1983

41. MC68120, intelligent peripheral controller, product preview. Motorola 1980

42. Männer, R.; Deluigi, B.: 16-Bit-Prozessoren im Vergleich, 1. Teil. Elektronik 30 (1981) H.5, 77-83

43. Männer, R.; Deluigi, B.: 16-Bit-Prozessoren im Vergleich, 2. Teil. Elektronik 30 (1981) H.6, 119-124

44. Männer, R.; Deluigi, B.: 16-Bit-Prozessoren im Vergleich, 3. Teil. Elektronik 30 (1981) H.7, 101-107

45. Bell, R.K.; Bell, W.D.; Cooper, T.C.; McFarland, T.K.: The big three - today's 16-bit microprocessor. SIGMICRO NEWSLETTER 11 (1980) H.3, 126-138

46. Grappel, R.; Hemenway, J.: Comparing the newest 16-Bit μPs to evaluate their potential. EDN 25 (1980) H.16, 197-201

47. De Prycker, M.: A performance comparison of three contemporary 16-bit microprocessors. IEEE Micro 3 (1983) H.2, 26-37

48. Z8000 CPU Technical manual. Zilog 1980

49. MC68008 16-bit microprocessor with 8-bit data bus, advance information. Motorola 1983

50. MC68010 16-bit virtual memory microprocessor, advance information. Motorola 1982

51. The MC68020 enhanced M68000 microprocessor, product preview. Motorola 1982

52. Components data book, 1983/84. Zilog 1983

53. Microprocessor applications reference book, vol. 2. Zilog 1983

54. iAPX186, high integration 16-bit microprocessor. Intel 1983

55. iAPX188, high integration 8-bit microprocessor. Intel 1982

56. Introduction to the iAPX286. Intel 1982

Index

Microcomputer System Design

An Advanced Course

Editors: **M. J. Flynn, N. R. Harris, D. P. McCarthy**

Springer Study Edition
Reprint. 1984. VII, 397 pages
ISBN 3-540-13545-6
(Originally published as "Lecture Notes in
Computer Science, Volume 126")

Contents: Perspective on microcomputers. – Integrated circuit physics and technology. – Computer aided design for microcomputer systems. – Properties of instruction set processor. – Customized microcomputers. – High level sequential and concurrent programming. – Microcomputer operating systems. – Notes on distributed systems of microprocessors. – LILITH: A personal computer for the software engineer.

In order to use microcomputers effectively, system designers require a broad knowledge of computer hardware, interfacing, software, and design tools.

Covering both theory and practice the microcomputer system design course described in this volume integrates the hardware and software sides of microcomputers. It includes the revised notes of a course which spanned development from silicon technology to software. It brought together current techniques in LSI/VLSI design, computer structures and languages, showing their application to, and implications for, microcomputer system design.

Springer-Verlag
Berlin
Heidelberg
New York
Tokyo